Žižek and Heidegger

Continuum Studies in Continental Philosophy
Series Editor: James Fieser, University of Tennessee at Martin, USA

Continuum Studies in Continental Philosophy is a major monograph series from Continuum. The series features first-class scholarly research monographs across the field of Continental philosophy. Each work makes a major contribution to the field of philosophical research.

Žižek and Heidegger

The Question Concerning Techno-Capitalism

Thomas Brockelman

For Tyler +
the entire crew)
of Honors, Fall
2010.

"Oh... the horror!"

Best,
Tom Brockelman

continuum

Continuum International Publishing Group

The Tower Building   80 Maiden Lane
11 York Road   Suite 704
London SE1 7NX   New York NY 10038

www.continuumbooks.com

British Library Cataloguing-in-Publication Data
A catalogue record for this book is available from the British Library.

ISBN-10: HB: 0-8264-9777-2
ISBN-13: HB: 978-0-8264-9777-2

Library of Congress Cataloging-in-Publication Data
Brockelman, Thomas P. Žižek and Heidegger: the question concerning techno-capitalism/Thomas Brockelman.
   p. cm.
Includes bibliographical references (p.).
ISBN 978-0-8264-9777-2
1. Žižek, Slavoj. 2. Heidegger, Martin, 1889–1976. 3. Technology–Philosophy.
4. Capitalism–Philosophy. I. Title.

B4870.Z594B76 2009
199'.4973–dc22   2008021980

Typeset by Newgen Imaging Systems Pvt Ltd, Chennai, India
Printed and bound in Great Britain by the MPG Books Group

Contents

Part III: The split subject of history

Preface
Le Style Žižek and the question of finitude

Beginning from style?

In the last years of Martin Heidegger's life and the first years after his death the power of the philosopher's future legacy emerged through the phenomenon of the "pious Heideggerian." Serious Heidegger readers would mimic the style and tone of the master, speaking of the "fourfold" difficulty of interpreting his texts or producing forced gerundives as philosophical concepts (the "thinking of the thought," etc.). And there was certainly no shortage of "earthy" tones in philosophical writing to honor the Swabian master's peasant rhetoric. Indeed, it was really only with the gradual emergence in international circles of what has been called the "French" Heidegger, the Heidegger of post-structuralism and particularly of Foucault and Derrida, that Heideggerian "piety" began to fade. My point here is that this fading corresponded precisely with the emergence of a meaningful *criticism* of Heidegger's work, that it was only when Heidegger could be properly "read" that possibilities beyond summary dismissal or abject discipleship began to emerge. Just as had been the case a century and a half early in the Germany of Hegel and his followers, so also now reception of an important thinker demanded a *double* event – a first "blow" to record the *fact* that something important was happening/had happened; the second to unravel the nature of that occurrence.

Plus ça change . . . of course, Slavoj Žižek is today very much alive (and still burying potential commentators in a mountain of writings produced at a faster clip than many of us can *read* them) and the issue with Žižek is not so much that everyone wants to *sound like* Žižek (though, hey, why not? He certainly writes better than Heidegger did!), but, still, today we find an almost obsessive emphasis upon his *style* marking the difficulty of *critically interpreting* his work. Indeed, three important books on Žižek, Tony Myers' *Žižek*, Ian Parker's *Slavoj Žižek: A Critical Introduction* and Rex Butler's *Slavoj Žižek: Live Theory* all *start from* the question of *Žižek's style*, and for all three, to one degree or another, this beginning point accompanies (and perhaps underlies) an argument about the incoherence of Žižek's positions or his work as a whole. [1] Even Butler, who is a sympathetic and careful reader, argues that Žižek "ultimately believes in nothing except the 'inherent correctness of theory itself,'" and also that, seen in a certain light, he "has nothing to say" (Butler 2005, p. 3, 123).

On the other hand, for Parker, Žižek's style doesn't so much open a path of interpretation as challenge the very possibility of forging such a direction. We are, he claims, too "easily sidetracked or swept along by his anecdotes or jokes," a tendency to bewitchment that distracts us from the fact that his "interventions around different issues are inconsistent and his theoretical position is contradictory" (Parker 2004, p. 2). For Parker, the trick of reading Žižek is not to be "seduced" by the Žižek "reading machine," by its production of this powerful illusion that there is a "treasure" hidden in Žižek's writing, awaiting the busy hermeneut willing to uncover it. We must resist the temptation to find a "true Žižek," beneath the dance of many veils into which he offers to draw us.

Though he is the least sympathetic to Žižek of all his "introducers," I would also like to suggest that Parker is also, in a sense, the best of those who begin from style; for he is most honest about where we end up if we make this the starting point of our investigations. That is, through this window we can only see Žižek's inconsistencies and shifts – which do, of course, exist and make up a part of the "picture" – but we miss the passionate cause that binds both the path of his development and the system of exceptions within it. Furthermore, Parker simply carries to an extreme the *judgment* that naturally follows from the "stylistic" starting point. He really speaks for a broad consensus in the academic world that admits it's *important* to write about Žižek (thus, the steady stream of books and journal articles on his work) but important, also, to dismiss him. [2]

An interesting fact of contemporary publishing-economics reinforces this tendency to assert Žižek's incoherence, namely the call for "introductions to" contemporary thinkers and, particularly, to thinkers in the fledgling discipline of Cultural Studies where, for reasons having to do with the institutional history of Philosophy in the Anglophone world, Žižek has largely been housed. The literary form of the "Introductory" text produces certain demands which reinforce the "incoherence" accusation, namely for a structure which emphasizes either the various scholarly disciplines and debates in which the writer (Žižek) has participated or the chronological sequence of his writings. Thus, introductions to Žižek (Myers, Kay, Parker, even Butler) all segregate the Slovenian thinker's work into convenient topics (Žižek and Lacan, Žižek and theology, Žižek and political theory, etc., etc.). Given his remarkable intellectual range, it's not surprising that such an approach should suggest the impossibility of reducing Žižek to any limited context.[3]

At least in its form, *Žižek and Heidegger: The Question Concerning Techno-Capitalism* is *not* an introduction to Žižek. In tracing Žižek's thought, I've discovered, rather, a single narrative within which at least much of what Žižek writes makes sense, a unified *context* for understanding his work, even if – profoundly aporeitic in its nature – it doesn't provide us anything like what we look for in a traditional philosophical system. Indeed, the remarkable thing that emerges when one examines Žižek's work through the lens of such a reading is how profoundly *irrelevant* the various discourses and disciplines that he crosses over time are for his thought. In this sense, Žižek is very much a philosopher, even in the most frightening and Platonic sense. At the same time, of course, my "core sample" of Žižek's work reveals an equally terrifying "trans-disciplinarity" at work, one implying a simple *irrelevance* of the provincial disciplines and discourses that it crosses: Žižek's is a philosophy for a cynical age, for an age enmeshed in what I call (see Chapter 3) the paranoid fundamental fantasy and the perverse reality it constructs. From my viewpoint, we should take the rush to hold Žižek in an "introductory" format (with its prejudice for disciplinary pluralization) as just that, a symptomatic effort at containment of a thought which is threatening and anxiety-producing in what it reveals about *us*.

No doubt, my book, in refusing a reduction of Žižek to style (though occasionally I discuss this style), will be taken as retrograde – as a reactionary effort to win back Žižek's *oeuvre* for a traditional disciplinary perspective, and, what's more, for the *worst* such discipline: Philosophy. I have little doubt that many representatives of *new* orthodoxies within the postmodern academy will want nothing to do with my Žižek. But, so I would argue, these same interests also dismiss *Žižek* or, worse, attempt to contain his thought within the pretty postmodern cage of a play of signifiers, a kind of "glass bead game" of cultural theory. But, as Žižek is fond of saying, the real venture of critique is the willingness to put forward some theses, to take the risk of *saying something*, even if it proves wrong or needs later revision. Here it might be worth remembering his attempt at the beginning of *Tarrying with the Negative* to defend Lacan against postmodern nominalism:

Lacan, however, is not part of this "postmodern theory": in this respect, his position is homologous to that of Plato or Kant. The perception of Lacan as "anti-essentialist" or "deconstructionist" falls prey to the same illusion as that of perceiving Plato as just one among the sophists. Plato accepts from the sophists their logic of discursive argumentation, but uses it to affirm his commitment to Truth; Kant accepts the break-down of traditional metaphysics, but uses it to perform his transcenden-tal turn; along the same lines, Lacan accepts the "deconstructionist" motif of radical contingency, but turns this motif against itself, using it to assert his commitment to Truth as contingent. (Žižek 1993, p. 4)

My claim is to correspond in some sense with what Žižek is trying to do, and, that being the case, I've tried to make *my* text "philosophical" in the sense in which Žižek's writing is – a sense of "philosophy" that we should not confuse with mere Platonic universalism. To illustrate, let's consider for a moment what seems *objectionable* about philosophy from Plato onwards, namely it's *hubris* in claiming to have discovered "The Truth." Isn't this, after all, precisely what upsets people in Žižek's work, a kind of *presumption* in the face of various understandings or political projects? "How dare Slavoj Žižek claim to have 'the Truth!'" And, we might continue, "how dare you, Tom Brockelman, claim to have 'the Truth' about Žižek!?" We are all, such is the logic behind this indignation, finite beings lacking access to such divine verity.

That such indignation is precisely mis-placed when it comes to Žižek can emerge if we return for a moment to Ian Parker's exaggerated effort to pro-tect readers against or prevent them from reading Žižek. Consider the social context eliciting Parker's text: At a recent conference featuring Žižek I noticed an odd uniformity in the dress of a large part of the audience. All of them (they turned out to be a group of graduate students) wore identical red tee-shirts announcing, "Žižek Rocks." Indeed, as the overfull room, the distinct buzz of anticipation, the presence of television cameras, etc., should have made clear, I really was at a rock concert rather than a mere academic meeting.[4]

Surely, Parker's rather exaggerated warnings against the temptation of being "sucked in" by the Žižek-phenomenon, his concern to introduce a kind of prophylaxis between the would-be reader and her text all respond to something like "Žižek Rocks." The need for protection – he warns against "getting drawn in" by Žižek's style – shapes the very meaning of "introduce" in Parker's *Critical Introduction*, which comes to mean something like "con-textualize" rather than "understand" (Parker 2004, p. 4). Thus, eschewing the temptation to pursue what Žižek means by interpreting his elusive and manic texts, Parker gives us a series of connected essays noting the choices Žižek has made in relationship to various traditions and interlocutors. "Don't read this at home alone, folks!" is the not-so-subtle message of his book.

But isn't there something odd, something disturbing, about the choice suggested by this frame in a text about Žižek's work? By, that is, the either/ or of those "groupie" graduate students and the dour Parker, playing the traditional father in warning the youth against seduction by the enjoyments of Žižekian dissolution? Why won't Parker *read* Žižek, choosing instead to inoculate readers against him? The extreme set of precautions against seduction that determine Parker's strategy is precisely worked out so as to obscure the one possibility that Parker refuses to entertain – that we might *think through* Žižek without being "converted" by him, that we might remain critical while acknowledging a coherent intellectual project.

Now, of course, I've given away my *own* ambition in *Žižek and Heidegger*, which is to provide the "critical introduction" that Parker (and others) fail to give us and to do so *precisely by refusing the elementary gesture of introduction*. However, my primary motivation in presenting Parker's book as a response to those students is to meditate briefly on the *attitude* underlying such an approach. Philosophers have *always been* seducers, always presented a pied-piper's tune with the potential to lead the "youth" off of the straight and narrow and leaving them with nothing in the end. In this, Žižek's work is no different than Socrates' was. So, what for Parker makes Žižek so particularly dangerous? Here we should depart from what he would "say" and pay atten-tion to what his book *does* – which is primarily to reveal a basic anxiety about the possibility of uncovering any *truth* when faced with Žižek's dazzling the-ory. Today – such is Parker's secret *suspicion* revealed in his hesitation to read Žižek – there really *is* no possibility of critique, just a series of exchange-able "viewpoints" shored up with more or less strong rhetoric (and Žižek is nothing if not a great rhetorician). In other words, "Žižek Rocks!" and "Don't Read Žižek!" actually express the same philosophical position – one which secretly rejects the possibility of genuine *criticism*. Either one is drawn in . . . or not. We are back with those dangerous Sophists and their worried Athenian parents.

In other words, any "debate" between Parker and the groupies *presupposes* something like a shared *cynical* universe, a universe constituted precisely as an infinite and homogeneous field of exchangeable "viewpoints." And, moreover, it presupposes a strange, unacknowledged knowledge *of* that uni-verse, of its basic structures, sufficient to fuel at least an anxiety that truth will never "out." Žižek speaks of this secret knowledge both as the Spinozis-tistic "wisdom" "*sub specie aeternitatis*" (Žižek 2003, p. 217) and the hidden truth of the pseudo-Buddhist "New Age." In either case, though, we have a position of extreme presumption – one which implicitly declares the very structure of reality – masquerading as *humility*. To understand this, picture a situation familiar to every contemporary philosophy professor, where a student proudly ends all debate by claiming that "it's true, if it's true for you." Beyond the logical problems which philosophers delight in discovering in such assertions, the really annoying (and revealing) thing about them is the way that, behind a mask of subjective humility (how can I know the truth of other minds? etc., etc.), they really amount to a complete construction of a solipsistic universe, a universe without *universality* and thus without the possibility of criticism. Or, to put it differently, what that student with his moral relativism is really doing is asserting a kind of power play, breaking off the possibility of any meaningful discussion with her/him. To combine these ways of explaining "it's true if it's true for you" is to see that the "wisdom" of the cynical universe *is* an assertion of power.

Thus a startling accusation against Žižek's critics (which is, of course, a *Žižekian* accusation): the *apparently* humble position is not the one that is genuinely so. Žižek's position (and *my* position as a "philosophical" reader of Žižek) doesn't lie in the apparently chutzpahdic assertion that he/I/has/have the "Truth" *a la* Plato. Or, to be more precise, what's in question here is an effort to rethink the stakes as they were in such assertions of philosophical insight. Rather than being Faustian assertions of power, Žižek's truth comes about as an *evasion* of the genuine hubris involved in cynicism, of the "wisdom" of asserting that "there is no truth." Staking a philosophical claim amounts to a dialectical negation of the cynic's world. That's why Žižek writes that "Lacan accepts the 'deconstructionist' motif of radical contingency, but turns this motif against itself, using it to assert his commitment to Truth as *contingent.*" And that's why, too, Žižek's writing is so easily distinguishable from that of his "post-structuralist" predecessors, like Derrida, in its *assertiveness*:

> I believe in clear-cut positions. I think that the most arrogant position is this apparent multidisciplinary modesty of 'what I am saying now is not unconditional, it is just a hypothesis,' and so on. It really is a most arrogant position. I think that the only way to be honest and to expose yourself to criticism is to state clearly and dogmatically where you are. You must take the risk and have a position. (Žižek and Daly 2004, p. 45)

The very concern for the finitude of the human being which leads to a rejection of "philosophical" assertions of truth turns out to demand, in fact, a deeper embrace of philosophy, a challenge to the common sophism of today's postmodern critics. But how to think in a fashion that is *genuinely* humble, that genuinely evades an inauthentic hubris? Obviously, if every-day attitudes entail such vain pride every bit as much as does Platonism, then what is demanded is a deeper reflection on possibilities for honest commitment to finitude. And that's exactly what Žižek's work, in its broad-est scope, sets out to do. That's what, according to my reading, Žižek's work is "about."

Reading Žižek(,) reading Heidegger

Žižek and Heidegger begins with precisely the demands of finitude and from the site where Žižek historically learned to raise the question as to the extent and nature of those demands. In tracing his biography back to his years as a Heideggerian in Tito-era Yugoslavia, one begins to glimpse also the ori-gins of the concerns that animate his work after his admittedly radical later transformation in Paris with Lacan's designated "successor," Jacques-Alain Miller. In particular, one sees the emergence of precisely *this* question: what are the *genuine* demands of a philosophy of finitude? How can we live our lives in a way that acknowledges the limits of human experience and, espe-cially, of knowledge? More than a mere exercise in historical reconstruc-tion, such a starting point in examining Žižek corresponds with his own most extensive efforts to outline his project as a philosophical one. That is, to the extent that Žižek *is* a philosopher, he himself would insist that we begin from the question of finitude in understanding his work.[5] And, more than that, we must start out from Žižek's relationship to Heidegger, a thinker to whom he refers as "connecting" all serious contemporary philos-ophers; for, "almost every other orientation of any serious weight defines itself through some sort of critical relation or distance towards Heidegger" (Žižek and Daly 2004, p. 28).

Thus, commencing with a consideration of Heidegger as philosopher of finitude and examining Žižek's immanent critique of the early Heidegger, the opening chapter of this book sets out from its wager on a philosophical Žižek down the Heideggerian path. Starting from the most important Heideggerian text of the 1920s, *Being and Time*, I reconstruct Žižek's Heidegger – his demand for a way of acting in and seeing the world answer-ing to finitude – as well his challenge to Heidegger. To begin with the credit Žižek feels that he owes Heidegger, we must note the odd, almost unspoken acknowledgement of the modern world implicit in the "pre-turn" Heidegger. With "finitude," we're not simply dealing with the Medieval theme – the need for humility before God, the equation of human self-assertion with "pride" and original sin, etc. Surely enough, something of this attitude survives in Heidegger and reemerges as dominant in calls for "*Gelassenheit*," etc. in the later work. However, the insight underlying the theme of finitude in *Being and Time* and other work from the late 1920s and early 1930s is that what seems a mere *epistemological* limitation in such medievalism, is, in fact, an ontological truth: if finitude first tells us that *we*, finite mortals, cannot have the kind of knowledge of reality that we attribute to an omniscient observer, then the Heidegger of this period insists that we conceive this as a limitation of *reality itself*. The real world is the kind of thing that structurally disallows *any* such knowledge. In other words, God is dead: there is no external or eternal order to be known.

Now, Žižek seconds Heidegger precisely up to this "ontological" completion of a finitude that initially seems a merely epistemological insight; but the two diverge in their understanding of what such a completion implies – what ethical attitude and what political stance follows from it. If there *is not* a measure for our lives, what does that mean for how we should live? It is in answering that question that the "master" and his "disciple" differ radically.

Allow me a self-reflexive trick in order to explain just *how* Heidegger and Žižek diverge in the way they respond to finitude: let's take, as a kind of laboratory experiment from which we might obtain a picture of their differing *ethoi*, the concrete manner in which each thinker approaches the task of *reading another "master" philosopher*. My justification for starting from such a point is, first of all, that the very task of dealing with another major philosopher forces the thinker of finitude into a methodological bind. Precisely what defines a text of Hegel or Thomas Aquinas is its ability to produce a *demand* on the reader to "make sense" of its insight: we know that Aristotle had an important way of understanding reality, so that any inability on our part to put a finger on that meaning indicates *our* failure to measure up to the text. Of course, implicit in that demand is the assumption that the text *does* make sense – the assumption of what Žižek calls "the position of the Last Judgment" – and that the interpreter's obligation is to struggle toward its meaning. As he puts it in an essay on Maximilian Robespierre, we are beholden to "the idea that somewhere – even if as a thoroughly virtual point of reference, even if we concede that we cannot occupy its place and pass the actual judgment – there must be a standard which allows us to take the measure of our acts and pronounce their 'true meaning'" (Žižek and Robespierre 2007, p. xxiv). Every philosophy student must be familiar with the psychology of "humility" and guilt with which we typically face theoretical "masterpieces."[6]

The problem for *both* Heidegger and Žižek is that *finitude* directly contradicts such a hermeneutic attitude and thus invalidates the task it sets. The key to this conclusion is that the "perspective of the Last Judgment" is *false*, that "there is no Other," no position corresponding to the illusion created by the master-philosopher's text (Žižek and Robespierre 2007, p. xxiv).

To return to the question of how Žižek diverges from Heidegger, we might compare the way that they deal with the concrete interpretive task of facing off against the texts of another "master." Now, of course, as I've already implied above, the starting point here is held in common between the two of them – which is, namely, the need to reject any slavish rehashing of another thinker's arguments and insights. For a philosopher to interpret a serious philosophical work is precisely *not* to re-present it, to give us a mere *exposition* of what it says. In a famous essay on Nietzsche ("The Word of Nietzsche: 'God is Dead'" [1943]), Heidegger insists on the necessity that any genuine interpretation of an important philosophical text must "give to the text something out of its own substance," a practice which "the layman," comparing the new interpretation to "what he holds to be the content" judges to be "an arbitrary imposition" (Heidegger 1977a, p. 58). Žižek, in a recent confrontation with the work of Gilles Deleuze (*Organs without Bodies*), similarly suggests in his introduction that there can be no "dialogue" between philosophers – a fact that he further elucidates as the necessity that philosophers "misunderstand" one another. Because each philosopher's work is only (in Žižek's paraphrase of Alain Badiou) a "consequent deployment of a fundamental insight" a genuine philosophical "encounter" will always involve the translation of the axioms from another thinker onto the ground of one's *own* insight (Žižek 2004a, p. ix).

But, starting from this common ground between Heidegger and Žižek, we can also catch sight of the abyss separating them. If both take the task of finitude to necessitate using a "violent" hermeneutics, the nevertheless significant differences between the way that Heidegger reads Nietzsche and Žižek reads Deleuze are telling. Let's begin from Heidegger's Nietzsche interpretation, whose very violence Heidegger immediately softens; he admits that "a right elucidation never understands the text better than the author understood it" but still justifies approaching Nietzsche at all (given this limitation) by explaining that his hope is "to touch upon the Same [*das Selbe*] toward which the elucidated text is thinking" (Heidegger 1977a, p. 58).

The notable thing about these last interpretive gestures is the way that they seem to readmit the very perspective of the "Last Judgment," which

Heidegger and Žižek had agreed to be wrong. This is the case, even though, in claiming to be working from "the sphere of the one experience from out of which *Being and Time* is thought" – a "sphere of experience" which would seem to forbid treating Nietzsche's work as *whole* at all – Heidegger implicitly confirms finitude (Heidegger 1977a, p. 56). That is, Heidegger's defense of his Nietzsche-interpretation takes a problematic turn by reinstating the ideality of the text's meaning: Nietzsche and Heidegger may not be saying the same thing, but both *are saying something*, both texts *have* a meaning, and it is this, I take it, that constitutes the "Same" allowing interpretive "dialogue" between them. If nothing else, they share a *structure* of meaning – precisely insofar as each text demands to be read in terms of that hidden "treasure" demanding the reader's interpretive labor.

Heidegger slants everything, in other words, so as to *defuse* the violence of his confrontation with another thinker, to reinstate an ethic of humility before, or at least circumspection about, Nietzsche's text. But isn't Heidegger's language here revealing in reinjecting an attitude of "openness to the other?" In order to push back against the implicit charge of intellectual hubris, Heidegger reinstates precisely the one thing that finitude forbids – the totality of the meaning system in the text. A fatal step, then, and one whose repercussions are both immediate ("the Same" turns out to be the implicit totality of the history of metaphysics which thus snares Nietzsche even in his anti-platonism, thus producing the infamous picture of the "last metaphysician") and far-reaching; we have an anticipation of Heidegger's ethical attitude after the war, of, that is, the "path" that will take Heidegger through the "Question Concerning Technology" and to "Letting Be" (*"Gelassenheit"*). In every case, Heidegger only continues his "strong" interpretation ("the path of thinking") while all-the-while advocating an end to the violent erasure of alterity in Western metaphysics.

In contrast, Žižek's approach to Deleuze in *Organs without Bodies* is unapologetically violent. Indeed, strangely, the *model* for Žižek's philosophical misreading of a philosopher is Deleuze himself who, in an interview from *Negotiations*, characterizes such an interpretive encounter as "buggery." His tendency is

> [t]o see the history of philosophy as a sort of buggery or (it comes to the same thing) immaculate conception. I saw myself as taking an author from behind and giving him a child that would be his own offspring, yet monstrous. It really was important for it to be his own child, because the author had to actually say all I had him saying. But the child was bound to be monstrous too, because it resulted from all sorts of shifting, dislocations,

and hidden emissions that I really enjoyed. (Deleuze 1995, p. 6/ Quoted in Žižek 2004a, p. 46)

So enthusiastic is Žižek for Deleuze's idea of "philosophical buggery" that he brings his critique of him to a head by proposing his own theater piece, a dramatization he calls "taking Deleuze from behind with Hegel."[7] Beyond the comedy of this scene – a matter to which I will return – we should be struck by Žižek's peculiar fidelity to finitude at precisely the site where Heidegger retreats from it.

I refer here not only to Žižek's gleeful celebration of textual violence but, more importantly, to the presence of *Hegel* here – a presence calculated to underscore the impossible openness of Deleuze's thought. That is, Žižek introduces Hegel as a sort of Deleuzian repressed: of all the "bad" philosophers in the canon (Plato, Descartes, Kant, Hegel), Deleuze is able himself to re-appropriate the thinking of every one – to find some redeeming point of intersection with their work – *except* Hegel (Žižek 2004a, p. 46). First of all, this means that Hegel marks a kind of "constitutive exception" to Deleuze's thought, the figure he *must* exclude in order to maintain his polemical opposition to all totalizing, universalizing inattention to virtual multiplicities, etc. However, Žižek's point is also and importantly that Hegel is far more *intimate* to Deleuze than such a figure of exceptionality would indicate – an intimacy that, so Žižek, would make any "cohabitation" of the two into a kind of "incest" (Žižek 2004a, p. 49).

For example, Deleuze's most famous "anti-Hegelianism" comes in his rejection of negativity, his "Spinozist" assertion of pure positivity. In Deleuze's polemic "Hegelian negativity is precisely the way to subordinate difference to Identity, to reduce it to a sublated moment of identity's self-mediation" (Žižek 2004a, p. 52). Žižek, on the contrary, proposes that it is precisely the threat that such is *not* the case which leads to Hegel's repression. Deleuze's pure positivity constantly divides and complicates itself. The properly Deleuzian "monster" is thus a negativity which functions in the same way. That is, "what remains unthinkable for Deleuze is simply a negativity that is *not* just a detour on the path of the One's self-mediation," and *that* is precisely what Hegel, so Žižek, does – "the unheard of 'positivization' of negativity itself" (Žižek 2004a p. 52).

In the non-dialogue between Žižek and Deleuze, Žižek attempts to rip open Deleuze's thought *precisely at the point* ("Hegel") where he, famous advocate of a non-totalizable, Nietzschean "pure becoming," seems to retreat to a finite and closed polemical meaning. Žižek forces Deleuze to be more Deleuzian than he wants to be. Here we have a "hermeneutics of finitude" with a vengeance, an interpretive operation designed to insist upon the incompleteness of a symbolic field which otherwise would present itself as closed.

This difference between the freedom of Žižek's exuberant "taking Deleuze from behind" and Heidegger's shameful and apologetic "rape" of Nietzsche bears witness; I would claim, to precisely the "ethos" of finitude to which Žižek aspires and from which Heidegger retreats. Not only does Žižek demand that we give up on all "piety," all guilt and submission to an onto-logical totality which we only imagine, he also does so in a manner which is both open and even funny! Indeed, as we will see when we turn to Žižek's critique of Heidegger in the first chapter of *Žižek and Heidegger*, the voice of finitude is *not* the anguished cry of Dasein facing its "being-toward-death" in anxious honesty: instead, we face our finitude, so Žižek, when we shrug off the guilt and anxiety which can only emerge when we take being as a whole. Nor is the subject of finitude closeted in narcissistic solitude: if we are to believe Žižek, there's a great deal of "buggering" going on, a great deal of, admittedly weird, sociality happening. Weird, yes, but also, in an odd sense, public and open – a coupling whose "monstrous" offspring becomes the subject of ongoing debate and discussion. In any case, Žižek pulls Heidegger away from his Swabian solitude and demands that he take a joke.

Let me take the question of interpreting a philosopher further, applying it to *my* reading of Žižek. *Žižek and Heidegger* is an *essay* on Žižek's thought, my effort to make sense of Žižek from the horizon of my *own thought* – which means, of course, that it raises all those questions about what precisely such a "making sense" implies, the very ones with which we've just been strug-gling. We might start in addressing those issues again by distinguishing my effort to write an "essay" on Žižek from either that slew of "introductions" to Žižek from which I began or, on the other hand, from the systematic scholarship of Adrian Johnston, whose *Žižek's Ontology* provides a deep and thorough interpretation of Žižek's philosophical position in relationship to the history of German thought (see, Johnston 2008). My own engage-ment with Žižek is both more modest but also more presumptuous than Johnston's – since my starting point (finitude) necessitates, as we've had ample opportunity to see, following Žižek himself in eschewing any herme-neutical measure based on completeness. No, this essay is just that, a try or attempt – the fruit of years of struggle with Žižek's writing whose success or failure must lie in whether or not it actually manages to say something about Žižek, to make some sense of his dense writing in the terms by which I myself understand the world.

But wait! Haven't I just written above that Žižek's radical hermeneutics of finitude argues precisely against the kind of "humility" I've just posited for myself – showing it actually to betray my cause? How can I claim to "make sense" of Žižek when it is precisely the question of a "sense" to be made that haunts my footsteps?

In answer to these questions, let me suggest that Žižek is not honest, or at least not *completely* honest in describing his relationship to Deleuze. Perhaps, the best way to put this would be simply to say that *Organs without Bodies* is (despite the negativity of its reception by Deleuzians) a *good* interpretation of Deleuze, a much more compelling interpretation than Žižek lets on. Indeed, what he accomplishes in his Deleuze book – a reading which takes certain aspects of the Deleuzian project and pits them against the "Spinozist" Deleuze who collaborated with Guattari and whose political project has inspired a movement within political theory – is compelling *both* in itself and in the access that it gives us to certain texts of Deleuze.

Which is just to suggest that Žižek himself may owe more to the kind of interpretation we found in Heidegger's Nietzsche than he lets on, an interpretation which, admitting the "sense" of the text, tries to find it or to find its equivalent within the thinker's own thought. Given that Žižek writes about Deleuze from an irreducibly hostile Lacanian perspective, it's not only the failure of any "dialogue" that should strike us in *Organs without Bodies*, it's also manner in which his elucidation of Deleuze indicates a fertile "Same" *shared with* Deleuze. And once we admit this, two additional observations force their way on us: first, we must note again Žižek's disdain for post-structuralism with its refusal to "say just what it means." Žižek's embrace of a critical discourse based on the Hegelian-Marxist tradition is precisely a resistance to our direction when we choose only to avoid the "closure" of meaning. The name, "Derrida" stands in Žižek's writing for the problematic I'm indicating here. Secondly, and consistent with Žižek's desire to avoid all post-structuralist affectation, we must recall that one of the great pleasures in reading his texts is the lucidity they bring to their subject matter – the way that Žižek helps us to understand what Marx *really* meant by "dialectical materialism" or Heidegger by "anticipatory resoluteness." However problematically isolated these passages within an otherwise overwhelming *oeuvre*, Žižek himself knows them to be vital, his *invitation* to read his work. Žižek "hooks" his readers (or auditors) in the moment when they realize that he has just, in three sentences, opened up their understanding of Lacan in a way that nobody else can.

All of this leaves us without the firm methodological directive that we had hoped to find in finitude. But it also suggests another principle, one anchored not in what Žižek *says* about how we should engage in philosophical interpretation but rather in what he *does* – a distinction that is, as I've already hinted, essential to his own critique of ideology.[8] Isn't the real key to understanding Žižek the *irresolvable tension* between what I've called the "Heideggerian" and the "Žižekian" hermeneutics – between an approach which assumes the text to be closed and thus to contain an interpretable meaning and another approach which insists on the impossibility of such closure? Indeed, we might almost speak of a generative battle between these two impulses in the unfolding of Žižek's discourse.

If I'm right about that, then perhaps the reader will forgive my "exegetical" moment in *Žižek and Heidegger,* as well as the way that I stretch it onto the framework of my own violence toward Žižek, my own "philosophical buggery." In hopes of winning such forgiveness, let me remark about my theme, the odd relationship "Žižek/Heidegger," that, even where the story in my book doesn't explicitly concern Heidegger, precisely in the necessity for an irreducible moment of textual "humility," Heidegger is always there. He remains, indeed, in my unwillingness to accept Žižek's efforts to smooth over his debts to Heidegger, to the past, to the closure of meaning. The reader can find Heidegger in the ultimate victory of paradox and even aporia in "my" Žižek.

Acknowledgements

This project has been several years in the making, though I would trace its inception to the 2000 session of the International Philosophical Seminar, a meeting devoted to Žižek's *The Ticklish Subject*. My thanks to Dr. Hugh Silverman for his invitation to participate in that, the venue which led to *Žižek and Heidegger*. A semester spent with the Circle for Lacanian Ideology Critique at the Jan van Eyck Academie in Maastricht, The Netherlands, was extraordinarily helpful in completing *Žižek and Heidegger: The Question Concerning Techno-Capitalism*. In addition to William Day, Chair of the Philosophy Department, and Linda LeMura, Academic Vice-President and Provost at Le Moyne College, who facilitated my sabbatical application, let me thank Marc De Kesel and Dominiek Hoens as well as the rest of the administration of the JvE for making my residency possible. The members of the Lacanian group at the JvE provided useful criticism as well as personal support. I should mention in particular Sigi Jõttkandt, Dominiek Hoens, Ozren Pupovac, Jillian St. Jacques and Bruno Besana – all of whom helped materially in the final formation of the manuscript. Thanks, also, to Edward Casey and Gail Hamner for their support and encouragement of the project. I am particularly grateful to two colleagues who provided valuable responses to parts of *Žižek and Heidegger* – Richard Boothby of Loyola College in Baltimore and Adrian Johnston of The University of New Mexico. Finally, let me thank Caila Hilbert and Monica Sondej, who provided invaluable administrative support.

Parts of this manuscript appeared previously. I am grateful to the following journals for permission to reprint the following:

Some material from Chapter 1 appeared in *Continental Philosophy Review*. (Vol. 41, no. 4) under the title, "Laughing at Finitude: Slavoj Žižek reads *Being and Time*."

Parts of Chapter 3 appeared in *S: Journal of the Jan van Eyck Circle for Lacanian Ideology Critique*. Vol 1., no. 1.

Excerpts from Chapter 6 appeared in *Contemporary Political Theory*. Vol. 6, Issue 3, in an article entitled, "Polemical Ambivalence: Modernity and Utopia in Žižek's *The Puppet and the Dwarf*."

Chapter 3 of *Žižek and Heidegger* contains several diagrams adapted from Hubert Damisch's *The Origin of Perspective*. My thanks to MIT Press for permission to reprint figures 6, 16 and 17 from that text. Thanks, also, to the Biblioteque National de France for permission to use their copy of the image of "Les Perspecteurs" engraved by Abraham Bosse.

Part I

Žižek and Heidegger: the alpha and the omega

Chapter 1

Thinking, finitely: Žižek on Heidegger on finitude

One might define the distinctive quality of late nineteenth and twentieth-century European thought with the term "philosophy of finitude," meaning by that something like the effort to think the human situation without reference to a Platonic viewpoint from and for which human life is to be lived. As a project, such a philosophy also aims to allow not only a more honest individual life but more open relationships between individuals and between the individual and society – relationships not shaped by metaphysically imposed expectations and imperatives. As Žižek puts it in *The Parallax View*, echoing more than a century of Continental thought, "there is no transhistorical absolute knowledge" (Žižek 2006b, p. 274). And the task of philosophy must be to help us live with and in the situation constituted by this insight. Seen thus, existential and phenomenological traditions would share a commitment to a radical historicity, perhaps best announced, as Heidegger himself pointed out, in the famous slogan of Nietzsche, "God is Dead." Neither history nor any other dimension of human existence affords us – or anyone else – the possibility of dispensing with immersion in the midst of things. No viewpoint from "nowhere." No eternal verities. Finitude.[1] Though in theory it cuts equally against premodern, "cosmological" philosophy, the commitment to finitude arises largely as a rebellion against the hubris of modern philosophy and science, a rejection of the *abstraction* of modern life. With finitude must be inscribed the impossibility of self-transparency *á la* Descartes, the necessity of a constitutive blindness at the level of the conditions allowing us to live in a meaningful world.

Now, the Heideggerian provenance of Žižek's work has often been noted, though, for all of its currency, the significance of the younger Žižek's discipleship to the Yugoslav Heidegger school has occasioned little real reflection.[2] With finitude, however, we can specify the aspect of Heidegger's thought which earns him the position for Žižek as the "unavoidable" reference point of all contemporary philosophy (see, Žižek and Daly 2004, p. 28).

Of course, Heidegger is not the only significant "existential" thinker, the only thinker to thus thematize finitude, and we must acknowledge the presence of both Kierkegaard and Sartre as influences on Žižek. In some ways, as we will see, Kierkegaard's notion of a "leap of faith" draws him closer to Žižek's emphasis on the "act," than to Heidegger; while Sartre's negative subject – his maintenance of an Hegelian perspective on human life – is certainly more Žižekean than is Heidegger's "Being in the World." [3] Nonetheless, Žižek's struggle about finitude is, both historically and textually, primarily a struggle *with* the Heidegger of *Being and Time*; and, for this reason it's important to follow out this relationship.[4]

Being and Time and modernity: the insight

The first step here must be to recall the way that the Heidegger of *Being and Time* underscores the finitist theme – which is, namely, through the existential thematic of "thrownness" ("*Geworfenheit*") and related concepts. We find our finitude in experiences where we are overwhelmed by our situatedness, where we find it impossible to scrabble up beyond the way that our situation shapes us. As Žižek puts it, "A human being is always on the way toward itself, in becoming, thwarted, thrown-into a situation, primordially "passive," receptive, attuned, exposed to an overwhelming Thing" (Žižek 2006b, p. 273). But, of course, this seems to be an experience of limitation or determination. Thus, it's essential from the outset to understand that Žižek refuses to limit *his* Heidegger to such a "negative" dimension of experience. As Žižek puts it, "Heidegger's greatest single achievement is the full elaboration of *finitude* as a positive constituent of being-human" (Žižek 2006b, p. 273). In what sense, "positive"?

In *The Parallax View*, Žižek suggests this "positive" side through a contrast between Heidegger's *Being and Time* and *The Discourse on Method* of Descartes. In Chapter 3 of that latter text, Descartes proposes a kind of "provisory morality" to help him live while he entertains radical doubts about the foundations of his thought. He will simply follow the modes and customs of his country and will act according to those rules in a consistent and persistent manner, "imitating in this the example of travelers who, when they have lost their way in a forest, ought not to wander from side to side, far less remain in one place, but proceed constantly towards the same side in as straight a line as possible" (Quoted, Žižek 2006b, p. 274.)

While, as we will see, Heidegger, will himself fail to live up to this insight, Žižek's interpretation of the implicit ethics of finitude opposes it to

Descartes' view. Heidegger's most direct answer to thrownness, "anticipatory resoluteness," (in Section 62) shares an apparently "provisory" status with Descartes' morality for the doubter, but it also differs essentially. Recall that Heidegger proposes in *Being and Time* that we should make an ungrounded, abyssal decision to live resolutely. For Heidegger, to "decide" without guarantees (based on resolute thrownness) is not simply to "make do" with what we're given (the impossibility of knowing the way things "really are"), as it still is for Descartes. Rather, as Heidegger writes, resoluteness creates the "situation" in which Dasein is ("The situation is only through resoluteness and in it.") (Heidegger 1962, H. 300/J&M, p. 346). Furthermore, such resoluteness also produces a primordial self-understanding: "Dasein is brought face to face with its own uncanniness," its irreducibility to any substantive identity that might later be disclosed for it (Heidegger 1962, H. 296/J&M, p. 342).

Following Žižek's interpretation, we might say that, in so deciding, I take the "as though" in "I act as though" and make it into my reality. I "assume" an incomplete reality not just in the way that a *reductio* argument assumes a conclusion but also in the way that a leader "assumes" her post. Everything that I do from that time forward is based upon that assumption – to the extent that we can't really imagine the possible context in which we might reverse it. Unlike Descartes' doubter, the subject of anticipatory resoluteness makes a commitment.

As Žižek sees it, that commitment is to the idea that the condition demanding resoluteness is the way things really are – that is, that there is no order to the cosmos, that the universe is essentially and inherently incomplete and without a totalizing position from which one could make sense of it. It is a resolution, as Heidegger himself puts it, that Dasein "gives itself the current factical situation," that "the situation cannot be calculated in advance or presented like something present-at-hand which is waiting for someone to grasp it." Or, as Heidegger claims, that resoluteness is a form of "holding oneself free."[5] In other words, for Descartes, "provisory" morality amounts to a *skepsis*, a doubt about the way things are; however, for Heidegger, the "resoluteness" of the one deciding itself amounts to an insight about the constitution of reality.

It's not exactly a factual knowledge, however, that this Heideggerian disciple of "anticipatory resoluteness" enjoys; for, the only fact to which someone who "takes responsibility for" the need to act answers is that *I don't know* the ultimate nature of reality. On the other hand, when I take responsibility for my life, I embrace its groundlessness. In resoluteness, I don't calculate about actuality and, thus, Dasein in such an attitude is as far as can be from "risk assessment." Quite the contrary, in "betting" that I will never discover a justifying framework for life, I also *decide* such meaninglessness *must* characterize reality itself and so determine it as such. More profoundly, the content of that transcendental "what must be the case" is that the universe is not simply without meaning but incomplete, lacking ultimate order and closure.

For Žižek, Heidegger's philosophy of finitude is thus a kind of transcendental articulation of the conditions of possibility for a being without support in a cosmos. As Žižek puts it in *The Parallax View*, Heidegger here "accomplishe(s) the Kantian philosophical revolution, making it clear that finitude is the key to the transcendental dimension" (Žižek 2006b, p. 273). For Žižek, when Heidegger writes of "fundamental ontology" he means, at least in the first instance, not a science of Being as a whole but rather a kind of science of the non-existence of the Other – of any "perspective" from which Being can be adequately conceived (in the manner that metaphysics conceives it) as a totality.

It's worth following Žižek's argument here in a bit more detail, something we can do if we ask about the relationship between fundamental ontology and "world disclosure." Recall Heidegger's famous thesis on truth, already announced in Section 44 of *Being and Time*, according to which "truth" is derived from the Greek word, *a-lethia*. Heidegger, of course, reads the "a" as privative and suggests that we hear an echo of "Lethe" (the river of concealment) in it. Thus, for Heidegger, truth is "un-concealment," a horizonal or world-disclosure which always contains its limit or opposite (the "un") with it. Dasein is always "in the untruth" just to the extent that it is also "in the truth" (Heidegger 1962, Section 44). This transcendental limit to our access to truth translates finitude into the dimension of world-disclosure.

Still, if we leave it at that, Žižek suggests in a recent article, we haven't yet understood the full Heideggerian bond between finitude and truth. Certainly, we can say that un-concealedness only exists alongside inauthenticity, our failure to inquire about or be alive to the truth of the world in which we live. "Proximally and for the most part," Dasein just ignores the possibilities for truth in its self-understanding, preferring instead the comfort and simplicity of the "They-world," and even at times forgetting that it has forgotten anything in so doing. Or, in Žižek's example, we might take the decay of Greek thought under the Sophists, a situation under which "confrontation with the very foundation of our Being turns into a trifling play with different lines of argumentation with no inherent relation to Truth" (Žižek 2007, p. 21).

The stakes in such a departure from truth, however, remain merely skeptical; for the structure of such a debased philosophy suggests that there *is* a truth, a structuration of Being adequate to Dasein's *authentic* understanding (see, Heidegger 1962, H. 221/p. 264). Dasein's "untruth" lies simply in having ignored the transcendent disclosure of its world: we just "don't know" what this truth is. The insufficiency of such a view to Heidegger's intention emerges if we ask ourselves about the foundation of his certainty *that* we are "in the untruth." Isn't it, insofar as we assume that we might authentically pay attention to our un-concealment, possible by definition that Dasein *could* attain to the truth of its world? Why *should* Dasein be primordially "in the untruth"?

Žižek argues, in answer to these questions, that Heidegger's insight about the disclosure of Being also contains another meaning, and a meaning, indeed, necessitated by his insight about finitude. The limitation of unconcealment doesn't *only* emerge when we fail to inquire after the truth of our world: quite the contrary, alongside such failure, Heidegger persistently finds another kind, a failure or "untruth" linked to precisely those moments in which Dasein *is* attuned to truth. Here, the "concealment" at the "heart of unconcealment" emerges precisely in the way that a world only exists insofar as *we* produce it in our very "way of seeing."[6] Even when we are attuned to our world, we miss *our* contribution to the constitution of worldhood. The world is "not" at least at one point, at the point *for which* it appears. Or, to use a language more in tune with Heidegger's, with worldhood comes necessarily the danger of "falling" implicit when we pay attention to "the world" and ignore our own Dasein (Heidegger 1962, H. 221–222/p. 264). That is, the "concealment" here lies in the way questions of truth already are filtered through the "pair of glasses" actively producing our world-horizon. Or, to put this in another way, such an horizon is not only transcendent, organizing Being into a totality to which we lack access but, rather, at the same time is also an "immanent horizon of this disclosure itself, invisible on account of its excessive self-evidence" (Žižek 2007, p. 22).

In other words, to the extent that, as Žižek insists, we must take the grounding of unconcealment in concealment in *both ways*, a sufficient understanding of Heidegger requires that we *also* take Being itself to *lack* truth, to lack another, broader horizon to which one might appeal for the way "things really are." Which means that the ontological horizon doesn't only indicate "something else/more/beyond" Being which organizes it as a whole but also the immanent "finitude" of the world itself, a finitude beyond which there is, literally, "nothing" – only Dasein itself in its subjective nullity (Žižek 2007, p. 22). This site of "concealment" in our unconcealment is precisely the point *from which* we (as Dasein) see the world, an immanent blind spot, and, as Žižek puts it, "the difference between beings/entities and their opening, their horizon of meaning, always also cuts into the field of beings themselves, making it incomplete/finite" (Žižek 2007, p. 22).

While Žižek's emphases in the above argument might strike the reader as unusual, there's nothing about this approach that openly challenges Heideggerian orthodoxy. However, from this starting point, Žižek draws conclusions that cut across the grain of mainstream Heidegger scholarship and even of Heidegger's self-understanding. The most important of these is that, precisely in his commitment to finitude, Heidegger pursues a kind of modernist project. That is, to the extent that modernity is defined by a "disenchantment" of reality, by the challenge to the great premodern and medieval synthesis asserting reality to be a meaningful whole assigning each and every being or act an appropriate "place," any assertion of finitude belongs to the modern project. In taking finitude to be a structure of ontology itself, Heidegger's analysis of Dasein and the ethics of authenticity that accompany such an analysis stand squarely in the modern tradition.

Now, there are good reasons why Heidegger himself would resist the "modernist" label, but there is also one merely semantic issue here that produces the appearance of disagreement where none may exist: and that is, namely, the parochial tendency within academic philosophy to label "modern" that body of philosophy that runs from Descartes through Kant and underlies the cultural movement called the "Enlightenment." While the waters are historically muddied by the intra-philosophical debate between empiricists and rationalists, the modernist project here emerges as something like the ability of the philosopher, given a basic skepticism about the subject's immersion in its world, to offer secure (certain) foundations for knowledge of that world. To label someone a "modernist," within a philosophical context is to suggest that they believe in the possibility of an epistemological foundation. Heidegger explicitly rejects such a project. Indeed, basic to his existential analysis of Dasein, is a rejection of the very picture of the human being as "*res cogitans*" (thinking substance) representing a world of "*res extensa*" (extended substance) for itself.

If there is a "modernist project" in pre-*Kehre* Heidegger, then, it is clearly not *that* modernism but rather a commitment to the doubt and uncertainty that originally elicits efforts at foundation-building from Descartes through the Enlightenment. Perhaps we would best explain Žižek's understanding here by dispensing with the whole, over-freighted language of the "modern" and speaking instead of Žižek's *subjectivist* Heidegger. And, indeed, it's fair to say that what this Heidegger represents is the modern subject as basis for *critique* – a beginning point that Žižek dates back to German philosophy from Kant to Hegel.

What if, Kant asks in the preface to the B edition of *The Critique of Pure Reason*, the failure of philosophy to establish itself as a basis for knowledge lies in the foundational metaphors by which metaphysics seeks to develop a science? What if it is a mistake to treat knowledge as a kind of journey from one "thing" (the subject) to another (the object) – an error that guarantees the end of all philosophical inquiry in skepticism? Whereas, previously, modern philosophers had been stymied by our inability to overcome the limitations created by our consciousness, to escape from "inside" the mind to gain a knowledge of objects "as they really are," Kant turns the tables, demanding that we see the perspectival representation of the object, its "imperfection" for us, as the precondition of objectivity itself. As Žižek puts it in *The Ticklish Subject*, Kant forces us to see that "the preconditions for knowledge are also the preconditions for an object of knowledge" – that when there is knowledge there must also be an object represented for a subject, and that what we therefore mean by "object" is nothing other than this being for a subject (Žižek 1999a, p. 55). In this way, the shift to a consideration of knowledge in terms only of the "perspectival" structure of the subject's representations marks a decisive attack on the very idea of a "meta-physical" or supra-sensible realm necessary to guarantee human existence, a transcendental space of omniscience beyond perspective. As Žižek puts it, the essential thing here is the self-assertion of modernity as a force of radical negativity, dissolving the secure boundaries that previously guaranteed reality to be a whole (Žižek 2003, p. 87). There is no space "in common" between subjectivity and the object because that is not their relationship.

Still, on the other hand, for Žižek Kant necessarily fails to live up to his own revolution, re-ontologizing the conceptual space of objectivity (reality) as both the "in-itself" of epistemology and the noumenal of practical philosophy. In making his "Copernican" turn from "objects" to our "faculty of intuition," Kant reinforces the very metaphor that he overcomes – suggesting a movement "inward," one that puts us firmly back in the *camera obscura* of the mind from which we had hoped to escape. For Žižek, the inevitable "form" of Kantian metaphysical thought operates in the necessity of thinking the "negativity" of the modern subject in opposition to objectivity. That is, metaphysical categories still shape or, even better, haunt Kantian transcendentalism. Even if the object becomes the "object of representation," "reality" remains independent of these perspectival structures, an opaque remainder of wholism.

Rejecting the common interpretation which sees Kant as the thinker who affirms that it is "impossible to conceive of the universe as a Whole" and then sees Hegel as "deploying the last and most ambitious" "ontological" and metaphysical totalization of Being, Žižek turns the tables: for him the problem with Kant is that he remains too committed to an essentially metaphysical project, unable to complete the "Copernican Revolution" in thought for which he calls (Žižek1999a, p. 55).

Hegel, in Žižek's view, completes the modern revolution by attacking this residual whole. He simply repeats the Kantian move with regard to the objects of consciousness/knowledge by applying it to reality itself: "what if," asks Žižek's Hegel, we double Kant's insight that "the conditions of possibility of our knowledge are at the same time the conditions of possibility of the object of our knowledge," by positing that "the limitation of our knowledge (its failure to grasp the whole of Being . . .) is simultaneously the limitation of the very object of our knowledge." Or, in other words, "the gaps and voids in our knowledge of reality are simultaneously the gaps and voids in the 'real' ontological edifice" and, therefore, "the insufficiency of this knowledge with regard to reality signals the more radical insufficiency of reality itself" (Žižek 1999a, p. 55).

Oddly enough, by Žižek's reading of him, the Heidegger of "anticipatory resoluteness" would amount to a radical modernist in the Hegelian mold, one who would insist upon translating the epistemology of finitude back onto the reality before which we admit our limitations. In other words, it is no accident that Heidegger's version of the ethics of finitude here demands an implicit assertion of reality's nature rather than simply an admission of our limitations in knowing reality. To live finitely is to assert oneself about the world in which we live, or, at least, to commit oneself to the world's incompletion and our freedom in it. It is precisely in this sense that Žižek speaks of Heidegger as "accomplishing" "the Kantian philosophical revolution," with his transcendental analysis of Dasein's finitude, an accomplishment that eluded Kant himself.

Heidegger's retreat

Now, most of Žižek's criticism of *Being and Time* and the work following it through the mid-1930s dwells on the impoverished social and political structure underlying it. But Žižek never fully explains his own path from Heidegger's subjectivism to social and political questions. When pressed to complete the critique of Heidegger's philosophy of finitude, both *The Parallax View* and *The Ticklish Subject* turn immediately to the social and political stakes of Heidegger's thought – the question of Heidegger's Nazism, the possibility of an Heideggerian politics, etc., etc. In other words, Žižek leaves out a step in his argument, and an essential one at that – namely, the explanation of why Heidegger's great social/political "error" doesn't stem from his subjectivism at all and what it does stem from. It's to the task of filling out that unarticulated moment in Žižek that I now turn.

Let me offer what is admittedly a mere "reconstruction" of Žižek's argument, an effort to fill in the missing step.[7] While such a method demands that we strike out a little from what he has explicitly written or said, it will not only allow us to bind Žižek's political critique of Heidegger with his (Žižek's) position on finitude but also help to clarify several cryptic Žižekian statements about the limits of a philosophy of finitude and of *Being and Time*.

While Žižek does a good job of underscoring the radicality of "anticipatory resoluteness," Heidegger's three chapters (at the beginning of Division II) which prepare the way for that concept present more difficulties. This is a key section of *Being and Time*, the part of the book in which Heidegger increasingly concretizes ways in which Dasein might be said to experience its own Being *in toto*. First in the famous analysis of Being-towards-death (resolved into its "authentic" understanding as "anticipation") and then in the discussion of guilt and resoluteness by which he claims to give an experiential pinpoint to such pre-theoretical self-understanding, Heidegger builds his bridge between fundamental ontology and existential philosophy; and it is obvious that, if this bridge fails, so does the basic project of *Being and Time*.

My claim here is that a careful Žižekian examination of these chapters in Heidegger would indicate a misplaced keystone: we might, in fact, use either or both of Chapters 1 and 2, but, for the sake of brevity, I'll stick with the clearer case here, the discussion of existential guilt and resoluteness in the second chapter of Division II. In attempting to connect the existential concepts of Chapter 2 with concrete (existentiell) experiences, Heidegger starts out from the "call of conscience," a call which he reduces to its essence as the existential accusation, "Guilty!" with which Dasein is always faced. Heidegger carefully dissociates this "call" from any specific remorse over deeds or intentions. Indeed, he argues compellingly that existential guilt *underlies* the possibility of the more familiar and everyday "pangs" which we usually associate with the, "call of conscience" (see, Heidegger 1962, H. 281–284/R& M, pp. 327–329).

Whence comes this omnipresent and foundational affect? As Heidegger's analysis reveals, Dasein is guilty in having evaded its "own" voice and thus being seduced by the comforting everydayness of the "They," with its elimination of ambiguity and uncanniness. Thus, for Heidegger, "Dasein itself," though only in its uncanny "nothingness," is the "caller" who breaks up the party of inauthentic definiteness, who challenges our identification with our publicly defined "selves" and their projects (Heidegger, *Being and Time*, H. 276/R&M, 321). The key moment of guilt here is one that happens to us (a "situation" into which we are "thrown") and its force seems to come from the tension between inauthentic "common" understandings and those which are my "own-most" possibilities.[8]

Heidegger characterizes "resoluteness" in the face of such guilt as "wanting to have a conscience," that is, as understanding and aligning one's Dasein with the indefiniteness of "care." While, given the sordidness of the life I have lived by following the "accepted" self- and world- understanding, my guilt will always, in the first instance, take the form of self-accusation, I respond resolutely – authentically – to this raggedness by acknowledging its *inevitability*. And I do *that* by choosing some coherent subset of concrete life projects, understandings and relationships. The "existential" choice here amounts to what I called "commitment" above, a complete investment in, and transformation through the situation in which it occurs. Certainly, we can make sense experientially of why somebody acting resolutely might speak of "finding themselves," but, really, what's at stake is *projecting* or even *producing* a "self." Recall here Žižek's emphasis upon the way that the *commitment* of anticipatory resoluteness attacks any conceptual space (ie., the world, the self) constituting a limit to finitude. To affirm resoluteness is to act in a manner "beyond good and evil" or beyond, in any case, the remorse by which such moral categories of selfhood are enforced. Thus, the chapter on "the call of conscience" gives us a second moment, a "resolution" of guilt, in which authenticity is defined not by the pair "theirs/mine" but rather "determinate/open" and openness is realized through a "determining" act of choice.

In fact, the issue here is, in the final analysis, the role of the authentic "self" itself. Heidegger's concept of "authenticity" has two antecedents: on the one hand, from its introduction in the first chapter of *Being and Time*, the term, "*Eigentlichkeit,*" (authenticity) is associated with "mineness" (*jemeinigkeit*), with, then, an honesty to oneself as "individuated" – even if this "self" must be conceived as irreducibly "worldly" and even insubstantial. On the other hand, Heidegger also associates authenticity with Dasein's ability to *decide* or *choose* (Heidegger 1962, H. 42/J&M, pp. 67–68). To this extent, the issue of authenticity is not so much one of "individuality" versus "group think" (falling, idle chatter, etc., etc.) as it is a kind of "understanding" of its world which frees it from even internal measures of its being. Which is just to affirm Heidegger's own insight that, with such resoluteness, we find an essential *freedom,* a spontaneity.

In the light of this ambiguity, we might say that, Heidegger, unacknowledged, "changes the subject" of his analysis between the Dasein of experience in general and authentic Dasein – moving from a Romantic, "individuated" self to a chosen, created subjectivity. And, in retrospect, doesn't Heidegger's own forced description of the categories in both Chapters 1 and 2 of the second division hint at this shift? Since it is "ready for anxiety," anticipation is no longer *simply* anxious Being-towards-death, a state into which Dasein is *born.* Since it "wants to have a conscience," resoluteness is no longer *simply* the existential "call to conscience" in its traumatic presence ("Guilty!") (see, Heidegger 1962, Section 45). Indeed, one might go so far as to suggest that "anticipatory" Dasein is *no longer* anxious and that her "resolute" doppelganger is *no longer* guilty.

Now, of course, it's important not to exaggerate this division in *Being and Time* between two Daseins. The very convincingness of the image of the "resolute" individual, authentically facing her own death and nullity, forbids such exaggeration. There is, after all, a certain intuitive rightness about the existentialist ethic that largely explains the enduring influence of Heidegger's early book. At a psychological level, nobody would deny that such an individual, as master of anxiety, still experiences something of it. Fortunately, though, a Žižekian understanding of the dialectical relationship between the two subjects of existential analysis allows us to understand this psychology, while also moving beyond it.

Recall that *Being and Time* introduces the concepts of "care" and "Being-towards –death" as figures for, more or less, the "uncanniness" of Dasein's Being – the way that its "existence" is never present-at-hand to it as a mere object for analysis. Now, the value of existential conscience as a moment in Heidegger's thought is that it suggests a concrete dimension in which such uncanniness obtrudes upon our everyday consciousness *without* becoming such an epistemological object.[9] "Uncanniness" isn't missing from the first subject, "guilty" Dasein. As Heidegger is at pains to indicate, the virtue of authenticity is that, in it, Dasein is "in-the-Truth," namely, the truth that is constituted by its own uncanniness all along. However, neither the anxiety of Being-towards-death nor even the "guilty!" of the call of conscience directly thematize this indefiniteness *as* self-understanding. In existential guilt we know our "Selves" in being struck by what we are *not* – our everyday "they" selves with our definite self-understandings and projects. But to know that we are *not* the definite "person" we thought ourselves to be or even *any* such determinate character is not yet to understand ourselves *as* the indefiniteness of care or Being-towards-death. If such Dasein (admittedly, fundamentally inarticulate) were forced to give its self understanding, wouldn't it be something like, "I am *not* what I thought myself to be, nor what others think of me?"

Heidegger himself acknowledges that, while the true *meaning* of conscience is present from the start in the call of conscience, such meaning only *appears* when "the call is rightly understood" and that only happens when we "*hear it authentically*" in "a factical taking-action" (Heidegger 1962, H. 295/ R & M, p. 341.) In other words, we only really "know ourselves" in the moment of practice, the moment of authenticity. We might say that, lacking such a *praxical* response, Dasein remains wedded to a view of itself as that kind of subject tragically opposed to a meaningless world. *From the viewpoint* of the Dasein experiencing "guilty!" there is still a "court of appeal" before which my everyday self is accused: there, I am "call(ed) forth and summon(ed) . . . to being-guilty," forcing me away from my everyday self and world (Heidegger 1962, H. 295/R & M, p. 341).

In other words, I'm suggesting that the shift from the call of conscience to resoluteness mirrors the movement Žižek finds from *Kant to Hegel*, a "parallax shift" from an incomplete to a complete modern dialectic. The only difference in my example from *Being and Time* is that Heidegger does not, indeed *cannot*, acknowledge the shift whose assertion underlies Hegel. Rather than admitting the difference made by the movement *from* a Kantian framework wherein a finite subject faces off against the "noumenal" or the "in-itself" *to* a "finite" Being, Heidegger projects the characteristics of those "Kantian" structures (such as guilt) *onto* the viewpoint of the "authentic" subject – so that, the authentic person exemplifies a kind of dour Germanic individualism in its "reticence," "certainty," etc., etc. In Žižek's words, this side of *Being and Time* models an "ultra-serious heroic confrontation with our destiny" (Žižek 2006b, p. 110). For this reason, it remains unclear whether Heidegger suggests that we should not take the end of a philosophy of finitude to *be* a "tragic" situation in which a humanized subject confronts a "meaningless" universe. But, in any case, Žižek demands that we push our understanding of finitude in another direction. We must move away from the "utter seriousness", the "all-pervasive pathos" of the merely "existential" Heidegger (Žižek 2006b, p. 110).

To describe his differences with Heidegger's classical existentialist philosophy of finitude, Žižek suggests an alternative type of comedy to the classical one: such a comedy depends not upon the symmetrical and harmonious resolution of a potentially tragic situation but rather upon an a-symmetrical doubling of tragedy – upon the "infection" of the subject of annunciation by the negation otherwise reserved for "reality."[10] He reminds us of an old graffito from May 1968 in Paris. Somebody crosses out an original inscription, "God is Dead: Nietzsche," and writes over it, "Nietzsche is dead: God." Now, for Žižek this is not yet the alternative comic dimension and indeed represents the worst kind of ideology; for the implicit result of the joke would be that God is alive and able to have the last word on Nietzsche. Thus, Žižek follows Alenka Zupančič in suggesting that the joke really should have read, "God is Dead. And, as a matter of fact, I don't feel too well, either" (Žižek 2006b, p. 109: see, also, Zupančič 2006, p. 196).

Without this gesture oddly preserving subjectivity in a wavering half-existence, we necessarily "revive" God by maintaining the tragedy of existentialism: either God is dead, so that the tragic hero Nietzsche must suffer, or Nietzsche is dead, proving that he was never anything but a speck of dirt, manipulated by the divine consciousness. Whether we tell the story as the death of God or of Nietzsche the tone is Byronic, outsized, tragic. And isn't this just the symptom that the narrative's purpose is one of reassurance rather than exploration or challenge? In this overly theatrical subject of finitude we find an abandonment of the genuinely finite dimension.

Indeed, as Simon Critchley has pointed out in a series of writings about Lacan – and partially in conversation with Žižek – the virtue of a comic or "humorous" subject is the deflation of such a theatrical, tragic "self." For example, writing of Freud's late essay, "Humor," Critchley embraces the idea that in the humorous, the super-ego "makes the ego itself look tiny and trivial" with the result that "I find myself ridiculous" (Critchley 2007, p. 79). This deflation of the ego precisely allows the world itself to appear as "nothing but a game for children" – essentially incomplete, an appropriate field for the act (Critchley 2007, p. 80, quoting Freud).

It is obvious that reading Žižek is a very different experience than reading Heidegger, a difference which is quite intentional. In a recent interview, Žižek notes his "deep distrust" of the "Heideggerian pathetic style" – a distrust which, he insists, underlies his compulsion to "vulgarize" his own writing, filling it with references to German toilets, sex acts and reality TV (Žižek and Daly 2004, p. 44). My suggestion would be that the stylistic difference between the "anxious" but "resolute" Heideggerian and the oddly "comic" Žižek points to precisely what, in Žižek's analysis, finitude really demands. In other words, we have to pass beyond the "seriousness" of all existential accounts to do justice to the demand inherent to the finite call. Not in heroic quaking before the nullity of death but rather in quietly but systematically kicking away the crutches of everyday existence can we redeem the finiteness of human life. It's a process that even removes the comfort of the tragic self facing the void but which, for all that, reaches more deeply into the "nothing" which Heidegger rightly discovers at the center of human experience than could *Being and Time*.

All of which would explain why Žižek combines repeated *encomia* of Heidegger's philosophy of finitude (as summarized in anticipatory resoluteness) with warnings about its limitations – warnings that extend, indeed, to an imperative that we "resist" any "temptation" to rewrite a "good" *Being and Time* (Žižek 2006b, p. 278). That is, to the extent that the project of *Being and Time* as a whole demands we overlook or minimize the shift in perspective between the existential structures of Dasein's Being and the existentiell stances definitive of its authenticity, it cannot be saved. And such a demand is surely inherent in the very project of grasping the structure of Being as a whole from the pre-reflective experience of Dasein: that is, Heidegger's very project in *Being and Time* demands that he draw a straight line from the pre-reflective dimension of our "thrownness" to authentic understandings of that state.

History and political life: Nazism and will

Now we are finally able to turn to Žižek's criticism of Heidegger's politics and particularly to his shocking *embrace* of Heidegger's apparently Nazi rhetoric, or at least, his willingness to applaud elements of Heidegger's approach in the period where others see only symptoms of his great "error."

But the first step here is to reflect upon the implications of Žižek's Heidegger-critique, as we've constructed it to this point, for understanding the very relationship between individual and society. We might assert now that his warning against "rewriting" *Being and Time* speaks to the foundational limitation Heidegger imposes on any social or political thought – a limitation which returns us to the difference between Žižek's critique and Jonas' or Habermas' condemnation of a "formalistic decisionism" in Heidegger. To see Žižek's point, we might begin from the observation that the movement from guilt to resoluteness takes us from a subject which is necessarily defined by the categories of individuality (my-ownness, for the most part absorbed in the "They," etc., etc.) to one which, in Žižek's take, defies description by such categories. The "decision" of authenticity, redefining reality itself by projecting "that possibility which is essential to Dasein at that time" no longer fits the way that we normally understand individual identity formation. For one thing, such a decision can issue from the socially transformative collective or revolutionary group (see, Žižek 2006b, p. 278).

Let me clarify this: the point is not that resoluteness allows us to substitute a "larger" subject for the individualized Dasein of "the call of conscience." Quite the contrary, the key here is that there is an untranslatable shift of consciousness between the kind of subjectivity which "individuates" in structures like anxiety and guilt and the authentic enactment of these structures – a heterogeneity in continuity which *dissolves* the constituted relationship between individual and society. More specifically, the same movement which forbids *guilt* in the second moment also makes traditional *identity* obsolete: to act resolutely is to leave behind the effort to "find out who I *am*," or to enforce the strictures of social inclusion and exclusion from an identity.[11] We get the breakdown of precisely that distinction between the individual and the social that is conceivable as providing the "content" of individual Dasein's world through traditions.

Here we can see the basis for Žižek's scathing contempt for the discussion of individual and society which Heidegger introduces in Section 74 of *Being and Time*. There, Heidegger does indeed treat the individual's resolute decision as "merely formal," since Dasein's existential possibilities are "not to be gathered from death" (Heidegger 1962, H. 383/J&M, p. 434). In this situation, Heidegger proposes that the *content* of resoluteness derives from "the communal heritage in which Dasein's existence is caught up" (Heidegger 1962, H. 383/J&M, p. 435: Žižek's translation, 2006b, p. 278).

Indeed, Žižek's implicit insight is that the subject-switch producing the resolute individual also subverts the position of the social as providing the "content" of individual Dasein's world through traditions. Quite simply, when Dasein ceases to posit a "self" (against which the shared or common understandings emerge), the social, too, loses its pre-definition and opens up. "We" might do some things together, things that would change the set of possibilities facing "us," but "we" are no longer the "not I" which nonetheless provides the "I's" measure. We have at least the possibility of a new kind of *socius*, the self-producing, self-defining "collective." Indeed, such a collectivist theme, which his theological writing associates with St. Paul's decision to define Christianity as a practical orientation rather than an"identity," is essential to Žižek. Thus, as opposed to Judaism, where the "chosen people" could still conceive itself as a defined religious or even ethnic group, for Pauline Christians;

> "Holy Spirit" designates a new collective held together not by a master signifier, but by fidelity to a Cause, by the effort to draw a new line of separation that runs "beyond Good and Evil," that is to say, that runs across and suspends the distinctions of the existing social body. The key dimension of Paul's gesture is thus his break with any form of communitarianism: his universe is no longer that of the multitude of groups that want to "find their voice," and assert their particular identity but that of a fighting collective grounded in the reference to an unconditional universalism. (Žižek, *Puppet*, 130)

That Heidegger misses this possibility for understanding Dasein's social Being, that he settles instead upon the double inadequacy of "Mitsein" and the picture of traditions as providing the "content" for Dasein's merely "formal" existential decision, explains the broad force of Žižek's various political critiques of Heidegger: Heidegger is constantly retreating from his own insight in *Being and Time* – a retreat that begins *in* that book itself. Indeed, Žižek would ask us to take one further step and consider such retreat as definitive of Heidegger's path. Heidegger retreats *in order to* evade accepting the full "threat" of the "anticipatory resoluteness" he himself projects, *in order to* tame its disruptive force under what I might call a "personalist" ethic of authenticity, an authenticity defined as being "true to oneself." Heidegger is, in Žižek's Lacanian/psychoanalytic understanding, fundamentally an hysteric, someone who protests loudly precisely in order to be sure that nothing changes. In this, we will see, his hesitancy in *Being and Time* anticipates the great political crisis in Heidegger's life which is to follow its publication.

Perhaps the most puzzling but fascinating part of Žižek's Heidegger writing is his derision for most critiques of Heidegger's Nazi period. I've already alluded to the widely accepted interpretation of Heidegger's "error," the one which ties his temptation by Nazism with residual subjectivism. Numerous Heidegger-critics from Karl Löwith through Habermas and Wolin start by observing that it is no accident that the authenticity of Dasein is defined in classic "existentialist" terms; in "transcending" the "idle chat-ter" of *das Man*, in authentic "being-towards-death," as its "own-most possi-bility," Heidegger seems to assert a classically subjectivist *individual* activity defined against a shallow social world. To be authentic is to act without determination by the "They", in an immediate "decision."[12] If the problem with Heidegger's early thought is that it remains still too individualistic because it is too subjective, then the corrective might be a thinking which eschews the existential subjectivism of *Being and Time*. And then attitudes about later Heidegger will fall between those who see Heidegger as redeem-ing himself from subjectivism when he abandons the remnants of modern philosophy after the "turn" (Arendt, Heidegger himself) and those who take what Žižek calls the 'passive receptiveness' of the later work as still rooted in a subjectivist irrationalism (Jonas, Löwith, Habermas, Wolin, etc.)

In either case, these critics blame the residual subjectivism of *Being and Time* for Heidegger's failures, including, most importantly, his attraction to Nazism in the early 1930s. From this viewpoint, the language of his texts from this period indicates the untenability of the still subjectivist *Being and Time*. Numerous references to "will" and "resoluteness" as well as a rhetoric embracing "violence" in *The Introduction to Metaphysics* and other texts post-*Being and Time* indicate the ease with which Heidegger was able to slide from his existential subjectivism of the late twenties into Fascism, a Fascism which – for these critics – was nothing other than a philosophy of subjective Will transposed onto the larger "subject" of the people (the *Volk*) and their leader. Thus, having declared itself in the crisis of Nazism, the disease of subjectivism was (either successfully or not, depending on the critic) expunged from the later Heidegger, the Heidegger of the critique of mod-ern technology and of *Gelassenheit*.

For Žižek, on the other hand, it is precisely the ungrounded nature of Dasein's "decision" – Heidegger's radical "finitism" and even "subjectivism" here – that is worth saving – though, as we've already seen, "subjective" for him means neither "individual" nor "irrational."[13] This last point is worth underscoring, for it is vital to Žižek that the subject of anticipatory resolute-ness neither acts as a "formal" individual nor gains its "content" from avail-able traditions. Žižek's appropriately titled post-*Parallax View* engagement with the question of Heidegger's Nazi period, "Why Heidegger Made the Right Step in 1933," tells this story, a story in which the language of "will," used in a transpersonal sense, actually indicates Heidegger's closest approach to a thinking-through *Being and Time*. Indicating Heidegger's derivation of this language from his seminars on Anaximander and Heraclitus, Žižek demonstrates that the meaning of such willing is hardly subjective in the sense of a closed position from which and for which Being is framed. Quite the contrary, in Žižek's interpretation at least, Heidegger's "will" must be related to Anaximander's "disorder," a primal disturbance in the historicity of any "fugue of Being" which cannot be ironed-out (Žižek 2007, p. 37). Seen not as the hegemonic claim of power over the whole of Being, but rather as a primordial disruption of totality itself, "will" means something much more like what Freudians get at with "drive":

> The primordial fact is thus not the fugue of Being (or the inner peace of *Gelassenheit*), which can then be disturbed/perverted by the rise of ur-willing; the primordial fact is this ur-willing itself, its disturbance of the "natural" fugue. To put it in yet another way: in order for a human being to be able to withdraw itself from the full immersion into its life-environs into the inner peace of *Gelassenheit*, this immersion has first to be broken through the excessive "stuckness" of the drive. Two further consequences should be drawn from this. First, that human finitude strictly equals infinity: the obscene "immortality"/infinity of drive which insists "beyond life and death." Second: the name of this diabolical excess of willing which "perverts" the order of Being is subject. Subject thus cannot be reduced to an epoch of Being, to the modern subjectivity bent on technological domination – there is, underlying it, a "non- historical" subject. (Žižek 2007, p. 37)

When will is understood as Freudian/Lacanian drive, of course, the equation of a primordial "violence" with it no longer is quite so disturbing, indicating simply the irreducible event by which disorder must always reassert itself over that appearance of seamless totality that we call "reality." In other words, so Žižek, Heidegger's critics are mistaken when they point, for example, to the "strife" between earth and world in *The Origin of the Work of Art* as an indication of Heidegger's incipient political "error," something needing to be expunged. Heidegger *himself* may have later interpreted his own gestures in such a manner, but we should avoid it. It is precisely the presence of such violence which indicates Heidegger's greatest advance in articulating his insight.

Furthermore, Žižek's last point in the text I quoted above demands underscoring; for it is the key to his view of Heidegger's Nazi period that this advance marks an effort to *think through* the implications of the modern subject – to move beyond either Romantic or Rationalist appropriations of it toward a praxical, materialist understanding. As Žižek puts it at another point in the same essay, the persistence of the language of will in Heidegger's texts,

> demonstrates the insufficiency of Heidegger's critical analysis of modern subjectivity – not in the sense that 'Heidegger didn't go far enough, and thus remained himself marked by subjectivity,' but in the sense that he overlooked a non-metaphysical core of modern subjectivity itself: the most fundamental dimension of the abyss of subjectivity cannot be grasped through the lense of the notion of subjectivity as the attitude of technological domination.(Žižek 2007, p. 34)

What, according to Žižek, *was* Heidegger's error in 1933? Precisely the one which typifies our response to the possibility of revolutionary change, change disruptive of reality itself – namely, anxiety and retreat. Or, to be more precise, Heidegger gives us the kind of retreat in the face of anxiety which *seems* like no retreat at all, a kind of "acting out" pretending to be a decisive "act." In its embrace of both an extra-individual "people" and a basic disruption of modern reality, Nazism *seems* to follow through on the promise of "will" and "violence," the promise of a "non-metaphysical core of modern subjectivity," but this appearance is *false*. Nazi "will" is, of course, merely the self-assertion of a larger, corporate but all the more metaphysical subject. Nazi violence is directed against people (Jews, Gypsies, etc.) who *represent* what cannot be integrated into a totalized reality and *precisely not* against totality itself. As Žižek puts it, perversely, in his essay on Heidegger in 1933, "the problem with Hitler was that he was not violent enough, that his violence was not 'essential' enough" (Žižek 2007, p. 39).

Nazism, like all Fascism, remained a kind of show, a "pseudo-Event" filled with the appearance of change, but designed in the end to ensure that "nothing will really change" (Žižek 1999b, p. 21). On, the other hand, while the Soviet experiment may have failed dismally to transform the fabric of society, with horrific human consequences, that was not a problem with its intention. Quite the contrary, the Soviets really *tried* to overturn the existing social order, and it was their initial success in doing precisely that which produced the vehemence of the Stalinist backlash.[14] Above all, the Soviet experiment tried to transform the very relationship between individual and society in the terms of the collective. Thus, for Žižek, we can express Heidegger's breakdown before his own conception of finitude as his failure to see that he really should have embraced the Soviet opportunity rather than the Nazi pseudo-alternative. For Žižek, "it was only Soviet Communism which, despite the catastrophe it stands for, did possess true inner greatness" (Žižek 2006b, p. 285). Had he remained "in the truth" of his own insight, Heidegger would have had to become a Communist!

Which, of course, indicates for Žižek not only how far Heidegger would have had to go to live up to the task given by anticipatory resoluteness, but also how effective the strategy of "acting out" proved; for Heidegger's staunch postwar anti-Communism could be taken to indicate the *continuity* between his choice of the 1930s and the "peace" of the later Heidegger. While Nazi-period Heidegger hides the radicality of his own insight about subjectivity from even himself by equating it with the Nazi pseudo-revolution, later Heidegger achieves the same result by erasing the very space *for* that insight. Indeed, the eventual effect of the entire Nazi episode for Heidegger was to make disappear the really disturbing possibility unearthed in his earlier work and brought to its most daring formulation in the crisis-period of the thirties . For the later Heidegger, as for Heidegger's followers, the *only* choices are between the violence of metaphysical subjectivism (the "danger" of modern technology) and a "thinking" which leaves the modern subject behind.

What drops out, of course, when we have only a choice between "self-assertion" and the open acceptance of destiny, is *finitude* itself, except as a residual skepticism demanding that we accept the cards dealt us. That for *Heidegger himself* (at least the Heidegger of *Being and Time*) we cannot sustain a philosophy finitude on the basis of the later, anti-modern position, indicates not only the content of Žižek's immanent critique of Heidegger, but also the role that Žižek takes for himself. *His* work can refuse the retreat from finitude that proved fatal to Heidegger's thought, can complete the task that Heidegger began, doing so by pulling the Heideggerian *corpus* in the direction of a subjectivity which is both collective and praxical.

While, as we'll see in the next chapter, things get more complicated for Žižek when we turn to the apparently marginal question of technology – the question by which Heidegger hid from the possibility of such a radicalized modern subject – still, the project here seems clear enough. Žižek suits himself up to play the "knight of finitude," to face the abyss of the Other's fictionality, in a way for which his first "teacher" remained unprepared.

With such a project in mind, we now turn from Heidegger's essays in finitude to the rigid structure of thought he eventually adapts in defense *against* the shock of his own insight. In doing this with an eye to understanding *Žižek's* path of thought, though, a second set of concerns must collect in the background: "technology" may be a mere symptom, a fundamentally mistaken direction in Heidegger's thought, but it also haunts Žižek, taking an increasingly important role in his recent writing. Indeed, Žižek seems to be spooked by *Heidegger on technology*, structuring whole sections of recent books as implicit critiques of "The Question Concerning Technology" – and this despite (or perhaps *because*) he has never developed an extended and careful reading of any of Heidegger's technology writings. In other words, the next chapter, which examines these flailing efforts to grapple both with technology and Heidegger *on* technology, amounts to a first step in figuring out the structure and meaning of this odd symptom in Žižek's *own* work.

Chapter 2

Žižek and the other Heidegger: technology and danger

Žižek on Heidegger on technology

Given my argument in the first chapter, the reader might be excused in wanting to skip a chapter on Žižek's response to the later Heidegger, and particularly to the Heidegger of "The Question Concerning Technology" and related writings. I wrote earlier that a distrust of the "hubris" of modern science, technology and philosophy often accompanies the basic existential impulse of philosophies of finitude. Many, if not most, thinkers who emphasize the transcendental limits of human knowledge do so because they mistrust the apparent hegemony of human reason or our unwillingness to conceive the a priori limits to human mastery of nature. Heidegger seems the most extreme of a group of thinkers that includes Weber, Adorno, Horkheimer, Arendt and Marcuse – the most willing to dismiss modernity *tout court* by tying the emergence of "modern technology" to Cartesianism. That is, it is Heidegger above all who, in his technology writings of the 1940s and 1950s, traces back the project of modern technology to the transformation wrought when all of being is conceived as *res extensa* for a representing *res cogitans.*[1] From such an anti-Cartesian position, the Heidegger of "The Question Concerning Technology," (1951) can project the development of modernity as a project of domination based upon the prior transformation of nature into an appendage of human representation.

Of course, as we've seen, *something else* – namely, a radical insight about human freedom – could actually be found in the "finitist" Heidegger of the late 1920s and 1930s; however, it's easy enough to understand how Heidegger himself could allow this other insight to disappear behind the façade of a thoroughgoing anti-modernism. It's easy enough to believe that, when, after the "turn" in his thought, Heidegger develops his argument concerning "modern technology," he does so simply to *prevent* the "thinking" he apparently advocates. Isn't it clear from Žižek's understanding of Heidegger on finitude that the technology essays are of interest primarily as *symptoms* of Heidegger's flight from the insight of his earlier work? In Žižek's writing, isn't "technology" just a name for Heidegger's retreat?

The answer to these questions and the justification for this chapter and, indeed, the remainder of my book lies in a peculiarity of Žižek's own work and particularly of his more recent writings. While, as one would expect, Žižek himself has not developed a reading of "The Question Concerning Technology" in any detail, reserving for that text and for Heidegger's thought on technology in general only the most dismissive comments, still the issue of technology and of technology *in Heidegger* has become an almost obsessive site within his writing. It's important to note several facets of this "obsession": on the one hand, since *The Ticklish Subject*, Žižek returns over and over to the theme of Heidegger on technology, almost always to dismiss Heidegger's concerns. The title for a section in *The Parallax View* is typical of this attitude: writing of Heidegger's famous invocation of "the danger" of modern technology, Žižek flippantly gives it the heading, "Danger? What Danger?" On the other hand, though Žižek so ostentatiously rejects his approach, the gesture of dismissal is almost inevitably accompanied by some serious tangling with the issues raised by Heidegger. That tangling has even recently expanded in scope and weight, to the extent that fully a third of *The Parallax View* concerns the technological "question," admitting that developments since Heidegger's day (virtual reality, genetic engineering, artificial intelligence) exacerbate the urgency of the issue. Finally, one must balance Žižek's rather glib dismissals of Heidegger with several places where he insists that Heidegger was in some way *right* in his technology critique.[2] In one of the *Conversations with Žižek*, he asserts that Heidegger was right to speak "about *Gefahr* (danger)," then adding that "there is something in . . . (the) . . . type of radical self-objectivization" suggested by today's science and technology, "which threatens at a fundamental level our very understanding of humanity and the human being" (Žižek and Daly 2004, p. 60).

In other words, Žižek reveals an important ambivalence about Heidegger on technology. What makes such ambivalence particularly odd is that it emerges precisely where Žižek clearly intends straightforward polemic, where he would encourage us, indeed, simply to pass over Heidegger on technology. Žižek *himself* seems, in other words, trapped in a classic philosophical "symptom," a place where we find a combination of assertions of clarity combined with actual intellectual entanglement. The more that Žižek urges us to "forget Heidegger" (or, at least, Heidegger on *technology*), the more that he gets himself entrapped by both technology and Heidegger's thinking *about* that question. Heidegger's technology writings seem to provide a kind of irresistible flypaper for Žižek.

To provide further evidence for my assertions about the place of Heidegger on technology in Žižek, let me offer a particular text for the reader's consideration: the opening of *The Ticklish Subject* is typical in its sneering dismissiveness about the traditions flowing from the Heidegger of technology-critique. At the end of the book's introduction Žižek presents an image that he intends to serve as warning against "Heideggerian" anti-technologism. He suggests an emblematic photograph for our time, a press image from 1997 of indigenous Borneans attempting to put out an enormous forest fire, a fire that indirectly was caused by global warming and the resultant El Ninō effect. What strikes Žižek about the image is the mismatch of scale indicated by tribesmen passing small plastic bags of water with which they vainly strive to put out a blaze whose smoke plume covers "the entire area of northern Indonesia, Malaysia and the southern Philippines" (Žižek 1999a, p. 4). In other words, enormous forces today are at work, forces that dwarf and foredoom the efforts of individuals and communities to control their own fates.

Having introduced this image, Žižek asks what this force looming over us is. The next passage in *The Ticklish Subject*, deeply enigmatic, demands to be quoted in full:

> This catastrophe thus gives body to the Real of our time: the thrust of Capital which ruthlessly disregards and destroys particular life-worlds, threatening the very survival of humanity. What, however, are the implications of this catastrophe? Are we dealing merely with the logic of Capital, or is this logic just the predominant thrust of the modern productivist attitude of technological domination over and exploitation of nature? Or furthermore, is this very technological exploitation the ultimate expression, the realization of the deepest potential of modern Cartesian subjectivity itself? The author's answer to this dilemma is the emphatic plea of 'Not guilty!' for the Cartesian subject. (Žižek 1999a, p. 4)

Despite its apparent polemical lucidity – it is certainly a polemic against the anti-Cartesianism definitional for postmodern theory – in fact, it is not entirely clear quite what Žižek is polemicizing *against* here: one thing *is* clear in this text: Žižek intends to shift blame for what is happening in our world today away from rampant subjectivism – the "usual suspect" since Heidegger. We must register Žižek's "Not Guilty' plea with full clarity.

Beyond that, however, the text is puzzling. In dismissing subjectivism as cause for our impotence today, does "the author" (Žižek) mean to suggest that "merely" "the logic of Capital" stands to blame for global crisis and not "the predominant thrust of the modern productivist attitude of technological domination over, and exploitation of, nature"? While it's certain that, as a defender of a certain radical Cartesianism, Žižek rejects the assertion in the next sentence – Heidegger's argument that such exploitation is "the realization of the deepest potential of modern Cartesian subjectivity itself" – his willingness to apportion blame *simply* to Capitalism, to take up a traditional (pre-Frankfurt-school) Marxist stance is more puzzling and less clear. In other words, the middle question in the above-quoted passage, the one about whether to lay blame also with techno-productivism *as well as* capitalism, seems to hang ambivalently between the clear answers to the first and third questions (in sequence, "Yes, we are dealing the logic of capital," "No, Cartesianism is not to blame.")

If you like, Žižek raises and fails to answer the question of the relationship between capitalism and technological productivism: but that relationship is precisely what his various efforts to come to terms with contemporary technology amount to. Given his obvious concern with this issue, why both raise the issue and fail to respond to it? Most obviously Žižek doesn't say more about techno-capitalism in that opening passage of The Ticklish Subject because what he has to say doesn't fit the polemic he constructs about postmodernism and the modern subject. Lengthy studies in ambivalence simply don't belong in the context of Žižek's clarion call to battle against the sophism of contemporary thought.

Particularly from a thinker who both delivers razor-sharp analyses of social phenomena and is deeply committed to restoring philosophy as the defense of finite critical theses, such ambivalence cannot but strike readers as disappointing. Indeed, Žižek's obsessive return to this intellectual *topos* where he seems mostly to have nothing more than this basic ambivalence to express seems *odd*. Is it a coincidence that this is also the site marked off by that middle possibility from the passage at the beginning of *The Ticklish Subject*? Recall that Žižek there asks: "Are we dealing merely with the logic of Capital, or is this logic just the predominant thrust of the modern productivist attitude of technological domination over and exploitation of nature?" – and leaves this question unanswered.

So, on the one hand, I want to suggest that Žižek's list of rhetorical questions at the beginning of *The Ticklish Subject* includes the *actual* (non-rhetorical, non-polemical) question of techno-capitalism precisely because he feels the *demand* for a univocal thesis like Heidegger's, the demand for a definitive answer to the question of modernity's status and value. On the other hand, his work demonstrates that precisely *this* question evades such resolution. We will always *need* a clear and definite answer to the question of how we should feel about the world ushered in by the modern subject. And we will never be able to respond to this imperative. Indeed, we *should not* cave into it. In the final analysis, we must take Žižek's *silence* in this passage as containing his real answer to the "question concerning techno-captialism" – which is that the question should have priority over any answer, that any answer is necessarily false.

Seen thus, that middle suggestion in the passage from *The Ticklish Subject*, an unaddressed question nested within an otherwise confident and even disputative passage boldly setting Žižek against the entire community of postmodern philosophers, seems a classic example of the phenomenon suggested by Edgar Allen Poe's "The Purloined Letter." There it is, literally in front of our noses but unseen, the thing about which Žižek *won't* (and, I will argue, *can't*) present clear theses. Even and especially in a passage where he obviously has so much to say, indeed, more than he *can* say: but, what if – and this will be my contention – really this innocuous "purloined letter," against all appearances, actually *produces* that "too-much-to-say?"

Technology is *not* the question

Now, the first thing to be said from Žižek's perspective about the view of modern technology emerging in "The Question Concerning Technology" is that it seems precisely structured so as to *avoid* that *act* whose conceptualization Žižek draws from earlier Heidegger. Instead of moving from the "receptive" moment of finitude to a radical and world negating spontaneity, the technology lens makes such an act into a form of "original sin" and fetishizes the inviolability of the world-horizon. It is, of course, no coincidence that the *image* accompanying Heidegger's technology writings is that of a *whole* nature, a nature whose Aristotelian *physis* grants the possibility for a redemption of human practice through *poiesis*. In other words, Heidegger not only insists upon a "court of appeal" but even moves this court back to its pre-modern *locus* in a position of transcendence. The ethic of "humility" (*"Gelassenheit"*) opposed to the "pride" of technological domination forces us into an implicitly *religious* posture, one that betrays the fundamental impulse of Heidegger's earlier work.

Recall here Žižek's analysis – already discussed in Chapter 1 – of the double meaning of the Heideggerian assertion that Dasein is always primordially "in the untruth." At a first reading, Heidegger simply seems to be asserting what traditional Christianity assumes about human finitude – that our "untruth" comes from our failure to notice a wider horizon of Being, one which forms a whole not apparent to us. This interpretation aligns nicely with Heidegger's "pastoral" analyses of Dasein's inauthenticity, its absorption in the petty concerns of the "They World," its "Falling," etc., etc. Dasein's untruth therefore coincides with a tendency to "miss the bigger picture," and the modern technological obsession analysed in Heidegger's later work simply marks a newly predominant version of such human fallibility.

Still, for Žižek, Heidegger's assertion of *certainty* in Section 44 of *Being and Time* (and many times thereafter) that Dasein is "in the untruth" is *ontological* rather than merely moral; while it might be the case that human beings tend to "miss the forest for the trees," there's no a priori reason on the face of things why such *must* be the case. Not unless, that is, we consider our "untruth" to manifest itself beyond when we ignore the wider horizon of our ontological constitution but also, and most of all, *when we pay attention* to that horizon. That is, at an ontological level Dasein's untruth is not that "bigger picture" but the very *illusion* that there is such a picture to be found, an illusion which hides the stain of subjectivity.

Isn't the problem with "the question concerning technology" (the question itself), that it is a precise itinerary for elimination of that second "untruth," that second finitude which Heidegger himself had previously understood to be structural to Dasein? In his technology writings, Heidegger presumes from the start that the fatal "untruth" today lies in the way we miss a broader horizon. Such conception of error is foundational to Heidegger's project in "The Question Concerning Technology," where the antidote to the dumb obviousness of modern technology, the project of "gain(ing) a free relationship to the essence of modern technology," is translated into the necessity of seeing such technology in terms of the wider "destining of Being" indicated by the transformation from Greek technology to its modern avatar (Heidegger 1977a, pp. 6–10). In other words, Heidegger equates "questioning" technology with seeing the limited "truth" of calculation in relationship to the broader horizon of *poietic* un-concealment, of which it is, nonetheless, an interpretation.

In this way, of course, Heidegger's thought here is not only mistaken but *dangerously* so, since it marks a *powerful* temptation. Take, for example, what Yannis Stavrakakis calls the dominant fantasy of contemporary "Green" visions, a fantasy that has frequently been tied back to Heidegger's technology-critique.[3] This fantasy, beginning from the now-problematized foundations of "Ecology" in systems-theory, posits nature as a harmonious interdependent system, always tending toward "a balance or equilibrium state" only disturbed by human activity (see, Stavrakakis 1997). Such a view of the *ecos* is posited of the planet itself in Lovelock's "Gaia" hypothesis. In this way of seeing things, the dynamic but essentially orderly "becoming" of nature provides a model for human activity. Furthermore, such an ideology also mirror's Heidegger's technology writing in the treatment that it gives to human spontaneous activity, which potentially *disrupts* natural order. Indeed, as Stavrakakis points out, if nature is by definition harmonious, "all imbalances" can be attributed "to humans" and specifically to "industrialism" or "industrial man" which "destroys nature's equilibrium" (Stavrakakis 1997, p. 127). We have a fantasmatic system in which everything has a place, everything except our "fallen" capacity to will – and this fantasy dominates a certain kind of ecological response to environmental crises, dictating that we eschew, for example, the possibility of "technical" responses to problems produced by technological civilization.

To the extent that Žižek follows *this* criticism, the criticism leveled by Stravrakakis, we could simply say that the problem here is that Heidegger, for symptomatic reasons, has pursued precisely the *wrong* question, that "the question concerning technology" with its entire motivation located in a suspicion of modern self-assertion, is what Heidegger himself called a *Holzweg* – a false path. And a subset of Žižek's scattered responses to Heidegger on technology amount to pointing this out. To begin with, such "ecologism" simply blinds us a priori to a startling facet of nature, one that Žižek emphasizes in *Looking Awry*, where he writes that,

> The very notion of man as an 'excess' with respect to nature's balanced circuit has finally to be abandoned. The image of nature as a balanced circuit is nothing but a retroactive projection of man . . . 'Nature' is already in itself turbulent, imbalanced. (Žižek 1992, p. 38)

That is, the very view of nature implicit in Heidegger's "answer" to the technology question – the very "piety" carried in his "questioning" – blinds to us *another* nature. The modern subject, that lack or gap in reality, brings with it as its obverse an incompletion of nature itself and an incompletion that is, necessarily, always "in process."

Indeed, following this line of Žižek's thought would lead us to assert not only that, when it comes to finitude, technology is the "wrong" question but that it is *precisely* the wrong question – that today's science and technology, far from being pacifying or quieting social forces, demand we confront the fantasmatic character of every nature-wholism, demand we face this very "turbulence" and "imbalance" in nature itself.

Perhaps Žižek's clearest exfolliation of such a position makes up the main argument of Chapter 3 in *The Parallax View*, the chapter entitled, "The Unbearable Heaviness of Being Divine Shit." Here, he returns to Freud's famous reference to psychoanalysis as a third great scientific "blow" to pride – the other two being Copernicus' assertion of the heliocentric model and Darwin's theory of evolution. Taking these three moments as traumas or "blows" to human narcissism, Freud compared the effects of psychoanalysis on the defenses erected by the human psyche with the realization that "our earth was not the center of the universe but only a tiny fragment of a cosmic system of scarcely imaginable vastness," and the insight that human beings do not enjoy a "privileged place in creation," but are instead "ineradicably" part of the "animal kingdom." The obvious question here, and the one Žižek raises, is in what way Freud's insight that "the ego is not master in its own house" marks not just *another* blow, equal to those delivered by Copernicus and Darwin, but the *heaviest* blow (see, Žižek 2006b, p. 163).

The answer lies in a transformation which, in hindsight, Freud *shares* with a kind of natural science new to the twentieth century: if both Copernicus and Darwin forced us to divide nature from its *appearance*, "reality" from the way reality "appears to us," then the new science of which Psychoanalysis serves as exemplar forces another adjustment. The first two "blows" amount to a challenge to a "higher" view of the human, a challenge which substitutes a "lower" relationship to "nature" for a previously dominant relationship to God. We learn that what we thought to be determining reality (our place at the center of the cosmos, our special role in creation) is merely the way things *seem to us*, and that, "beneath" this level *really* we are determined by blind natural forces. Of course, part of the shock here is that there are *multiple* such "points of view," hiding the single truth of mechanical causation.

With the "new" sciences of the twentieth century, though, our "humiliation" is of a different kind. Here, with the phenomenon of the Freudian unconscious, it is *appearance itself* which is split, bifurcating between "the way things appear to us" and "the way things *really* appear to us" (Žižek 2006b, p. 172). We have, in other words, a division, not between a blind, mechanistic nature and a unified subjective world of human meaning, but an abyss within the subjective itself. And when appearance is split in this way, "nature" too, the reality behind appearance, suddenly loses its wholeness. Using Lacan's concept of a "fundamental fantasy" to explain the Freudian unconscious, Žižek suggests that the trauma of psychoanalysis lies in this – that the analyst challenges what previously had remained impregnable in subjective experience, despite all the humiliations caused by modern science:

> According to the standard view, the dimension that is constitutive of subjectivity is that of phenomenal (self-)experience – I am a subject the moment I can say to myself: "No matter what unknown mechanism governs my acts, perceptions, and thoughts, nobody can take from me what I see and feel now." For example, when I am passionately in love, and a biochemist informs me that all my intense sentiments are merely the result of biochemical processes in my body I can answer him by clinging to the appearance: "All that you're saying may be true; nonetheless, nothing can take from me the intensity of the passion I am now experiencing . . .." Lacan's point, however, is that the psychoanalyst is the one who, precisely *can* take this from the subject – that is to say, his ultimate aim is to deprive the subject of the very fundamental fantasy that regulates the universe of his (self-)experience (Žižek 2006b, p. 171).

To understand this threat, consider the odd conceptual space within which it is located. On the one hand, we misinterpret the Freudian unconscious – according to Žižek and Lacan – if we take it merely as some kind of "complex network of mental causality and behavioral control" which transpires outside of experience (Žižek 2006b, p. 172). On the contrary, Žižek insists that the unconscious belongs to the *phenomenal*. On the other hand, though, we must remember Freud's elementary distinction between the "unconscious" and the "pre-conscious": we distinguish the unconscious because it is foundationally constructed so as to evade consciousness. It *cannot* become conscious. In this way, of course, *Urverdrängung*, primordial repression, is simply an underscoring of the idea of the unconscious itself.

Thus, when Žižek follows Lacan in interpreting the unconscious through the device of a "fundamental fantasy," a fantasy (appearance) which *cannot* appear to consciousness without dissolving it, he is simply offering a technical vocabulary adequate to the idea of a split *in* appearance. The fundamental fantasy *is* the way "things really appear to me."

But what does that mean? The vital clue lies in the bond between appearance and reality within modern thought. Surely it is no coincidence that modernity brings us *both* the emergence of "perspectivism" – of the *subjective* constitution of a world made of up of an infinite number of "viewpoints" – and the causal "closed circuit" of classical modern views of nature. That is, we can *afford* to distinguish various "inner realities," various forms of personhood, etc., etc., precisely to the extent that all of these are contained by their reference to a single world: they are all points of view on a single reality. Nor is this limitation a matter of "choice," of a kind of psychological cowardice, since it reflects the very structure of representation. As long as I remain with a "picture" of the world (as containing/being constructed from multiple viewpoints, etc.), I also re-posit the unity of a "natural" reality underlying it. But what of the "story" telling us how and why we thus always "map"subjectivity, anchoring it in a totalized reality? What about the story telling us of the opening of "dimensionality" per se, the space of conceptual space?

The third chapter of *Žižek and Heidegger* explores the nature of such "fundamental fantasy" in more detail, but suffice it for now to note that exposure to such a narrative would "undermine" the very way we construct experience. Which means that psychoanalysis is a basic response to – a basic rejection of – the picture of the world which conceives of it as a "constructed" dimension of "points of view" or "stories." The crisis of an analysis, then, amounts to an exposure to this "impossible" truth, a truth that divides appearance itself. Or, to put the same thing in other words, psychoanalysis, forces us to challenge the apparent dimensionality or coherence of reality.

A science which "follows" the Freudian revolution, then (we'll see that really it's not a matter of Freud's historical precedence), will be one which *embraces* that challenge to the causal closure of nature that Žižek announced above. Paradoxically, Žižek uses Darwin, or Darwin as he appears to the late twentieth -century eyes of Stephen J. Gould, to exemplify such a view (see, Žižek 2006b, pp. 198–199). *Gould's* masterful interpretation of Darwin (Žižek refers to Gould as a genuine "dialectician") refuses to rest with Darwin's challenge to theology – his insight that "man" has no privileged position in creation – and goes beyond this. This means that various ideologies of "natural selection," ideologies which re-import an apparently non-theological "direction" to evolutionary processes, are wrong. Life does not move toward "greater complexity" or "hardiness" or anything else. As Gould explains it, the rudiments of Darwin's theory (some sort of genetic variation, inheritance of traits, failure of some offspring to survive) are extremely simple and basic to *The Origin of Species*. Evolution occurs when selection in the long run favors changes in the gene pool better adapted to the environment in which particular organisms live.[4]

But note that, once it is understood based upon the *interaction* of mutation and an unpredictable environmental change, evolution *cannot* have
a direction. Variation in the environment constantly shifts the "favored"
traits, so there really cannot be anything like evolutionary "progress" or "ascent."
Indeed, as my choice of the word "variation" – the same word that Darwin
uses to describe the genetic process whereby species mutate – indicates, it may
be *definitional* that environments change at the same time that individuals
and species do. "Variation" occurs at every level of evolution, not only
renewing the game but also shuffling the deck and even changing the rules!
In such a situation the idea of any scale or ladder of evolution – any fixed
set of characteristics that might be judged "superior" or "more advanced" –
is silly. As Žižek puts it, for Gould, "the New emerges not as an element, but
as a structure. In an aleatory way, all of a sudden, a new Order, new har-
mony, emerges out of chaos" (Žižek 2006b, p. 199).

His reference to "emergence" in relationship to Gould indicates also
what Žižek sees as Gould's other radical thesis – namely, the idea of
"ex-aptation." That is, since every organism only emerges in relationship to
the feedback loop between itself and its environment, there is no "univocal
agent" of evolution, as Žižek puts it. To the extent that such emergence
governs evolutionary processes, it's impossible to speak of a "survival of the
fittest" (the dictum of Darwin himself in a different mood) as a *purpose* or
end of evolution. Nature is fundamentally self-disruptive and creative. As
Žižek puts it, "An organism evolves to survive, but it cannot emerge in
order to survive: it is meaningless to say that I live *in order* to adapt myself"
(*Parallax*, p. 199).

In other words, "splitting of appearance", as focused by Gould, suggests
precisely the view of nature – self-disruptive, aleatory, etc., etc. – which Žižek
posits over and against "ecologism," or against Heidegger's own fantasy of a
"poietic" history of Being. There is no "dimension" of points-of-view, no
"underlying reality" to the multiple possibilities of appearance. A vital
insight, this; for, "at a single blow," as it were, we must give up on all the
various fatalisms that the popular imagination puts in the form of techno-
dystopia. If nature is as Gould's science suggests it to be, then there can be
no question of our entrapment within a "closed loop" of perfected science
wielding the laws of nature.

I wrote above of the process of an analysis, with its "threat" to subjective
integrity as what, for Žižek, Freud "meant" in his 1917 lecture. Up to this
point, we've only explored one aspect of this threat – namely, the danger to
our view of *nature* as totality. Still, to follow the metaphor of the analytic
session is also to understand a possibility for human change: after all, it is at

least the *hope* of every analysis to bring the subject, the analysand, to a point of transformation. Moreover, the provocative claim that Žižek underscores when he suggests that the analyst's "ultimate aim is to deprive the subject of the very fundamental fantasy that regulates the universe of his (self-) experience" is that such "theft" can transform *reality itself* and not simply its appearance. Think here of the way that evolution transforms "reality" itself – the "environmental" combination of organisms and inorganic elements stabilized at a given moment – within which mutations strive to adapt. Subjective change is not just "mutation" within a fixed environment but transformation of and by the environment, too. The Freudian revolution (even in its "Darwinian" moment!) brings us to a place where subjective and objective revolution collapse into each other, what Lacan calls the "impossible Real," a "dimension" constitutive of dimensionality per se. It is an "unimaginable" transcendental function producing the very possibility of synthesis or coherence. And the analysand can sometimes be brought to "touch the Real."

Still, Žižek's clearest explanation of what he's getting at with Freud's "third blow" to humanity's narcissism comes not in his discussions of psychoanalysis but in his example from that natural science which best mirrors the Freudian revolution: Žižek accounts for that emergence of a "new" structuration of reality in the wake of the splitting of appearance by turning to Quantum Physics and the basic concept there that "the "appearance" (perception) of a particle determines its reality" (Žižek 2006b, p. 172). Indeed, such Physics provides Žižek's best explanation of what is implied by the "splitting of appearance." In particular, defending against the idea that he is simply locating another conceptual "dimension" or space for the play of different "realities," Žižek writes:

> The very emergence of "hard reality" out of the quantum fluctuation through the collapse of the wave function is the outcome of observation, that is, of the intervention of consciousness. Thus consciousness is not the domain of potentiality, multiple options, and so on, opposed to hard singular reality – reality previous to its perception is fluid-multiple-open, and conscious perception reduces this spectral, pre-ontological multiplicity to one ontologically fully constituted reality. (Žižek 2006b, p. 172)

In other words, we have here a marker for the transformation of science in the past century, a change which turns on the mutual imbrication of observer/subject and observed/object. Prior to observation the realm of quanta is a "spectral, pre-ontological multiplicity," a nature which is precisely the opposite of the stable ground for subjective interiority and multiplicity implied in classical modern understandings. In this, as in Heisenberg's uncertainty principle, Žižek finds a perfect analogue for the peculiar change in the status of appearance underlying contemporary thought.

Another point in *The Parallax View* offers yet another demonstration of the oddly redemptive effects of consciousness upon reality. Consider Žižek's compelling analysis of *Minority Report* (both the Spielberg film and the story by Philip K. Dick). The central conceit of this science fiction story, which takes the form of a crime-drama is that "precogs," psychics working in teams of three, are able to predict (and thus prevent) future murders. When he suspects the identity of the man who has raped and murdered his own child, the cop enforcing the decisions of the precogs, John Anderton (Tom Cruise, in the film), is caught up in a web implicating himself. The precogs issue a report predicting that he (Anderton) will himself commit a murder. What complicates the situation, as we learn in the film only at the very end, is the time between each of the three precog "reports" *to Anderton* and the next report. In each case, when Anderton comes to know what is predicted *of him*, this knowledge changes the very course of destiny. For example, soon after the prediction is made, Anderton comes to know that the first precog ("Donna") predicts that he will murder "Kaplan"(the bad guy). This causes him to decide *not* to commit such a crime – a decision that is then reflected in the second report (that of "Jerry") where Anderton is predicted (based on his now altered decision) *not* to commit the murder, etc., etc. (See, Žižek 2006b, pp. 207–208.) In each case in *Minority Report*, it is knowledge of what Anderton *will* do that changes the actual course of events, a diversion of history, which, like "nature," is shown to be fundamentally incomplete and open to transformation.

Still, something else in both *Minority Report*, and in Žižek's account of it, should give us pause, namely, the fact that this openness of reality is inseparable from – only forms the reverse of – its complete closure and determination. It is not *simply* the case that nature (or history, in this case) is ontologically incomplete. Rather, it is precisely because it *is* complete at any given moment with regard to any particular object or event – because an adequate prediction of Anderton's actions *is* possible – that Anderton is able to change his behavior. In other words – and we will return to this thesis – it is only in the context of techno-scientific "objectification" of reality that nature can, in a second moment, emerge as indeterminant, etc.

For the moment, let's just focus on what Žižek calls the "opportunity" hidden behind the "danger" of such technological objectification. In *Conversations with Žižek*, we are asked to consider a case of cloning: I am faced with a perfect copy of "me," a clone, or, indeed, the "formula" for producing such a thing. Žižek argues that such an experience, while no doubt "uncanny" and even "monstrous,"[5] will nonetheless, have the virtue of forcing us precisely to an *authentic* confrontation with our own subjectivity. Such will be the case, argues Žižek, "because, in the very experience of 'that's me', you will, as it were, look at yourself from the outside. And so this dream of total self-objectivization will also confront us radically with its opposite, with the gap of subjectivity" (Žižek and Daly 2004, p. 57).

In other words, the prospect of total objectification forces a confrontation with the role of consciousness in *articulating* itself. This idea of a persistent remainder in the face of technology, of a confrontation with an uncanny "Real," is perhaps clearest in Žižek's line of thought about affect and virtuality. Once again, *Conversations* gives a good example, this time a consideration of how "VR" technology realizes an old dream of cinema – to grant access to a "real" affect for which there is no representational equivalent. He suggests this to be a kind of realization of Hitchcock's fantasy in which,

> in future, a director will no longer have to invent intricate narratives and shoot them in a convincingly heart-breaking way in order to generate in the viewer the proper emotional response; he will employ a keypad connected directly to the viewer's brain, so that, when he presses the proper buttons, the viewer will experience sorrow, terror, sympathy, fear . . . he will experience them for real, in an amount never equaled by the situations 'in real life' which evoke fear or sorrow. (Žižek and Daly 2004, p. 99)

Far from associating the affects of virtual reality with the *representations* it produces (computer animations, etc.), Žižek sees the possibility of direct neuronal stimulation, and therefore of an experience *disconnected* from and *disruptive of* the totalized appearance that makes up "reality." He notes that in such a case "the Real of, say, the sexual pleasure generated by direct neuronal intervention does not take place in the reality of bodily contacts, yet it is 'more real than reality', more intense," with possibly jarring results for our commitment to such reality itself.[6] Or, differently put, Žižek suggests that such a virtual, precisely in delivering us a direct experience that is "too much" for reality can force us to confront what remains "unbearable" in our own construction of reality from the Real –helps us move beyond the limits of ideology (Žižek and Daly 2004, p. 101). It is with such revolutionary potential as this in mind that Žižek mocks Heidegger in that key section of *The Parallax View*, "Danger? What Danger?"

Right question. Wrong answer: the crisis of technology rehabilitated

Still, this rather simple story of reversal – this mockery of "The Question Concerning Technology" – doesn't yet give us Žižek's *whole* account of that very "question." The limitation of my story up to this point can be made clearer by reference to a similarly toned passage from that third chapter of *The Parallax View* to which I've already referred extensively. Having discussed both the dream and the nightmare today associated with the possibilities of "full digitalization" – of our transfer into some sort of "software" form of ourselves – Žižek dismisses the problem:

> What if both the utopia – the perverted dream of the passage from hardware to software of a subjectivity floating freely between different embodiments – and the dystopia – the nightmare of humans voluntarily transforming themselves into programmed beings – are just the positive and the negative of the same ideological fantasy? What if it is only and precisely this technological prospect-that fully confronts us with the most radical dimension of our finitude? (Žižek 2006b, pp. 195–196)

In the return to finitude in Žižek's last sentence here, I want to claim a deeper problematic. So, say that contemporary techno-utopias and dystopias are simply variants on a single "ideological fantasy"; Žižek still admits that this perverse fantasy is *essential* in that it "confronts us with the most radical dimension of our finitude." In other words, in moving from the logic indicating that technology is the wrong question to a logic suggesting that it is *exactly* the wrong question, Žižek has subtly ratified Heidegger's focus on the technological problematic, even while sharpening his condemnation of what Heidegger has to say *about* it. Isn't there a sense in which "modern technology" is anything but the "wrong question" for Žižek, but instead represents precisely the *right* question today?

Return for a moment to *Minority Report* and Žižek's use of that film to indicate the intertwining of consciousness and causality. Recall, also, as I already indicated, that Žižek's point with regard to the film is *not* that the openness of the future is somehow a "direct outcome of some radical indeterminacy or 'ontological openness' inscribed in the fabric of reality" (Žižek 2006b, p. 208). Quite the contrary, it is vital to the possibility of Anderton's success in overcoming his fate (that he will kill Kaplan, etc.), that this fate is, in fact sealed – that natural causality does, in a sense, form a "closed loop" from which there can be no escape. There is *no* "realm" of exception to techno-scientific control. Furthermore, Anderton's free act here *depends upon the knowledge* made possible by reductivist science: that is, we note that, in addition to a deterministic universe we must assume an *effective knowledge* of that universe's laws. As Žižek says in the case of *Minority Report*, "the ontological 'fork,' the alternate path of future reality, is, rather, generated when the agent whose future acts are foretold gets to know about them; that is to say, its source is the self-referentiality of knowledge" (Žižek 2006b, pp. 207–208).

To put the matter provocatively, freedom can *only* occur in the light of knowing what *must* happen. And this insight carries far beyond Žižek's discussion of *Minority Report*. Among other places, in *The Plague of Fantasies*, Žižek confirms the unavoidable necessity of precisely such fatal knowledge for the liberating moment Lacan calls "traversing the fantasy." Praising Nietzsche's "eternal return of the same," Žižek argues that its point is precisely to produce such a knowledge of closure, such a demand to "renounce every opening, every belief in messianic Otherness" (Žižek 1997, p. 31). Which is to suggest that, to quote the title of a recent anti-technological screed by Bill McKibben, we should never declare "enough." Only in developing objectifying knowledge to its full extent do we open the possibility of freedom.

First of all, Žižek here rings the changes on an idea I've already suggested – that technological totalization forms the *subjective* precondition for the development of any new and liberating insight. Only when we *know* that we are not and cannot be free can we . . . free ourselves. Indeed, this is a key concept in Žižek's interpretation of history in *The Puppet and the Dwarf, For They Know Not What They Do* and elsewhere: in *The Puppet and the Dwarf*, indeed, Žižek *praises* the Heidegger of the technology writings (along with Horkheimer and Adorno), for his fatalism, his projection of history as a kind of "checkmate" (see, *Puppet*, pp. 164–165). The argument, is that such thoroughgoing "determinism" actually leads not to quietism but to action. It is precisely when we know that there is "no way out" that possibilities for escape emerge.

Furthermore, the technological, totalized view of nature (and science in relationship to it) is not only *useful*, it is also, in a sense, *true*. To put this in another way, no matter how *ideological*, it is, Newtonian or modern nature as homogeneous infinite totality doesn't, can't, really just disappear – to be replaced by a newly dialectical science. Recall that the space of Newton and Kant is only secondarily a physical dimension (to be contrasted with time, etc.) insofar as it is also the precondition for any real science at all: since Ptolemy was joined at the hip with Aristotelian physics, the main Galilean and Newtonian arguments against the Ptolemaic system didn't have to do with helio-centrism so much as with the homogeneity of nature. The real Copernican revolution (though Copernicus didn't propose it) concerned *that* issue, the precondition for a new method of hypothesis and verification. This "space" is really the presupposition of homogeneous lawfulness (everywhere and at all times) and thus the basis of *scientific method*, a method that makes possible contemporary as well as classical modern science. Simply noting the ways that contemporary science moves to the verge problematizing its own foundations doesn't dispense with their continued necessity for the operation of that science. In other words, given that it is immanent *within* even the most revolutionary of versions of contemporary science, the problem of two "natures," here corresponding with two "sciences," won't just disappear.

In some sense, furthermore, what Heidegger identifies as the "essence of modern technology" – the "enframing" of all phenomena within an assumed total space of universal, mathematical law – is intimately bound up with the formation of our reality itself. Or, to put it slightly differently, we might suspect that such a Newtonian "universe" (the word already lets us know of nature's pre-totalization) is not simply a "choice." Žižek vehemently *rejects* the postmodern out, wherein we would claim that this reality is reduced to an artificial and non-binding "social construction." Quite the contrary, as he writes in *The Plague of Fantasies*, Heidegger was *right* in arguing that "modern science" is "the *Real* of our historical moment, that which 'remains the same' in all possible ('progressive' and 'reactionary', 'technocratic' and 'ecological', 'patriarchal' and 'feminist') symbolic universes" (Žižek 1997, p. 38).

All of which is just to suggest that at some basic level, we *do* live in something like the world of Heidegger's "modern technology," or at least of the science to which it is bound, to an objectification without limit. The success of science in determining not just "external" nature but human language and thought certainly provides a kind of horizon of contemporary experience – an horizon *within which* alone cultural phenomena can play.[7]

Finally, Žižek is quite clear about *why* Heidegger's anxiety about our everyday "technologism" is important. Take another passage from the very chapter in *The Parallax View* where we've seen his dismissal of the technological problematic. In discussing the ability of computers to displace the "functions" of a conscious person (inter-computer communication, thinking computers), Žižek comments that "the prospect of radical self-objectivization brought about by cognitivism cannot fail to cause anxiety" (Žižek 2006b, p. 198).

In explaining why this must be the case, he suggests, first, that the benefit of such technology is that it *threatens* the very space within which we imagine ourselves to be "free." That is, such technology fills out the implication of Newtonian space, according to which there can be no "beyond" to, no transcendence of, reality. Thus, increasingly we can imagine neither a substantive "humanist" sphere of dignity, nor a comforting story of evolution, granting such a transcendent guarantee to reality. But, and this is the *hidden* source of that anxiety for Žižek, the real threat here comes in the way that such technology confronts us, ironically, with our *freedom*:

> On a first approach, anxiety emerges when we are totally determined, objectivized, forced to assume that there is no freedom, that we are just neuronal puppets, self-deluded zombies; at a more radical level, however, anxiety arises when we are compelled to confront our freedom. (It is the same in Kant: when we are able to identify a pathological cause of an act of ours, this cannot but be a relief from the anxiety of freedom; or, as Kierkegaard would have put it, the true horror is to discover that we are immortal, that we have a higher Duty and responsibility – how much easier would it be to be a mere natural mechanism . . .) Consequently, cognitivist self-objectivization causes anxiety because – although, in terms of its enunciated content, it "objectivizes" us – it has the opposite effect in terms of the implied position of enunciation: it confronts us with the abyss of our freedom, and, simultaneously, with the radical contingency of the emergence of consciousness. (Žižek 2006b, p. 198)

In other words, the importance of technology, revealed in our (and, of course, Heidegger's) anxiety about it, lies in its ability to make us confront our very subjectivity, our freedom. Here Žižek makes the same point that he made in *dismissing* technology, only now in reverse. Above, I showed how technology amounted to a mere "chimera" in that, as new, "materialist" sciences demonstrate, *nature itself* is incomplete. Here, on the contrary, technology *is* a real issue (or a real *perceived* question, a "real appearance") in that it forces us to see wherein that incompletion of nature emerges. Nature is incomplete at one point alone – the point of the subject with its free act, the point where this subject *contaminates* reality. Or, to put this in another way, today technology *is* the right question; for it marks a key sight at which such anxiety appears, at which the very "mask" of the reality guaranteed by modern science threatens to slip. That Žižek *gets* this about technology – that he sees Heidegger as asking the right question (but giving the wrong answer) in his technology writings – emerges powerfully in the context of a Lacan-interpretation in *The Plague of Fantasies,* where Žižek writes:

> Lacan's supplement to Heidegger would thus be: why should this utter "forgetting of Being", at work in modern science, be perceived only as the greatest "danger"? Is there not within it an already perceptible "liberating" dimension? Is not the suspension of ontological Truth in the unfettered functioning of science already a kind of 'passing through' the metaphysical closure? (Žižek 1997, 38)

It's precisely in this sense that Žižek says Heidegger is right, that technology marks a genuine challenge to "our very understanding of humanity and the human being" (Žižek and Daly 2004, p. 60).

The end of "Žižek and Heidegger": breaking up

And so, Žižek's ambivalence about Heidegger on technology points to an at least apparent tension between two constructions of reality. On the one hand, nature being incomplete, science, the *knowledge* corresponding to this incompleteness, is simply a boon and the sense of crisis or "danger" associated with modern scientific achievement an illusion. On the other hand, the crisis is genuine for Žižek insofar as it refers to the reality defined *by that science itself,* insofar as it indicates the impossibility of an *imaginable* way out of scientific objectification, a *limit* to knowledge. We have a real "apparent crisis," a crisis at the *level* of appearance.

Thus, in Žižek's grappling with technology (and Heidegger on technology) nature is both beyond totalization and thoroughly totalized.

I would suggest, we must stay with the "tension" between two incompatible views of nature in Žižek, tensing it, in fact, to the point even of contradiction. This is not, in the first instance, meant as a *criticism* of Žižek, though my eventual criticisms of him will grow out of it. Indeed, his work has the (admittedly unintentional) virtue of exposing it. First of all, it seems to me that these two understandings of nature (and science/techno-science in relationship to it) correspond closely with the way that the matter really does present itself in our world – a *phenomenological* virtue of Žižek's ambivalence. We are indeed stretched between a revolutionary new paradigm for science, one which suggests the possibility of a renewed alliance with dialectical materialism, and a sense of crisis based upon the ever-advancing frontier of scientific-technical control – a kind of paranoid limit of the closed reality of a mechanistic universe without exit. Contemporary science really does seem to divide unfathomably between these two paradigms, and that "fact" in itself is a worthy matter for philosophical reflection.

But I will also be concerned in the long run to discern with such splitting a limit to Žižek's thought, a limit at least to the manner in which it can attain a systematic coherence. In reading Žižek through his relationship to Heidegger, it's important to see that the point where Žižek places his *own* limit to Heidegger's worth, the point beyond which Heidegger no longer rewards interpretation or even reading, is also the place at which Žižek's thought enters *its own* crisis.[8] The "marriage" I've proposed in reading Žižek *through* his relationship to Heidegger, includes an apparently tragic final chapter: "if only you hadn't left me!" wails Heidegger in the background, "we both might have avoided trouble!"

Actually, it's been a successful divorce, and this for two reasons: first, on his own Žižek must shoulder the burden for a critical theory to *replace* Heidegger's critique of modernity – that *other* answer to "the question concerning technology" whose demand we've seen to lurk beneath the surface of the Žižekean anti-Heidegger polemic. That is, like Heidegger, Žižek must respond to the "crisis" that, indirectly, he himself admits – but he must come up with a *different answer* to it than did his partner. Of course, even the issue here is not exactly what Heidegger claims it to be. In some sense, Žižek is closer to Horkheimer, Adorno, Arendt, or Marcuse in insisting that the question is not so much with "technology" per se as with the social formation that produces it – with *techno-capitalism*, as I already called it at the outset of this chapter.

But it is the *difference* between Žižek's critique of techno-capitalism and the *anti-modernism* shared by Heidegger and other postmodernists that will prove most fruitful. When conceived in the light of Žižek's broader understanding of historicity and the modern subject, this insight yields what is, if unsystematically presented in his work, its most valuable contribution to philosophy – a powerful but *immanent* critique of our technological reality. Above all, Žižek gives us a novel and powerful understanding of what constitutes the "modern world," both its crises and its revolutionary potential. The next part of *Žižek and Heidegger* (Chapters 3 and 4) articulates this alternative answer to "the question concerning techno-capitalism."

Secondly, the confusing intertwining of *two* Žižekian views about technology (or, more precisely, about Heidegger and technology) in his apparently polemical texts also suggests another task, one that will find in this split the source of others. His odd ambivalence about the "question concerning technology" can lead us to reflection on a general and profound division inherent to Žižek's own thought – a division concerning Žižek's predilection for a certain kind of anti-historicist *historicism*.

The story Žižek tells in Chapter 5 of *The Parallax View* – the story of finitude in *Being and Time* as displacing an otherwise merely Cartesian skepticism about our access to the truth of existence – is typical of the accounts by which he explains himself. Such *displacement* forms a structure, indeed, that he justifies in his Hegel-interpretation. This Hegel emphasizes the *immanence* in dialectical logic of the second or "ontological" realization to the first (or epistemological) insight. The second moment is "for itself" what the first is only "in-itself," so that the entire process is conceived as a single history, apparently the realization of a potential already contained in the "content" of the epistemological revolution as the formal "frame" is invaded by that content[9] (see, Žižek 2003, pp. 85–87).

Still, my chapter's tale about Žižek, Heidegger and technology provides an example where the smooth operation of Žižek's historical, narrative-producing machinery gets gummed-up. Neither side of Žižek's *ambivalence* here could serve as "subject" of a history. Indeed, the *polemic* by which he frames his *actual* ambivalence about it would suggest that the continuation of Newtonian nature today, it's co-existence with its radically heterogeneous, "incomplete" double, might represent a deeper problem. And, more specific to the techno-scientific theme, we must also be struck by something else – namely, the *actual* proximity of Žižek's and Heidegger's understandings of why such contemporary techno-science is *important*. Žižek goes to great pains to hide his *intimacy* with Heidegger concerning the way that science today closes the window on any possible humanistic escape, any transcendence.

The final division of *Žižek and Heidegger* will return to both the general and specific questions thus raised by the technology-problematic – to both the odd inscription of a methodological historicism in Žižek's *anti-historicist* thought and to the specific place of a certain technological "fantasy" in that construction.

Part II

Slowing Žižek down: modernity and techno-capitalism

Chapter 3

Missing the point: Slavoj Žižek on perspective, modernity and subjectivity

The Cartesian specter and the ghost of perspective

There's something particularly wicked, particularly lovely, about taking a canonical text of Leftist academia ("The Communist Manifesto"), switching a word and re-presenting it with its original meaning changed and its full shock-value revived. Precisely that is what Žižek does at the beginning of *The Ticklish Subject,* a text which it's worth presenting in full:

A Specter is Haunting Western Academia, the specter of the Cartesian subject. All academic powers have entered into a holy alliance to exorcize this specter . . . Where is the academic orientation which has not been accused by its opponents of not yet properly disowning the Cartesian heritage? And which has not hurled back the branding reproach of Cartesian subjectivity against its more 'radical' critics, as well as 'reactionary' adversaries? Two things result from this: 1) Cartesian subjectivity continues to be acknowledged by all academic powers as a powerful and still active intellectual tradition. 2) It is high time that the partisans of Cartesian subjectivity should, in the face of the whole world, publish their views, their aims, their tendencies, and meet this nursery tail of the Specter of Cartesian Subjectivity with the philosophical manifesto of Cartesian subjectivity itself. (Žižek 1999a, p. 1)

Of course, what's most interesting about the opening of Žižek's *The Ticklish Subject* is the choice allowing this effect: echoing the Marx and Engels of the Manifesto, Žižek writes that the rejection of the modern subject (and no longer of "Communism") "forms the silent pact of all the struggling parties of today's academia," and he then endorses the very "specter" that this new Congress of Europe fears. Against the conspiracy of Deep Ecologists, Quack

New-Agers, Heideggerians, Deleuzians, Habermassians and deconstructionists (in short, against "postmodernism" in all of its guises), the Slovenian philosopher proposes a radicalized subjectivism, a subjectivism based upon the "forgotten obverse, the excessive, unacknowledged kernel of the cogito, which is far from the pacifying image of the transparent Self" (Žižek 1999a, p. 2).

Of course, what's at stake here is not really Descartes. Nor is it even just a philosophical position. To oversimplify a little bit, we might say that the issue here is the continued viability of the modern insight. Žižek means to defend something about the Enlightenment vision, something that gets all too easily passed over in various returns to wholism or even in rejections of modernism's "abstraction" or the violence of its technological search for control of nature and society. Having identified Žižek with modernity, though, we must immediately qualify that identification; for Žižek's Cartesianism stands for something about modernity so *uncomfortable* that even reliable modernists like Habermas have to reject it.[1] It is with this discomfort that I return to identifying just *what* the modern insight is, free of the distortion that accompanies its programmatic projection; for it turns out that the real "silent pact" of today's intellectuals is precisely a decision to ignore the subversive potential of the modern and to embrace or reject "modernism" on the basis of its distorted representation.

In the version of the *Cogito* that he includes in his *Meditations on First Philosophy*, Descartes argues as follows: while I *can* doubt the existence of all things up to and including dreams and the analytic results of reasoning ("2+2=4"), it remains *indubitable* that some "I" that doubts, that some function exists allowing doubting itself to occur, since it must be *for* a consciousness (Descartes 1968, Med, II.3). Of course, Descartes' articulation of this argument immediately adds something to the way I've put it, precisely distorting the *Cogito* into an instrument of traditional foundationalist metaphysics and blunting its revolutionary effect; for Descartes puts no scare quotes around the "I," claiming simply "doubtless, then, I exist, since I am deceived." Moreover, the central argumentative thrust of the second *Meditation* and, indeed, of Descartes' rationalist project, soon transforms this I into a fully substantial (albeit, impoverished) "self." Having posed the question of *what* precisely is thus made certain, he proceeds subtractively, eliminating all that hyberbolic doubt challenges. Beyond the body, this subtraction also removes those "mental faculties" that depend upon the body – that is, the "nutritive" soul responsible for its animation and the perceptive faculties responsible for gleaning information through it. The remainder here, of course, is the faculty of "thought" itself, the mind. Descartes writes:

"I am therefore, precisely speaking, only a thinking thing, that is, a mind" (Descartes 1968, Med, II.6).

Here we have already constructed the universally reviled Descartes, the Descartes whose "person" is an "abstract" subject, a "self" forever removed (unless one buys the sordid tricks of Descartes' proofs for God's existence) from the "extended" world (*"res extensa"*) by an unconquerable dualism. Thus, on the one hand, we can – as do, for example, Richard Rorty or Susan Bordo[2] – blame Descartes for both the abstraction and solipsism of the modern self, seeing it as alienated from both its own body and the natural world. Perhaps the nadir of such argumentation comes in Teresa Brennan's ironically "Lacanian" account, *History after Lacan,* a text in which she claims that the separation of the subject from its world leads to an "hallucinatory" regime, a dominant fantasy in which human creativity is squandered in maintaining a representational control over nature and society.[3] In fact, Brennan's version of Descartes' tale ties the "distortion of the person" version of anti-Cartesianism to the anti-technological argument that is its complement and that emerges in Adorno, Horkheimer and Marcuse as well as in Heidegger. In all of these writers, the "Cartesian" sin is traced back to an inability to accept finitude and death and a compensatory demand for an unconditional control of nature and human nature. In this story, the representational "distance" evidenced in Descartes' dualism (between subject and object, *res cogitans* and *res extensa*) is simply a dialectical step in the effort to entirely remove the world's alterity. What counts is that representation for a subject in theory removes the "otherness" of the other – nature or person. Thus, for Heidegger the "age of modern technology" realizes the Cartesian project precisely when the objectivity of the object fades behind a general ordering of nature as "standing reserve" for human uses and, for Horkheimer and Adorno, today's "totally administered society" is symptomatized by the disappearance of the last traces of a natural *"mimesis"* from culture. In either case, Descartes stands in for a technological domination without boundary.

The peculiar thing, of course, is that all of these critiques of Descartes accept as canonical what acute readers ever since – beginning with Kant[4] – have seen clearly was a mistake in Descartes' own understanding of what he had accomplished in the Second Meditation. The basic argument there demands only that we admit there *is representing* going on. To put this in Kantian language (and it is Kant upon whom we rely here), when Descartes subtracts everything that he can doubt, he transforms being itself into a field of representation – things taken by the act of "doubting" to be mental constructs. "Subject" names the precondition for that subtractive operation, a condition that, as transcendental, cannot appear *within* the field it makes possible. This does not, in any full way, however, necessitate that this subject really "exists." Descartes' full assertion, "*Cogito, ergo sum,*" is certainly unwarranted. As Mladen Dolar puts it, "in the place of the supposed certainty of the subject's being, there is just a void. It is not the same subject that thinks and that is; the one that is is not the one that thinks, even more, the one that is is ultimately not a subject at all" (Dolar, in Žižek 1998, p. 18).

Thus his argument does *not* necessitate the direction Descartes subtly introduces with his very "what" question ("what is it that "I" am in doubting the existence of anything?") and his consideration of the problem in terms of "faculties" of the soul. It does not yet presuppose that the "I" *of whom* I think in the *cogito's* self-reflection is the same as the "I" *that* thinks – the hasty elision underlying the characterization of "me," the self, as "*res cogitans*" ("the thing that thinks") In other words, "Cartesianism," meaning the unarticulated "enunciative position" hidden by the rationalist argument, suggests a view that is "far from the pacifying image of the transparent Self" (Žižek 1999a, p. 2) – that Descartes and the united forces of contemporary thought *want it to be.* It suggests a subject of representation that is precisely *not* the self and, furthermore, is not so much "outside of" the extended world as a heterogeneous *condition of possibility* for it. Or, as Žižek puts it in another context, Descartes forces us to think a "subject bereft of subjectivity" (Žižek 1998, p. 7).

Although this is not entirely clear before the 1960s – perhaps because of Lacan's earlier *Auseinandersetzung* with Sartre – Lacan's writings and seminars from the early 1960s onwards indicate an alliance with *this* Descartes. In fact, such Cartesianism runs implicitly through Lacan's work from the late 1940s onwards – in the distinction between the subject ("*je*") and the ego ("*moi*"), between the subject of enunciation and what it enunciates or, finally, between a "knowledge" suggested by the analyst but inaccessible to the analysand.[5]

This last distinction demands we address the peculiar way that a radicalized Cartesianism can be of use in psychoanalysis rather than simply in constructing a philosophical position. No doubt, Lacan's approach to Descartes is mediated by his interpretive transformation of Freud's science, by his insight that the "unconscious" is misunderstood when taken as a substantive but secret set of "contents," a "real me" somehow lying beneath my consciousness. Thus, in *The Four Fundamental Concepts,* Lacan asserts that the subject of psychoanalysis is "the Cartesian one" precisely insofar as it is *not* "the living substratum . . . nor any sort of substance" (Lacan 1981, p. 126).

Against psychoanalytic psychologism (most famously the kind of analysis embraced by Jung), Lacan insists that the unconscious is the *subject of representation*. As such, it is essentially inaccessible to a representational consciousness, heterogeneous to the very objectifying "form" imposed by representation. The subject ("I", or "*je*") cannot appear as a content of consciousness because it is not that sort of thing. Indeed, it is not an "object," a "what," at all and, indeed, strictly speaking does not even exist but is only the presupposition of every representation.[6]

But, on the other hand, just as the position of the observer in a perspectival pictorial representation is registered in the appearance of representation, so also the distortion of the analysand's discourse (in comparison to other discourses) *registers* this unrepresentable subject. Here we arrive at the specifically psychoanalytic dimension of Lacan's Cartesianism, but also at the site of his own dissatisfied continuous self-revision; for, even if we take as canonical the Freudian list of ways in which such distortion appears within an analytic therapy (gaps, lacunae, slips, neurotic symptoms, etc., etc.), the meaning of such registration is fundamentally unclear. Aren't these "gaps" in the analysand's discourse themselves, at least when cycled through the analyst's interpretation, *really* representations? That is, the danger emerges that the clarity of the Cartesian structure of subjectivity will break down, that "the subject who speaks" and represents will be reduced to a secret version of "myself."

One could argue that the tortuous unfolding of Lacan's theoretical work through the 1960s and 70s partially results from the difficulty of defending his Cartesian insight as specific to the analytic situation. Over and over, the task of analytic therapy (the transference, the role of interpretation, the short session, etc., etc.) is rethought along with the notion of the subject. The specific meanderings of this path of reinvention need not detain us, but one version at least must give us pause if we are to make sense of Žižek's Lacanian polemic. Lacan becomes increasingly convinced that at least some subset of the symptomatic material generated by the analysand is thoroughly resistant to interpretation, that analysis cannot undo its repression, resolving the symptom. Such material testifies, so Lacan, to the "fundamental fantasy," that primary repressed related to the structure of representation itself and resolvable only through the most radical means.[7] In other words, the eruptions of this fantasy will not allow a therapeutic process wherein we come to "recognize ourselves" in them.

We will eventually have to return to the idea of the "fundamental fantasy." but a detour could clarify things both in relationship to Lacan and to Žižek; for, the idea that the subject of psychoanalysis is Cartesian is inextricable from the related notion of its *perspectival* nature – a matter to which both Lacan and Žižek frequently refer.[8] That is, the ground for the purely "doubting" consciousness of the *Meditations* was laid two centuries before in the painting, architecture and theory of Alberti, Brunelleschi and Fillarette, Leonardo, Piero and others.[9] The key here lies in the notions of a "vanishing point" and "viewpoint," concepts which – particularly in the simplest (and most favored!) version of perspective, so called "one-point" perspective – correspond to Descartes' insubstantial subject.

If that's the case, if we can actually "model" the Cartesian subject on the perspectival one, then it should be possible to *think through* the relationship between subject and world or subject and self in relationship to that same model. Differently than in the case of Descartes, who so basically mistook his own insight that generations of thought were required to grasp it, consideration of Renaissance perspective-theory should help us to understand what *underlies* Žižek's polemic for the modern subject.

In what is arguably the initiating act of Italian Renaissance painting, Filippo Brunelleschi produced a famous demonstration. Painting in correct one-point perspective (a perspective system at the time not yet formalized in theory) the baptistery and piazza outside the duomo in Florence as they looked from a place inside the cathedral's door, he placed a pin-hole at the center of his panel. In order to complete Brunelleschi's experiment, the viewer was to stand inside the duomo at the very position from which the work had been painted. Holding a small mirror, he was to gaze through the pinhole, jockeying the mirror into such a position that it reflected the scene on the panel in perfect continuity with the *actual scene* that extended out visually from the mirror's edge. The picture in the mirror and the scene beyond its border blended into a single image. The "miracle" about which Manetti, Vasari and others later wrote lay precisely in the way that the represented and real scenes blended – that the actual piazza appeared as a continuation of the space of the panel's representation.

In *The Origin of Perspective*, Hubert Damisch has argued compellingly that the demonstration here concerns the relationship between perspectival space and subjectivity (Damisch 1994, p. 121). While Brunelleschi's accomplishment in this panel clearly belongs to a history of, if you like, "smoke and mirrors," of quasi-magical perspectival effects, that both predates and outlasts it, the *form* that he chose here for his trick bears thought. Why force his viewer to hold this awkward small mirror when Brunelleschi might have dispensed with the pinhole and the mirror, having the viewer look, from the privileged "viewpoint," directly at the panel superimposed on the scene?

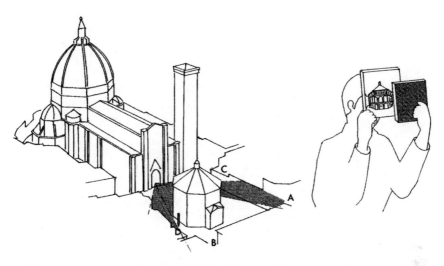

FIGURE 3.1 Brunelleschi's First Demonstration: According to Damisch

Why not look *at* the painting instead of *through* it? Such a technology would have been simpler and would also have demonstrated the "blending" of representation and visual space just as well as the preferred scheme.

As Damisch demonstrates, the reason for Brunelleschi's preference of the pinhole view and the small mirror has to do with an, as yet, unarticulated – and, in the forming language of the *quattrocento* still *unarticulable* – sense about *subjectivity* and spatial representation. Cutting the viewing hole in the painting precisely *at* the vanishing point collapses two representational functions, but in each of these, the effect of the pinhole and the mirror is to underscore the "subjective" nature of pictorial representation. On the one hand, a line perpendicular to the picture-plane behind the peep-hole itself contains the so-called "viewpoint" around whose symmetrical simulacrum *in the painting* the geometries of the representation are organized: otherwise put, jockeying the mirror allows Brunelleschi to demonstrate that the view represented is specific to a chosen viewpoint, that it is a representation *for* a viewer, and to that extent *of* a viewer. You picture your "self" in picturing where you are in relationship to the painted scene. The viewer of the pinhole device simulates putting her/himself "in the picture" to demonstrate this representational fact.

On the other hand, Damisch notes that the advantage of the chosen system is that it puts the vanishing point (located at infinity on that same "centric" line [as Alberti later calls it]) *behind the eye* of the viewer. In other

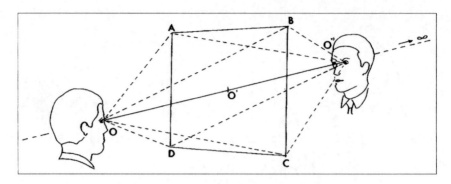

FIGURE 3.2 Reconstruction of the Vanishing Point in Brunelleschi's First Demonstration by Damisch: "Infinity: An Idea of What's Behind Our Heads"

words, it forces us to associate that vanishing point (where the parallel lines of spatial recession meet at the horizon within the painting) with what will later be called the dimensional, insubstantial *subject* of representation. Representation of space in correct "one point" perspective – translation of three-dimensional space into systematic two-dimensional representation – involves the projection of a *point of exception* to that representation, a subject point as "hole" in the totalizing representation of being as objectivity (See, Damisch 1994, p. 121.) In Damisch's words, the subject of one point perspective is "behind the eye" of the viewer at infinity.

Brunelleschi's first experiment thus proves an odd demonstration of the Lacanian subject; for, in superimposing vanishing and viewpoints on a single perpendicular line, at a single point, it both *excludes* that subject from the painting and *includes* it within it, indicating both subjectivity's heterogeneity to the field of representation (as insubstantial, dimensional, etc.) and the fact that representation is *for it* (as the spatially positioned monocular viewer). In other words, the structure of subjectivity is calibrated with the utmost accuracy, demanding both that we conceive representation in terms of a constitutive "hole" in it and that we be able to calculate precisely the position of this exception point in relationship to the geometry of a specific representation.

Fundamental fantasy and master signifier

Let me begin with a contrast, an image from Freud, one that he calls a "primal fantasy" (*Urphantasie*). In general, Freud wields the term *Phantasie* in various ways all of which have in common the notion of a psychically con-structed and coherent scene in which the subject or "dreamer" is present as an observer (Laplanche and Pontalis 1973, pp. 314–316). Beginning in 1915, moreover, Freud speaks of "primal fantasy" (*Urphantasie*) – using that term to indicate a "primal scene" (most typically the scene of witnessed parental coitus) that is present to the individual even when it represents no actual experience. Freud's various "*Urphantasien*" share a reference to "ori-gins"; in the case of the primal fantasy of the parental sex-act, this reference is quite literally to the subject's origination, and the "primal scene" here is a kind of staging or representation of one's own conception (Laplanche and Pontalis 1973, p. 332).

So, whereas Brunelleschi's demonstration offers us the image of a scene which is explicitly non-whole (broken at least at one point, the vanishing point) and dependent (on the subject viewing it), the Freudian primal fan-tasy suggests a universe closed on itself. Furthermore, if we take Freud's own most famous *entrée* to the primal scene/primal fantasy combination – namely, the "Wolfman" case, it's interesting to note that what leads Freud to such a scene of parental intercourse from the "Wolfman's" own dream of "wolves in a tree" is the obvious anxiety underlying it. Here we should shift from the perspective of Freud to that of Lacan who, less concerned than Freud with the idea that the "scene" captures an "actual" infantile event would comment, rather, on the peculiar combination of *fantasy* of a com-plete and reliably independent world and such anxiety. In other words, it is only at an *affective* level that the fantasy delivers its really "fundamental," unbearable content; it is only at that level that it is irreducibly unconscious.

To suggest *that* content, we might join Žižek and Eric Santner in return-ing to a different Freud, the speculative theorist of *Moses and Monotheism* who proposes that the myth of Moses the patriarch and, indeed, the accom-panying production of a patriarchal "God-the-Father" are responses to a repressed *murder* of the actual (Egyptian) Moses.[10] According to this account, the fundamental fantasy – that *we* are guilty of some horrible primal crime and thus must endlessly atone for it – *actually* aims to defeat anxiety, to transform it *into* guilt (Žižek 2003, p. 57). After all, Freud's deduced lesson from the death of the *actual* Moses, the "father," is that there *are no* external consequences, no divine retribution for murder. However, we prefer a state in which what overcomes us is a specific object demanding a definite atonement rather than an undefined "cloud" of affect. We prefer to have offended the gods, who demand expiatory sacrifices rather than confront a fundamentally meaningless universe where no punishment follows from our "wicked" deeds. Afflicted by paralyzing anxiety regarding the meaningless-ness of the world, we create an unconscious fantasy by which we owe a specific debt for breaking the world-order, we find ourselves in need of atonement for contravening God's will.

The fundamental fantasy, then, does two things: first, it accounts for that "subject" visible in Brunelleschi's perspective demonstration by expunging it "from the picture" – by attributing to it a basic transgression demanding compensatory atonement.[11] "We" are sinners (in the Christian vision, *original* sinners, guilty of disrupting the basic fabric of Being). In such a cosmos, we as human beings are primordially guilty of disrupting the fundamental order and therefore excluded from it. Of course, this way of explaining the unconscious fantasy already implies its *second* characteristic, namely, its *virtue* of totalizing being, guaranteeing a "meaningful" universe.[12] An ordered universe, essentially complete in itself, still holds "no place" for the sponta-neous human will, the *subject*. The cosmos is whole: only, short of the redem-ption posited by orthodoxy, *we* cannot belong to it.

In brief, the exchange enacted through the fundamental fantasy acts in a profoundly *pre-modern* fashion. Moreover, from a Žižekian perspective, the fundamental fantasy *produces* reality by means of this *proto-representation*, wherein, precisely, the "field" of experience is cast as a fantasmatic or imagi-nary totality.[13] That is, fantasy projects the social *qua* totality by imagining it as totalized from the position of transcendence, from a privileged subject's perspective. Reality emerges from the Real precisely when the world of human existence is conceived *as the perspective of an omniscient subject* – as what Žižek follows Lacan in calling the "Other." In order to conceive of the world as "ontologically closed" we imagine a "viewpoint" *from which* it appears as totality.[14] Reality is always conceived from and for such a totali-zing view, such an outside. As a result, reality per se is a product of an omniscient subjectivity *we* imagine. Žižek notes this explicitly:

> What psychoanalysis calls 'fantasy' is the endeavor to close this gap by (mis)perceiving the pre-ontological Real as simply *another*, 'more funda-mental', level of reality – fantasy projects on to the pre-ontological Real the form of constituted reality (as in the Christian notion of another, suprasensible reality). (Žižek 1999a, p. 57)

The pre-Copernican image of the cosmos familiar to us from medieval maps pictures the "universe" opened by the fundamental fantasy, wherein guilt is interpreted as resulting from our transgression of a lawful order.

Thus, such maps take the heterogeneity of the divine subject and give it a "place." Indeed, "place" is vital here in a couple ways: on the one hand, the medieval cosmos suggests, in the Thomistic or Neo-Platonic "Chain of Being" theories, that every being "has a place" within it. As Žižek puts it, the fundamental fantasy "provides a sense of ontological 'safety', of dwelling within a self-enclosed finite circle of meaning where things (natural phenomena) in a way 'speak to us', address us"(Žižek 1997, p. 160). On the other hand, of course, there is the divine place, the "Empyrean Heaven" which, appropriately, occupies the "highest" and outermost circle of being in medieval maps. This is, of course, the place of places; for it implies a position from which God can overview all of being, from which he can, in fact, constitute it as a whole.

The remaining piece of this Lacanian "genetic ontology," is provided by the so-called "phallic" or "master" signifier. Its function is easy to capture by returning to the scene of primordial guilt framed by Freud's interpretation of religion – a tableau which produces the master signifier in translating that "cloud" of anxiety resulting from remorse at a human crime not only into a crime against God but also into a specific path of atonement. Such a path also has the benefit of strengthening the bonds of the group, sharing guilt. The torturing, hectoring affect of the "superego" (the internalized, murdered father) is *not* pleasant and it can be *harmful* as well. On the other hand, the Freud of *Moses and Monotheism* notes a more straightforward affective benefit for the individual in belonging to the *community* of the guilty – namely, the sense of shared "accomplishment" in relinquishing immediate desires to follow the dictates of the Law. In a pre-modern context, the master signifier *builds the self*, helping the individual to become stronger by becoming a full and mature part of the community. Notice, however, that such a sense of accomplishment hinges upon the definite and shared nature of the "code" of Law. We can only overcome our immediate desires and needs to the extent that these are opposed by *specific* prohibitions. A vague sense of disquiet about a given act won't suffice.

In effect, the master signifier is responsible for the conscious effects of the unconscious fundamental fantasy: it paints that "cosmological" picture of the world *as* whole by creating the space of ideality (the "suprasensible," in Žižek's Christian example) which is the "picture" accompanying the repressed fantasy. How does it accomplish this?

Think of the way that a photographer or painter can accentuate a foreground image – say, the "subject" of a portrait – by limiting the function of focus to that figure and blurring the background. Perhaps, as is often the case, the artist will accentuate this effect (think of the darkness in so many of Rembrandt's backgrounds) with light and color, for example bringing the foreground, brilliantly accented, forward to grab our attention.

We should notice three separate phenomena at work in such an aesthetic effect: first, the subject of the photograph or painting in this way becomes something like a *place* of interest, a *topos* selected from amongst an indefinite but numerable set of possibilities. That is, in the language of structuralism, it marks a signifier, unattached to any particular meaning. In *The Ticklish Subject,* Žižek uses the example of Abraham Lincoln's statement, "You can fool all the people some of the time, and some of the people all of the time, but you cannot fool all the people all of the time." Ever since Lincoln uttered these words, people have lost themselves in the coils of the logical ambiguity they express: "does it mean that there are some people who can always be fooled, or that on every occasion someone or other is bound to be fooled?" (Žižek 1999a, p. 56). The point for Žižek, however, is precisely that these words just *sound good*, that they are "witty" enough to fascinate us. In other words, they provide a *focus* (and, in that sense, serve as a "signifier") for our attention and, like the foregrounded subject of a portrait, draw our attention away from an *unfocused* and meaningless background.

Of course, and this makes the second important phenomenon, both Lincoln's words and the portrait manage to provide such a focus because they are *enigmatic*, because, meaningless in themselves, they seem to be mysteries, to invite an endless process of interpretation. In this light, it's hardly surprising that, Žižek at one point suggests that an individual's feelings for someone with whom she/he has fallen in love provide a perfect example of such an enigmatic signifier. After all, our love refers to "an unknowable X, to the *je ne sais quoi* that makes me fall in love," and as a result, the place of the "master signifier" marks an endless effort to find a meaning adequate to it (Žižek 2003, p. 72).

Finally, moreover, the enigma of the master signifier gives birth to a kind of *transcendence* or *ideality*, figuring the limit or end of the search for a "solution" to the mystery it poses. In other words, around this signifier we are utterly convinced that there *is* a meaning to our love, to the portrait hanging before us or, for that matter, to Lincoln's words. This meaning is *out there*, beyond us, but in a position that makes sense, not just of some particular phenomenon (Lincoln's "sound bite," say) but, rather, of our lives as a whole. The promise of one's search for the meaning of one's love is that this meaning will "make sense" of all the absurdity in a life. Our fascination, indeed, is predicated upon this hermeneutical affect, wherein the very search for a meaning instantiates it. It all "makes sense," if we could just put our finger on how . . . Thus, it is not simply that the master signifier fascinates us; it does so in a fashion that retroactively provides consistency to our lives.

Herein lies the peculiar space of the fundamental fantasy attached to the back, as it were, of the master signifier. Its space corresponds to that peculiar transcendence that we posit when we take the solution to the enigma to "exist" "out there." Only one thing must be added: we must understand that a precondition of such ideality is *that we never actually achieve it,* that we are never able to occupy the space of the Other from which the meaning of our lives would be manifest. Žižek acknowledges this necessity, for example, with regard to the way love operates, noting that "the moment I can enumerate reasons why I love you, the things about you that made me fall in love with you, we can be sure that this is not love," or not any longer (Žižek 2003, p. 72). In other words, to be effective, the master signifier must remain an enigma, not only in the sense that it promises *transparent meaning* but also in the sense that it *promises* such meaning, that it never actually delivers it.

Modernity and fantasy

With these accounts of the fundamental fantasy and the master signifier, it is now possible to pose my basic, structural question – possible, that is, to see how the structure of the "perspectival" subject forces us to a deep problem in Žižek's thought. That problem derives from the observation that it's *no coincidence* that the Lacanian psychoanalytic subject is *also* the radicalized modern subject. In other words, there's a bond between the subject of psychoanalysis and modernity. We might articulate the problem itself as follows: on the one hand, the revolution apparent in Brunelleschi's perspective experiment (a revolution which becomes the "cause" of both modern philosophy and modern science) depends upon what seems to be an *exposure* of fantasy as "false". Recall that in the demonstration, and in systematic painterly and architectural perspective in general, the subject is revealed as both constitutive of the world's apparent totality and as a specific void or lack *in* that totality.

We needn't wander any further than Nicholas of Cusa's speculations (contemporary with Brunelleschi) on the perspectival nature of all truth and the resultant impossibility that we live in a "centered" universe to see contained in Brunelleschi's insight trouble for unconscious fantasy. Recall that, for Nicholas (and his disciple, Giordano Bruno), *because* all truth is constituted perspectively (that is, for a finitely positioned viewer), there can be no finitely locatable "center" to the universe. Or, as he also puts it in the *Docta Ignorantia,* in a perspectival universe, *every point* (and thus *no* point) is the center.[15] It remains for Bruno to draw the most outrageous consequences already implied in Cusanus' still "orthodox" thought – namely that such a universe reserves no special "place" either for any individual or for humanity as a whole. Thus, at a single blow, the entire *cosmos* of the master signifier is challenged. In the infinite, homogeneous space underlying perspective, we lose the sense of security it grants us.

Indeed, in its invisible subject-effect, perspective might constitute *the* exemplary historical moment within a Lacanian view of history, the moment when people were able to "traverse" the fundamental fantasy itself – to liberate themselves from its claim. In other words, representation was the primary hammer with which the cosmological worldview, with its closure and its Platonism, could be smashed. Perspective "subjectivized," forced us to live without a "place" from which and for which we were constituted. I might go so far as to write that what we mean by "subject" within the modern context is nothing except the structure necessary to conceptualize the real *without* transcendence, the structure necessary to escape the "cosmological" form of fantasy. The inception of the modern is thus an *experience of freedom,* a matter that we should not forget in the ambiguous history following from it.

To this extent, the *political* revolutions of the eighteenth century belong essentially to – perhaps one might even say that they provide something like a goal of – the subjectivism that makes such a representational transformation possible. Or, to put this in other words, the possibility of a genuinely political society, a society that would acknowledge and take responsibility for the freedom of itself and persons within it, lies in the loss of "our place" which ushered in modern space and modern science. Only a society that conceptually admits the freedom of its acts and the acts of its citizens – refusing all forms of arguments from nature – can provide the conditions to further that freedom. Modernity opens the possibility of political freedom, and such opening provides modernity's ultimate justification.

On the other hand, though, from a Lacanian perspective, the master signifier and its fantasmatic reverse are *constitutive* figures: reality itself depends upon their existence. In other words, nestled into what often seems a merely technical account, the Freudian-Lacanian tradition includes a profound transcendental insight: what we *mean* experientially by reality is something like an existence guaranteed by fantasy, an existence which we imagine to be totalized and which, *as* totalized, excludes *us* (that is, as *subject*) from it. It's thus not possible to suppose that the truth of the subject, the truth suggested by Brunelleschi's experiment, somehow does away with fundamental fantasy.

The problem with a modernist interpretation of Lacan should be obvious from my characterization of the fundamental fantasy. The "perspectival" moment, whatever its revolutionary potential, doesn't shatter reality itself: nor could it, fantasy being *constitutive* of reality per se. Leaving aside for the moment the question of the possibility and limitation of revolutionary change within a Lacanian framework, we must address the tension here between the claim of transcendental constitution assigned to the fantasy/ master signifier combination and the claim that the modern, perspectival moment (with its various Cartesian and subjectivist permutations) *exposes* the fantasy.

Žižek's resolution of that tension is implicitly to argue that fundamental fantasy and master signifier don't disappear within the modern world but that they are profoundly *changed* by it. For the most part, we discover the effects of the modern subject in the emergence of new forms of fantasy, forms that no longer follow the model of an exclusionary transcendence.

And, just as, as a kind of corollary to it, the pre-Copernican diagram of the cosmos gave us entrée to the fantasy-formation, we might here return to the *counter-formation* to such cosmology proposed by the founders of modern thought to understand the underpinnings of such a new formation of reality. Think here of the radical (and, of course, for its author, traumatic) immanentism of Spinoza's philosophy. In subtracting the very space of transcendence from the universe, in proposing his "monist" philosophy, Spinoza follows the most explosive potential of the modern revolution, but, oddly, he retreats in a characteristic way: in his *Ethics*, he posits a position, the "mind of God" which conceives all natural events in terms of their pure actuality – in terms, that is, of a completed causal chain. Indeed, the moment of retreat from the subversive potential of modernity comes precisely here, at the moment when *nature itself* is reconceived immanently from a totalized perspective. At first, powerfully, we conceive of all being as subsisting in a single plane, a plane of material causes. But then we add to that thesis *a closure* of the material dimension: all effects are already contained in their causes, so that the end of the universe is already implicit in the first events occurring within it. We are faced with a reductive causal determinism, a determinism without the possibility of freedom (See, Žižek 1999b, p. 26). Paraphrasing Hegel, Žižek tells us that, "teleology is the truth of linear mechanical causality" (Žižek 2004, p. 113). Is not such totalization of nature the almost invariable accompaniment of all early-modern, all "mechanistic" science?

It might also be instructive to recall a theoretical trope that emerged almost as soon as the perspectival metaphor established itself in the fifteenth century – the location of the divine at the confluence of all "viewpoints" constituting perspectival space. For, it turns out that modernity opens a *second* possible "position" from which reality may be constituted. Recall the philosophical view first articulated by Nicholas of Cusa, but reflected in Bruno, Leibniz and Newton. This argument starts in a radical de-centering of the medieval, cosmological, worldview. Space is projected as an infinite and homogeneous field amenable to purely quantitative understanding. Where in such a universe is God – still the "subject" for philosophy until Descartes? A universe without center can allow no places "nearer" or farther from him: nor (which is really the same thing) can it admit the image of a God out "beyond" space.[16] Cusanus' solution is to conceive God as present at *every* point, every position, *but only insofar as any such point is conceived as viewpoint.* In Newton's famous phrase, the universe is God's "*sensorium.*" In other words, the subject is in every place *qua* viewpoint. The "other space" of this fantasy, then, consists of the infinite (but complete) set of all points within objective space. It's the same space in which we live but now conceived as a web of subject points. There is, and can be, no distinguishing characteristic of such a space, since it is the *very same* space as the one we inhabit, but it is, nonetheless, functionally distinct from objective space. Thus, we get a sense of uncanny "closeness" to us, typical of a paranoid psychical economy.[17]

And this paranoid structure also informs the form of subjectivization at work here: for example, in a late work, "On the Image of God," Nicholas describes an icon that he gave to the Monks at his former home, Tegernsee: like those paintings with which murder-mysteries have made us familiar, the eyes of this icon had the odd quality of seeming to gaze *at* the viewer no matter where he positioned himself (Nicholas of Cusa,1997a, p. 235). If we admit that such subjection indicates a subject who is anywhere and everywhere, we are "subjected" to the gaze of the "Other" at any and every point.[18] Space itself seems to be alive with this (nonetheless) "obscene" gaze. Surely, though it emerges with early modernity, this idol seems remarkably contemporary. It captures that uncanny sense of a subject of the world that is no longer simply transcendent.

To understand the unconscious element of this "paranoid" construction of reality, the key transformation involves that closing off of transcendence

FIGURE 3.3 Bosse: The Perspecteurs/1648

which we've seen to be definitive of the modern fantasy. Instead of *outside* a closed cosmos, the Other now inhabits a space of unprecedented intimacy to the subject, right there, at the same "point of view" *as* that of the subject but still distinct from it. A paranoid intimacy, then.

The effects of this paranoid relationship are twofold and, to a large extent, historically ordered. Let me name them: obsessional neurosis and perversion.

The first, whose emergence I might date in the period after the Renaissance, retains the basic economy of guilt-before-law that we've already seen to have been definitive of reality in the *pre-modern* period. Still, without the function of that master signifier producing the Other's transcendence, guilt affects the individual differently. With the disappearance of the concrete site for guilt's atonement, we lose also the "communal" structure that reinforces individual identity *before* the modern period. To put this in Lacan's terms, modernity could be identified with the gradual disappearance of *ritual*, of those kinds of communal bonds founded upon a *symbolically shared* sense of guilt.[19]

The displacement of the pre-Copernican "map" is both symbol and cause of the decay of such a *public* law and, with it, of a public identity based upon shared guilt. For one thing, there's no longer a specific set of public rules sufficing to satisfy the demands of conscience. Think here of the great struggle of the Protestant Reformation, which follows the modern revolution by *internalizing* faith, making it a matter of "the heart" rather than of public rites. Increasingly, in the period of the seventeenth and eighteenth centuries, the individual is thrown back on herself in determining the "content of conscience," a position that, in turn, weakens identification *through* and *with* the social bond. In a series of arguments, Žižek associates the infinite demand of the Protestant, Kantian call to "duty" with the situation of Kafka's subject called "before the law," that is, faced with a legal demand never specified or, better, whose specific content we are never allowed to know.[20] We know we are supposed (not) to do something, but we can never really know what that something is. Our primordial guilt becomes, then, precisely the anxiety in the presence of a Law without possibility of a finite redress by "following the rules," since these rules are never specified (See, for example, Žižek 2003, p. 129).

Now, of course, the results of this change are themselves ambiguous and well-documented – on the one hand, the emergence of modern neurosis and the accelerated weakening of instituted forms of community, on the other, the development of the "genius," the self-creating person and the Romantic cult of individualism, but either end of the equation indicates that, when guilt is finally separated off from the symbolic apparatus of a specific set of requirements and prohibitions – when the Law ceases to form a potential identity – we face a transformed fantasy/master signifier combination.

We must ask what happens when the "object," the place of the superego, is occupied by the very "excess" of being that guilt intended to tame? This is in fact the strange condition controlling *our* reality today, the condition under which totality emerges as that strange, excessive thing, "life": "Are we really living?" we ask. Have we really "given our all?" or "enjoyed ourselves?" These Romantic questions begin to haunt humanity, to provide, ironically, the nexus of guilt ("I have not really lived, given my all, enjoyed, etc"), precisely at that moment, at the end of the Enlightenment, when the old institutions and specific demands of the Law fall. Less and less are persons tortured by guilt at moral transgression: at an ever accelerating pace our guilt now becomes *performance-guilt* about life, guilt that transforms life into a vague totality capable of providing a measure for our success or failure and a measure, of course, in terms of which we almost inevitably fall short.

The key transformation at that historical moment is the prominence of a *new* totalizing device, a device for the imposition of "reality" on the Real – now associated with "life" or in the term wielded by Lacan, Žižek and, Todd McGowan, "enjoyment." McGowan has recently hypothesized that increasingly since the nineteenth century we have become a "society of enjoyment," a society in which the commandment to "enjoy!" has largely displaced traditional moral imperatives. In other words, the society of enjoyment or, as McGowan specifies it, "the society of *commanded* enjoyment," is the visible symptom of the paranoid fundamental fantasy, the way that the "belief" in the big Other continues when we consciously claim to disavow it.[21] Guilt and anxiety – the weapons of the superego – still operate, but they do so by torturing us for *not enjoying ourselves*, not being "really alive" in response to the direct enjoyment of the Other.

And it is in this sense of a disavowed belief in the Other that we are justified in following Žižek's lead in finding the predominant master signifier of our world in *perversion*. The pervert is a false transgressor of the law, apparently radical in his/her willingness to engage in "forbidden" practices but secretly invested in maintaining Law *so as to leave room for the pleasure of breaking the rules!* The structure of this deception is a fundamental fantasy in which she/he imagines her/himself to be a kind of "bodyguard" for the Other, protector and facilitator of the *Other's* enjoyment rather than his own.[22] Consider the transformation of Kantian Moral theory first suggested by Lacan in his seventh seminar and much elaborated upon by Žižek and his colleague Alenka Zupančič.[23] The demand that a free subject heed the "call of conscience" – suggests an outcome today that's far from Kant's own moral rigorism. In *The Ticklish Subject*, Žižek even suggests that one can see this outcome in Michel Foucault's ethic of the "care of the self," (from his *History of Sexuality*) (See, Žižek 1999a, pp. 279–280.) Kant's moral philosophy demands that we distinguish the "inner" voice of conscience from the external and artificial imperatives imposed by tradition, religion, etc. We must not confuse the *form* of the categorical imperative with the *content* of specific duties. Foucault simply sees the necessity of completing this "formal" interiorization of morality. "The care of the self" demands that we avoid *all* socially imposed (and thus artificial) rules, *including the rules that Kant ascribed to duty or morality itself.* The new imperative of conscience is that one do "what one really wants to do," a task that first demands of the "moral agent" that she discern this "true" desire in a preconstituted and complete "self" – a self which here *plays the role* of the Other (one might determine what "it" wants by means of a *ouija* board or. . . by means of free association). To return to the preferred Lacanian term, the new formations transform the superego from an agency of *prohibition* to one of *enforced enjoyment.*

I referred above to perversion as a "substitute" for the traditional master signifier, an assertion that I would justify in part with the analogous way that perversion *diverts* or fascinates us, preventing us from "paying attention to what's behind the curtain" of fantasy. That is, here too, as in the traditional fantasy, reality gains its consistency by diverting attention from a fragmentary and senseless condition. As Žižek puts it, perversion allows the subject to treat life as "a childish game," one "unencumbered by the Real of human finitude" (Žižek 2002, p. 265).

In such a game, Žižek would locate all the varieties of frenetic activity that fill the space of post-Romantic cultural politics – from the Nietzschean cult of the "overman" and its reverberations in modern art to the "play of the signifier" embraced by Post-Structuralists, to the "Risk Society" of Ulrich Beck.[24] In each of these cases, "play," a kind of hyper-activity, is substituted for any challenge to the order of reality. Indeed, Žižek *defines* the "game" aspect here in precisely this manner – indicating the "perverse" nature of the culture it supports: the game is defined by the question, "what do we have to change so that ultimately nothing will really change?" (Žižek 1999a, p. 200)

And, finally, we must not forget the way in which paranoia itself betrays its foundational presence in our fundamental fantasy. That is, one of the definitive qualities of a reality guaranteed by the paranoid fundamental fantasy must be a certain fragility, brittleness – a tendency to dissolve at odd moments into a psychotic imaginary. Above all, such brittleness emerges in the continued breakdown of symbolic authority. Increasingly, the Other belongs not within the symbolic domain of traditional fantasy but in the domain of the impossible Real. As Žižek puts it, behind today's "cynical" disinvestiture from symbolic authority lies a more sinister investment:

> The distrust of the big Other (the order of symbolic fictions), the subject's refusal to 'take it seriously', relies on the belief that there is an 'Other of the Other', that a secret invisible and all-powerful agent actually

'pulls the strings' and runs the show: behind the visible, public Power there is another obscene, invisible power structure. This other, hidden agent acts the part of the 'Other of the Other' in the Lacanian sense, the part of the meta-guarantee of the big Other (the symbolic order that regulates social life). (Žižek 1999a p. 362)

The paranoiac experiences this Other in the Real as "too close," unpredictably eruptive, "always watching." Are these not precisely the metaphors suggested by Nicholas of Cusa's "Idol" or, for that matter, by the Wachowski brothers film, *The Matrix* (1999) – a movie that much fascinates Žižek? Though, as will be seen in the next chapter, for Žižek *The Matrix* is deeply ideological, its ideology, of course, contains a kernel of truth. Recall, the film's conceit: we are presented with a vision of the (near) future as a kind of "Virtual Reality" projected by a network of computers who have enslaved the human race. The film's plot turns upon the "discovery" by Neo, a young computer hacker, that his nominal "world" is not real, that there is another "reality" beneath the appearance of everyday life – the reality of the computers who, for their own enjoyment, maintain persons as a batteries immersed in amniotic fluid. The notion is that, in our apparently mundane lives within today's technological world (Neo is a computer programmer for a large and anonymous corporation appropriately called, "Metacortex"), we are really all victims of "the matrix" – this system so "close to the skin" that it hides itself by projecting a kind of "virtual reality" for us. Having accepted the challenge to "go down the rabbit hole" and face the reality beneath the virtual projection he has always lived, Neo awakens to find himself cradled in a "field" of human batteries tended by monstrous, insect-like machines. What interests Žižek here is this supposed revelation of the ultimate nature of "reality"; for, it demonstrates quite effectively, *not* our reality but the paranoid fantasy underlying it or, "what the film renders as the scene of our awakening into our true situation is effectively its exact opposite, the very fundamental fantasy that sustains our being." (Žižek 2002, p. 245).

In other words, the perverse activity and cynicism of the contemporary world hide a fantasy of the Other as "just beneath our skin," as omnipresent but also without limit and as in control from a dimension which is sickening in its anxious proximity.[25] Here the Law has no codes, no specific prohibitions or practices to direct the subject's activity. We have, instead, a fantasy in which our very bodies serve the Other's incalculable, obscene enjoyment.

Conclusion

Though its truth is *more* than this, too, we could say that Brunelleschi's "experiment" represents the insight of subjectivity: "nothing" is missing from reality – except the very act by which it *becomes* reality, the act of representation for a subject. Of course, the first thing to say about this "nothing" is that it is, non-coincidentally, *invisible*, indeed, largely undetectable. The function of the subject is to disappear, leaving the apparently seamless totality of the world it represents.

But that, of course, raises the question about moments like the one in which Brunelleschi conducted his demonstration – moments that we might provocatively call, "modern." That is, we must ask what happens when the fact of this disappearance and its cause *itself appears*, when we face just that truth of the subject whose tendency is to erase itself. In Žižek's view this is a story of trauma and reaction: the history of modernity has been one of adaptation: "how to maintain social stability in the face of an insight (the subject) with revolutionary potential?" That's the implicit question whose various answers have comprised the secret history of our present. In its ability to analyze the increasing extremity of the moves necessary to maintain the socially constituted Other in the face of its exposure as fantasy, such a theory can explain much that remains opaque within either conservative or traditional Marxist critiques, not only about the fate of subjectivity but also about the imaginary and social organizations with which a capitalist, technological world maintains its stability.

Now, of course, when seen in this light, Žižek's understanding of subjectivity and modernity provides an ambitious alternative to the anti-subjectivist critical theory of Heidegger or of the Frankfurt School. Heidegger is only the one of a series of critics of techno-capitalist society in the past century (Adorno, Horkheimer, Marcuse, Arendt, etc.) to underscore the *difference* between unfreedom in traditional worlds and the "danger" facing us today. The proposition that we *do* face a loss of freedom today, even in societies where consumer choices multiply or where few people face immediate threats of force or even direct interference with their lives, and *that* this threat above all robs us of the very language with which to criticize our contemporary reality or suggest alternatives to it, lends a common urgency to these otherwise various critiques. Žižek rejects the common starting point of such critical theorists, seeing that beginning point as *symptom*, of a paranoid fundamental fantasy rather than as access to the foundations of subjectivity. Still, for all of that, a central thrust of his work, too, is to picture what happens to reality in the wake of the crisis to transcendence by which the modern world emerged, to help us understand the way that the structures of our lifeworld developed from of crisis.

The great virtue of Žižek's account of the present in terms of a transformed "fundamental fantasy" is that it allows concrete and specific analyses of both discontinuities and continuities between the past and the present – the appearance of new modes of subjectivity, new social organizations, new social institutions. We have yet to see the force of Žižek's conceptual apparatus in full operation, its ability to explain various contemporary social and political phenomena, but we can already grasp at least its *potential*, for it leaps over the hurdle that had stymied the last generation of critical theorists. Breaking the bond between critical theory and *anti-subjectivism*, it allows a series of insights about contemporary personhood and worldhood that remained closed to earlier generations. That's because, in rescuing the "excessive" moment in Cartesian subjectivity, Žižek has redeemed the genuinely *revolutionary* potential of modernity. I would argue that this is a far more promising approach to critical theory than any philosophy (like Heidegger's) which allows itself to entertain nostalgia for a pre-modern world or truth.

Chapter 4

The techno-capitalist danger: ideology and contemporary society

Ideology today: re-calibrating dialectical materialism

Perhaps the most breath-taking of Žižek's many daring intellectual moves is his rescue of "dialectical materialism" from the "dustbin of history" where political consensus seems to have tossed it. Of course, at this point Žižek's preference for such a "lost cause" will hardly surprise the reader, but it is the *content* of Žižek's reading that can be shocking; for that interpretation claims that the "dumb" theory of history called "dialectical materialism" within the "really existing socialism" with which Žižek grew up is in fact not the real thing at all but merely a perverse version of idealism.

One has only to read Engels' later efforts to expound Marxist theory of history, to see how easily "materialism" can itself become a crypto-idealism: for Engels, the reality underlying the play of ideas in world history is economic class struggle. Everything reduces to material reality. However, what is such a reality – no matter how "concrete" its manifestations – but the central "idea" of history itself?

Setting out from the devastating effect of these questions for the "dumb theory," Žižek proposes an alternative. Since we cannot seriously conceive of the "material" as an all-encompassing, fundament, a totalizing basis for reality or history, Žižek proposes that, by "dialectical materialism," we mean simply the *non-existence* of anything else, anything that is *not* matter. In other words, the point is not to produce a positive theory of "everything" but rather to assert a limitation, a negativity. Žižek reminds us that "there is a fundamental difference between the assertion 'everything is matter' . . . and the assertion 'there is nothing which is not matter' (which, with its other side, 'not-all is matter,' opens up the space for the account of immaterial phenomena)" – and then proposes the truth of the second position over against the first (Žižek 2006b, p. 168).

Žižek's "dialectical materialism," in this following the logic of sexuation from Lacan's twentieth Seminar, both reaffirms the foundational impor-tance of the material and denies its metaphysical closure.[1] Though there is "nothing else," matter itself is "not-all." The key to dialectical materialism for Žižek is that it asserts the incompleteness of being, the fact that some-thing must be added to being to impose the totality we associate with either scientific socialism or idealism.

It is a truism of Leftist analyses of capital that the capitalist system is riven by inherent contradictions while presenting itself as a coherent whole: some-thing like that insight marks the foundation of all Marxist ideology critique. Now, if the appearance of totality concerning us here is the one we've explored above, the appearance induced by a deceptive idealism, then the important next question must be how it comes about. If, that is, "nothing is not matter" and yet, also, "not-all is matter," then we must ask what allows it to appear that "everything is matter." We must ask what allows this elision, this sliding.

To answer that question, let's turn to another moment of Žižek's reflec-tion on Marxism. In *The Fragile Absolute*, he argues for an intimate but unac-knowledged bond between communism and capitalism. Recall that the basic move of "scientific socialism" was to argue that communist revolution depended upon and would maintain the technological and social revolu-tion accomplished by industrial capitalism in production. In other words, under communism, "everything remains as it was: only the means of appro-priation have been transformed." In Engels' understanding of it, we might conceive communism formulaically, as technological *productivism minus capitalism*, with all its contradictions. The problem with such a formulation, of course, is that it turns out not to work in practice: as Žižek points out, the sad experience of "actually existing socialism" was that, without capitalist dynamism, productivism soon shrivels (Žižek 2000, p. 17).

What this reveals, so Žižek, is that the "communism" of "really existing socialism" was itself nothing, a construction of capitalism, the ideological "inherent transgression" of capital itself. How does a capitalist society justify itself, given the injustices it imposes? By seeing those wrongs as "tempo-rary," "merely local," exceptional, etc., etc. The basic ideology of capitalism is, therefore, the dream of a world of pure productivity, a productivity unchained from the "'obstacles' and antagonisms" generated by actual cap-italist practice. Communism is only a representation of this "ideological fantasy" of capitalism, that is, the "notion of a society of pure unleashed productivity *outside* the frame of capital" (Žižek 2000, p. 18). As such, the utopia of scientific socialism is simply an ideological expression of the world-horizon that capitalism produces. Indeed, we might say that communism marks the point of exception that sustains capitalism, removed safely from the body of capitalism so as to maintain the apparent closure of the productivist/capitalist fantasy. One can therefore remain sympathetic with the Marxist demand that we see capitalism as both based on a fundamental contradiction in material life and dependent upon repression of that contradiction through various forms of ideology – including Soviet-communism!

More generally, the "inherent transgression" acts here as a kind of *symptom* – to the extent, indeed, that we are tempted to say that for Žižek *communism is a symptom of capitalism*. The communist exception, in other words, is what allows the world of capitalism to appear as *natural*, as normal. It diverts our attention from the actual injustices and inequalities – the fundamental antagonisms – that disrupt productivist societies. Ideology functions here by exiling the point of social incompletion, antagonism or rupture to a safely *exterior* site, leaving the fantasmatic appearance of totality.

In the example of Marxist Communism, we have an ideology which, in one sense, remains quite traditional: it depends upon idealization, the positing of a better world somewhere (or, more precisely, "somewhen") which then deflects our attention from existing conditions. Contemporary ideology, however, transpires in a milieu where such idealization is increasingly rare and difficult to accomplish. If ideology continues today as a real force, then it cannot rely on *that kind* of belief.

Certainly such a change in the very form of ideology must be expected given the transformations Chapter 3 traced in the structure of today's fantasy. If, for Žižek, modernity ushers in a form of fantasy no longer guaranteed from "outside," then the price of such a new fantasy must be a *homogeneous* reality.[2] We don't need Newton to tell us that in modern space there is really only *one* place, since this is implied by the very construction of a fantasy in which reality is the confluence of an infinite number of "points of view." Because of this fantasmatic basis, furthermore, we find an increasing "homogenization" of human reality, a collapse of "dimensions" of human experience into the single field of technical manipulation. In such a situation, we increasingly become cynics, people who "know too much" to naively embrace any special identity or belief. Individuals cease to invest in causes (political, religious, artistic), understanding the "partial" nature of all such belief. Poisoned by the overarching homogeneity and reducibility of reality, they combine scientistic pragmatism with a self-abnegating cultural relativism. For Žižek, in this matter agreeing with the Peter Sloterdijk of *The Critique of Cynical Reason*, cynicism *is* the fundamental phenomenon occurring in techno-capitalist societies. That's a position which remains constant in Žižek's work from *The Sublime Object of Ideology* (1989) through today.[3]

Perhaps the strongest testimony in favor of cynicism's dominance lies in the subordinate power of the discourses, religious and political, by which it is opposed. To begin from the religious, think here of the anti-modern polemics of the last two Roman Catholic popes. In *The Puppet and the Dwarf*, Žižek approvingly cites Robert Pfaller's *Illusionen der Anderen*, praising Pfaller's argument that "directly assumed belief" is a modern phenomenon.

Let's take this step by step. Both Popes John-Paul and Benedict decry the failure of "belief" in modern Babylon, suggesting a retreat from a former world of faith, a universe where people "really believed." Pfaller demonstrates, however, that actual traditional societies rarely exhibit such a direct belief. Within actual pre-modern contexts, beliefs are known to be symbols derived from communal activities or rituals. In other words, such "beliefs" are more like "commitments" based on what we *do*. Žižek uses the example of Newton's wife in Edith Wharton's *The Age of Innocence*: she was "well aware" of her husband's love for Countess Olenska (she doesn't *really believe* in his innocence), but she "just politely ignored it, and acted as if she believed in his fidelity" (Žižek 2003, p. 6).

Pre-modern belief is like what she confirms in her actions: it depends upon the subtle complexity of "really knowing" – a category that, in this case, includes the private domain of her intimate understanding *subordinated to* the "polite," public world in which her "feelings" are entirely expressed by a series of conventional attitudes and actions. *Modern* belief, on the other hand, excludes such a hierarchy of realities. It accepts that things *really are* one way and asks that we believe *against our better knowledge*. Thus the very form of the anti-modernist's "faith" betrays his *actual* belief in the "reality" underlying cynicism. To the extent that faith fails to transform that reality itself (for Žižek, an open question), one cannot but think it amounts to a futile, rearguard activity, a hopeless effort to stem the tide of modernity.

Thus, cynicism is itself an answer to the question of *ideology* in our world. Indeed, it is with his understanding of cynicism as ideology that Žižek burst onto the international scene with *The Sublime Object of Ideology* (1989) and soon thereafter with *For They Know Not What They Do*. (1991) The title of this second book demands attention, since (in addition to referencing the words of Jesus on the cross) it repeats the classical Marxist formula for ideology from *Capital*, "they don't know it, but they do it." As this formula has traditionally been understood, it means something like, "because they don't understand (know) the nature of their reality, people act in ways harmful to their interests." Ideological distortion of reality, *misrepresentation* of its nature, is what, enforcing mass docility, prevents revolutionary change.

The problem is, as Sloterdijk had argued in *The Critique of Cynical Reason*, that ideology, so defined, seems to have disappeared from our world, a "technological" reality dominated by overwhelming cynicism. The fundamental assumption of ideology-critique, traditionally defined, *must be* that adequate knowledge will cause any ideological illusion to crumble. That is, *if* "they do it" *because* they don't know, then the obvious solution is to lift the veil of ignorance from "their" eyes. But, of course, the history of the Left in the years since the Second World War (and to some extent long before that) is written largely in the failure of such procedures of enlightenment. People can be shown, they can "come to know," but they keep right on supporting the positions underwritten by "false consciousness" – a phenomenon that only accelerates today. Or, to put the same thing in the language of cynicism itself, people really "know too much" to be swayed by any *particular* representation of reality. So, such was Sloterdijk's position, it must be that we today live in a "post-ideological" universe.

Building upon and radicalizing Louis Althusser, Žižek's earlier work amounts to an extended response to Sloterdijk, an effort to reinterpret what Marx *meant* by "they don't know it, but they do it" in such a way as to preserve the critique of ideology *within* a cynical reality. To put this in a different way, Žižek argues that ideology is not primarily present in a "set of beliefs" (eg. the famous "opiate of the masses" of *The Communist Manifesto*) (Žižek 1989, p. 31). To the extent that it were such a thing, ideology would, indeed, today be "dead" or, at least, dying; for, "people no longer believe in ideological truth; they do not take ideological propositions seriously" (Žižek 1989, p. 33).

What if, such is Žižek's gambit, we were to read Marx's formula for ideology more literally than it has been interpreted, heretofore? What if, instead of ascribing our actions to our beliefs (we act *because* of a failure of knowledge), we were to reverse causality? We know what we know because of what we do, because of the way that we act. Here it's worth citing Žižek at length:

we have established a new way to read the Marxian formula 'they do not know it, but they are doing it': the illusion is not on the side of knowledge, it is already on the side of reality itself, of what the people are doing. What they do not know is that their social reality itself, their activity, is guided by an illusion, by a fetishistic inversion. What they over-look, what they mis-recognize, is not the reality but the illusion which is structuring their reality, their real social activity. They know very well how things 'really are' but still they are doing it as if they did not know. The illusion is therefore double: it consists in overlooking the illusion which is structuring our real, effective relationship to reality. And this over-looked, unconscious illusion is what may be called the ideological fantasy. (Žižek 1989, pp. 32–33)

In traditional fantasy, as we've already had the opportunity to see, such ideological effects simply track the fascination we experience before "the ideal" and our endless effort to articulate its meaning. On the other hand, the cynic's tired assertion of "worldly wisdom," her removal from every lim-ited belief or commitment, is also a mode of ideological blindness. What structures her "effective relationship to reality" is still an "illusion"; only it is an illusion of a different kind, an illusion which does not imply any ideal. Yes, she knows "everything" – except the way in which this *assumption* of "everything" is itself what stabilizes her reality and prevents radical change. As Žižek puts it, "even if we do not take things seriously, even if we keep an ironical distance, we are still doing them," and such actualization of fantasy means that "at this level, we are of course far from being a post-ideological society" (Žižek 1989, p. 33).

The perverse individual

A first deduction from Žižek's translation of the Marxian formula – a deduc-tion particularly suited to explain its function *today* – might be that ideology subsists primarily in *actions* rather than in systematic beliefs. Or, to put this another way, our genuine "beliefs" are betrayed by what we *do* rather than what we *think* or *say*. In fact, this thesis follows naturally from Žižek's model of subject and world, a model in which the subject is what escapes represen-tation since it evades understanding as *something that subsists*. Reality emerges through the subject's activity, an activity which itself defies the representa-tional regime it produces.

And, here again we return to the territory made familiar in the previous chapter, to do justice to the "deed" whereby we constantly re-institute reality demands return to Žižek's concept of the present as an age of perversion.

Above all, we must focus on the peculiarities of individuality in a world where "ideology" can't be opposed to any "right thinking" – a world where the "ideologue" may spout all the properly "subversive" ideas, may understand full well the extent to which society is manipulated by corporate interests or imperial institutions, but in which subjective activity, nonetheless, prevents real change. It is a world in which the "radical" search for correct thought (one thinks of what Žižek calls the "bad faith" of "Political Correctness") hides actual conservatism. In short, for Žižek, to understand the historical present is to understand the world of the "pervert," the subject whose apparently transgressive behavior covers for a deeper interest in maintaining "the rules" in order to break them.

To deepen our understanding of the "perverse type" so vital to Žižek's analysis of the present, let me fulfill a promise made in the last chapter – a return to The Matrix in order to explain why Žižek's fascination with the film is ambivalent, why the film is deeply ideological for him (see, for example, Žižek 2002, p. 240). After the initial 20-minutes of the first Matrix film, where the focus is on the paranoid, dual structure of matrix-reality, the movie shifts, veering increasingly in the direction of an action film, with Neo (Keanu Reeves) as a classic action hero. Indeed, the film's popularity probably comes from its success within this genre, from its transformation of Reeves into even a kind of über-action hero, "the One" – a messianic figure supposedly destined to defeat the oppressive machine that we ourselves created.[4] Of course, the field of this battle, which takes place in the two sequels to The Matrix as well as in the rest of the first movie, is none other than the supposedly "virtual" reality of our everyday world. On account of some innate ability and the training administered by Lawrence Fishburne and his troop of guerilla renegades, Neo is able to defy what we take to be the laws of nature for bodies in space, leaping impossible chasms, flying, disapparating, and, above all, speeding up and slowing down time. This last set of tricks is especially important, since it produces Neo's video-game-like ability to defeat the "agents" of the artificial intelligence projecting our world. He can dodge bullets, ward off blows, attack multiple assailants simultaneously, etc., etc.

Now, with this picture of The Matrix as action film, we might rejoin Žižek's criticism of contemporary ideology in relationship to it; for, everything about The Matrix demands an investment in keeping our world as it is, in preventing real change from occurring. That's the case, first of all, in the very, technological nature of the "reality" that provides the space for Reeves' heroics. Within the conceit of The Matrix, Neo must remain within or return to the virtual reality that he supposedly escapes at the beginning of the first film. Only *there* is he a super-hero. More generally, *The Matrix* seduces *us* to invest in a reality which is similarly technical – the one that is translatable into the coordinates of modern space. Since what we *enjoy* about the film is Neo's ability to exceed normal humanity, *The Matrix* calls for a conception of reality allowing such manipulation – precisely a *technical* reality, a reality conceived in terms of a homogeneous, universal set of laws. In other words, for Neo's "powers" to "surpass" the limits we normally associate with reality, it must be something like a videogame, an avatar of Newtonian space.[5]

Which is as much as to remind us of why conscious projection of a ratio-nalized space provides the obverse – what is "in the picture," as it were – to the unconscious frame of the fundamental fantasy. But it also calls our attention to the "borderline" nature of paranoia itself, its location between neurosis and full-fledged psychosis: recall that, as a way of framing "reality," paranoia brings with it an alternative distancing device to the one produced by transcendence in traditional fantasy forms – namely, the two-storey struc-ture of a "normal" reality and the dark space of the "Other of the Other" beneath it. So conceived, paranoia can maintain a minimal consistency, a sense of reality even at the border of total psychosis. This "reality" presents the face of a "rational" space, but one also suffused with an organizing power, an organic and dynamic unity that asks for us to lose ourselves within the process of its unfolding.

The occupant of this paranoid space, who operates within a kind of "secondary symbolic" preventing her/him from simply falling into a psy-chotic suspension of symbolization, is, as we've seen before, the pervert. Perversion plays within the rationalized space undergirded by the paranoid fantasy, dreaming of an ability to "plug-in" to the "Other of the Other's" projection of that reality. Thus, the irony is that *what* we desire in watching *The Matrix* is the suspension of distance, overcoming the necessary "delay" produced by consciousness and decision, so that we might don the super-human strength of the Other.

One could say, indeed, that the set of genres involving "super-heroes" is itself perverse in exactly this sense: the superhero must become a "superior machine" able to combat machinic evil at its own level while he/she also preserves sufficient humanity (at the very least, he/she is "good") to allow identification. This is itself the precondition for our perverse relationship to the perverse hero; it allows us to both "enjoy," say, Neo's power and remain conscious of it.

Perversion is, in other words, a way of erasing "interiority" while main-taining its structure. The pervert remains a self but the "life" of this self, no matter how intellectual or sophisticated, involves no search for meaning, no sense of "self"-discovery, etc. A life of an almost pure exteriority, an intentional "shallowness." When, almost a century ago, Marinetti and the other Italian Futurists decried the decadent culture of humanism, who would have guessed that, in response to their critique, Western culture would give birth to the pervert, spawn of cynicism? But such is the possibility for maintaining the ideological closure of selfhood when the value of selfhood has been emptied of any support in the social.

In almost every Hollywood film that, like *The Matrix* series, projects an overwhelming technological apparatus, a technology "out of control," one also finds the figure of the "superhero" – the figure of the machine defeated by its own devices, overpowered *by* power, but potency spiced with a pinch of "humanity." However, the "face" of this humanity is always minimal and residual. The perverse enabler of contemporary reality must be an "individual," surely enough, but not *too* individual – more a *type* or token of personhood than a person. Beyond its implications *within* popular culture (substitution of one "Batman" for another, etc., etc.), we should treat this "de-personalization" of the literary hero as quite in line with an overall drift in today's culture.

Here we might recall another powerful example raised by Žižek from recent cinema – *The Mask*, where Jim Carrey, a fearful and insecure middle-management type discovers a mask which, when, placed upon his face, allows him to freely transform himself into all that he ever wanted but, previously, was too afraid to be, a kind of "superman" freed from the neurotic limits that had previously made him weak and docile. He robs banks, seduces women, etc., etc. But, from Žižek's viewpoint, the telling thing about this film is the way that the mask "coming alive" "takes possession" of Carrey (or whoever else wears it) (Žižek 1999a, p. 390). It liquefies and adheres to his face, seeming to suck him out of his own body. The mask quite literally covers the face of its wearer, substituting a fearless and essentially *cartooned* character for Carrey's middle-management banker. The mask is *immortal*, though with the peculiar, impersonal immortality of the cartoon: [6] it's wearer can be shot, hammered, dropped from high buildings, etc., etc., without being destroyed (Žižek 1999a, p. 389). Such immortality (the opposite of the "personal" immortality offered by Christianity) is a direct result of its "impersonality"; for the masked figure lacks the kind of investment in a meaningful, symbolic world that allows one to be a vulnerable person. Instead it is a kind of pure substance without personality, an outcropping of the Lacanian Real within reality – but in a fashion that

explicitly *preserves* reality, defusing the Real's revolutionary potential.[7]
We might, then, reformulate the pervert's perverse compulsion: he/she
wants to be a cartoon action hero.[8]

And, indeed, *The Mask* shows us with exceptional clarity the relationship
between the decline of the modern narrative of "full personhood" and the
rise of paranoid fantasy with its perversion. The peculiar way that the mask
grabs Carrey – explained in the Freudian language of the film as the victory
of the "Id" – reminds us of the problems we might associate with the fantasy
of the "bodyguard of the Other." The temptation, the desire, to take on the
power of the Other is literally irresistible. Who could resist the desire to
"channel" the power of techno-capitalism itself, to assume the position of
"life" per se? Above all, it overwhelms the weak voice of "desire" – of the
neurotic subject's need to discover "itself" through an enigmatic signifier. [9]

Thus, the pervert is apparently incapable of "commitment" because she/he
is differently placed in the economy of identification than is the traditional
subject. At a first pass, we might say that the cynic is *incapable* of identification; psychoanalytically speaking, as Žižek discusses at length in "Wither
Oedipus," the final chapter of *The Ticklish Subject*, the cynic evades the traditional superego. The key here is to remember how the *traditional* master
signifier already positions the moment of prohibition through desire. We
say, "I am X," where X is an *idealized* identity, both something I "am" and
something I "am not" but *wish to become*. In this formula, the superego acts
as the structural limit for the collapse of the "both/and." In fact, I can never
fully become X or the entire identification loses its efficacy. Guilt is the *force*
of the prohibition – what prevents me from fusion with my "self."

In perversion, the real shift is in the *nature* of identification. Having lost
the lure of the enigmatic "something" that we want/are, the subject splits
the tasks of "personhood" in two. Whereas earlier, the master signifier had
provided a single answer to the questions, "who am I?" and "what should
I do?" for the cynic, these questions are separate – though stable "identity"
requires a response to both. Identification itself becomes largely *fetishistic*:
a residual attachment to some signifier as opposed to others ("I am an
"urban guy" or a "cowboy," etc., etc.) That such identification works perfectly within a commodified culture – which offers identities for sale – is,
as will be seen, no accident. Think here of Patrick Bateman, the psycho-
killer in Bret Easton Ellis' *American Psycho* (later a film by Mary Harron),
whose weak identity is stabilized purely by the products and services he uses –
the "drinks at Harry's," the "wing-collard jacquard waistcoat by Kilgour,

French & Stanbury from Barney's," he wears along with "a silk bow tie from Saks" and "patent-leather slip-ons by Baker-Benjes," etc, etc. (Ellis 1991, p. 176). These fetishes, while "holy" in the sense of "taboo," are not a matter of curiosity or desire for the subject embracing them. The role of the fetish is *simply* to locate the cynic on the grid of possible "types" produced by culture.

Rather than with curiosity, we should associate the fetishistic identity with a kind of thin-skinned *annoyance.* I am constantly irritated by threats to my fetish, invasions of my "personal space," etc. Žižek reminds us here of the self-righteousness of the "anti-smoker," or, again, we might think of Bateman, whose meticulous indifference gives way to uncontrolled sadism on being challenged at all: when, in Mary Harron's film of *American Psycho*, a waiter interrupts Bateman to tell him the day's specials, Bateman smiles and threatens to remove his spleen.[10]

And it is the *assumption* of the cultural space "locating" the individual that answers the *other* question of identity, the "what should I do" question. The pervert is, of course, the ultimate inhabitant of the world of "commanded enjoyment," a phrase I already borrowed from Todd McGowan. Guilt and prohibition still operate for her/him, but now an ominous "substance of enjoyment," displaces previous "ego ideals" – subjecting her/him to the vague and oppressive totality of commanded *jouissance.* Above all, we must strive frenetically to "live." Thus, a first commandment here is that the pervert must labor on, exploring ever new modes of perverse enjoyment, deferring, always her/his ultimate failure to measure up to "life."

So, for Žižek, today's world is increasingly peopled by perverse, workaholic, thrill-seekers annoyed at incursions within the fantasy space of their "identity" and unknowingly committed to maintaining the reality in which this fragile economy of the "masked" person, the machinic "superhero" dominates. Today a new kind of person seems to be emerging from the cocoon of mass culture, a definitively post-Oedipal individual.[11] No longer afflicted by the neuroses of the humanistic individual but also no longer concerned with the interests or well-being of society as a whole, the time and energy of the new, the "perverse" individual is given over to a strange combination of frenetic "loss of self" (whether in "sex, drugs and rock'n roll" or 80-hour work weeks) and "defense of personal space." For Žižek the various permutations of the post-Oedipal person amount to a catalogue of the ways that cynicism transforms personhood.

Culture: de-materializing the social

If we return to the final question we addressed in the last section, the "what should I do" question, asked in the wake of the fetishization of identity – Žižek's work also suggests another response. Repeatedly, he insists that cynical belief is *stronger* than its "naïve" counterpart. For example, in *The Puppet and the Dwarf*, he mentions the universality of the Christmas Tree in every American home, despite the fact that nobody "believes in Santa Claus."[12] The more that we rid ourselves of "dogmatic" belief, the more we become cynics, the more that we grasp desperately to such disowned belief. For this reason, cynicism brings with it *conformism* – where, in the face of freedom to "do what you want," everybody actually does exactly the same things. What I should do, is precisely what everybody else does.

I raise this example here because it demonstrates the force of what we might call the "cultural" turn in societies today. In fact, Žižek suggests that "culture" is the name we give for the reality constructed of such "disavowed" but actualized beliefs – "for all those things we practice without really believing in them, without 'taking them seriously'" (Žižek 2003, p. 7). Such disavowed belief produces massive conformism, but that's hardly the last phenomenon for which its responsible.

Even given that ideology occurs first at the level of "what we do" rather than "what we know," and given, also, that systems of ideology based on traditional belief are increasingly in crisis today, still Žižek also demands that we consider the emergence of *second-level* ideologies in our world – ideologies controlling knowledge and belief. That is, the gradual weakening of traditional religious ideologies (including those of humanistic belief systems, such as, for example, "the nation") should not blind us to the continued generation of ideological *belief* within a cynical society. If presentation of the ways that a culture of cynicism transforms individuality seems to pull ideology critique away from its roots in dialectical materialism, Žižek's reflections on the ideas *generated* by the "lifestyle" of cynicism, and thus *ideological* at a second level, reinforces his Marxist allegiance.

Indeed, we owe to Žižek's reflection on the missing "material" element in contemporary academic discourse, perhaps his most famous polemic. For, Žižek's critique of "postmodernism" (in its various forms) as amounting to "*the* ideology of late capitalism" gives concrete meaning to his dialectical materialism and helps us make sense of an identification with Marxism that might otherwise seem farfetched (see, for example, Žižek 1999a, p. 216). In opposition to many of his Leftist colleagues, Žižek is fundamentally critical of the Left's "cultural" turn, the turn to "cultural studies." Not for him, then, endless demonstration of the priority of socially constructed language in understanding all human projects. This path leads to perhaps Žižek's most famous position, his rejection of the "post-Marxist" "cultural turn" in political analyses. How are we to understand Žižek's criticism of the cultural politics ascendent on the Left since the 1970s?

Working in the 1970s and 1980s, Leftist intellectuals felt it necessary to break out of the rigid constraints of orthodox Marxist historicism: typical in this regard is Ernesto Laclau and Chantall Mouffe's, *Hegemony and Socialist Strategy*, a text which attempts two things – both in an effort to defend the "new social movements" that, since the 1960s, have largely taken the place of traditional Leftist movements in politics: first, *Hegemony* completes a critique of the Marxist tradition aimed against its implicit essentialism. Under this project, Laclau and Mouffe attack both the specific "economism" of *Second International* Marxism – the dogmatic treatment of economic relations as an ultimate self-contained grounding "reality" impervious to other social/cultural spheres – and the general determinism implied by such a base/superstructure model. This part of Laclau/Mouffe's project is largely a rejection of the traditions of Marxist ideology critique and is aimed at legitimizing such movements as feminism or indigenous identity struggles, which cannot be reduced to a particular economic position (the "working class"). On the other hand, however, *Hegemony* attempts to remove the shackles limiting leftist theories (and, implicitly, the development of Leftist politics in relationship to such theory) by proposing the "radical democratic imaginary" as a non-totalitarian remainder of the utopian tradition.

In a series of essays and lectures, including, most famously, one published as an appendix to one of Laclau's books,[13] Žižek offers a devastating critique of this turn away from the "economism" of traditional Marxists, showing how the "democratic imaginary" poetized by Laclau and Moufe reflects the cynical universe backwards. In various versions of their "anti-essentialist" argument, Laclau and Mouffe are led repeatedly to introduce a homogeneous field coordinating possible differences of social or political understanding. The key to his critique, and to Žižek's overall rejection of the postmodern "cultural turn" is the way it perfectly fits a "cynical" reality. That is, the cynic "knows" a reality totalized without transcendence – in this case, without a privileged "base" for the explanation of social phenomena. "Culture," in this context, simply names the social stripped of any site of struggle or antagonism.[14]

Thus, where Marx had given us *class*-analyses of capitalist society, of the economic question always *excluded* from contemporary analyses, now we have a "thriving multitude of identities – religious, ethnic, sexual, cultural" based upon the "mantra" of "class, gender and race" as opposed to the earlier "class reductionism and essentialism." However, for Žižek the key to this multiplication of dimensions of identity is the way that, in practice, it *prevents* class analysis – analysis based upon a crisis-laden material/economic dimension. In the neutral space of "difference," class "sticks out, never properly thematized."[15]

That is, invoked in the interest of breaking the rigidity of economic determinism, postmodernist culturalism actually produces its own limitation of
trauma. It amounts to the cynical *realization* of the space where one "knows
everything." The very act of rejecting any exception to the space of compet-
ing and relative cultural truths, totalizes – prevents the emergence of any
genuinely challenging exception. What Žižek calls the "depoliticization of
economics" – the always implicit *exclusion* of the "material" from political
debate – is inseparable from the victory of "culture," of such a "homogeneous" field in which different truths can play. Culture – the "multiplication"
of differences – acts for the postmodernist as a *defense*, a protection against
the trauma of material *exception*, as much as it is an answer to a "materialist"
reductionism.

Strangely, then, Žižek, like today's reactionary conservatives, will criticize
the very forms of contemporary pluralism – moral relativism, deconstruc-
tive perspectivism and multi-culturalism. But he will do so for the opposite
reason: not because they indicate a threat to social order but because they
actually *stabilize* or *prop up* that order. In its various manifestations, from
post-structuralist perspectivism to multi-culturalism and political correctness, postmodernism throws out the "baby" of materialism along with the
"bathwater" of "scientific socialism." Postmodernism enforces a shrinking
of the social/political imagination – constructs a terrain for unquestioned
conformism whose "contents" are precisely those terms which are supposed
to challenge that landscape.[16] Which is to say that both multi-culturalism
and various other manifestations of postmodern "culturalism" amount to
renunciations of the possibility of more radical change. And Žižek's most
famous charge is that the emergence of postmodern and post-structuralist
theory is strictly correlative with retreat from any genuinely radical thought:

> It is in fact as if, since the horizon of social imagination no longer allows
> us to entertain the idea of an eventual demise of capitalism – since, as we
> might put it, everybody tacitly accepts that *capitalism is here to stay* – critical
> energy has found a substitute outlet in fighting for cultural differences
> which leave the basic homogeneity of the capitalist world-system intact.
> So we are fighting our PC battles for the rights of ethnic minorities, of
> gays and lesbians, of different lifestyles, and so forth, while capitalism
> pursues its triumphant march – and today's critical theory, in the guise of
> 'cultural studies', is performing the ultimate service for the unrestrained
> development of capitalism by actively participating in the ideological
> effort to render its massive presence invisible: in the predominant form
> of postmodern 'cultural criticism', the very mention of capitalism as a world
> system tends to give rise to accusations of 'essentialism', 'fundamentalism',

and so on. The price of this depoliticization of the economy is that the domain of politics itself is in a way depoliticized: political struggle proper is transformed into the cultural struggle for the recognition of marginal identities and the tolerance of differences." (Žižek 1999a, p. 218)

The dark force: violence and techno-capitalism

In my discussions of both the individual and culture in the age of the "paranoid" fantasy, we've felt the shadow of an unprecedented social violence. It's time to make such violence our explicit theme, to pursue Žižek's diagnosis of its origins in the construction of today's reality, understanding the bond between the fantasy responsible for cynicism and the forms of social violence we see emerging around us.

Whether analyzing the failure of forced bussing as an address to school segregation, the problems of punk and skinhead brutality or the brooding sense of threat behind the post 9–11 security state, Žižek has a single and remarkably powerful explanation. In a "thoroughly reflected" society, increasingly all social problems and issues are treated as *technical.* The individual is studied, her social condition quantified by experts and the system ill-serving her adjusted. Or, alternatively, "the market" is allowed to "solve the problem" by "satisfying the consumer." In these complementary ways, techno-capitalist societies maintain the fantasmatic illusion, the illusion that the world they dominate is ontologically complete. No change in the horizon *defining* that world is necessary.

What is missing, of course, from such a technological/bureaucratic vision is the political itself – a dimension for which the specific "case" is always the pointer to a lack or insufficiency in social reality.[17] In other words, the claim here is that "complaints" become political at that moment when we take them to symbolize some more universal cause: the construction of *this* nuclear power plant is taken by protesters to represent in general a bureaucratic and fossil-fuel based response to global warming or the Bush administration's bungled response to Hurricane Katrina becomes the symbol of Right-Wing indifference to the conditions of impoverished blacks. Without the possibility of "politicization" of particular problems and grievances – treatment of their particularity as symptomatic of broader failure of the social world as a whole – the inevitable result is "senseless violence." That is, subjects within techno-capitalist societies are *robbed of language,* robbed of the function whereby particular issues or questions point to a problematic in social identity itself. Thus, Žižek writes:

> What post-politics tends to prevent is precisely this metaphoric universal-ization of particular demands: post-politics mobilizes the vast apparatus of experts, social workers, and so on, to reduce the overall demand (com-plaint) of a particular group to just this demand, with its particular content – no wonder this suffocating closure gives birth to 'irrational' outbursts of violence as the only way to give expression to the dimension beyond particularity. (Žižek 1999a, p. 204)

In other words, "irrational" violence ("terrorism," etc.) is *the* symptom of a society where the political is foreclosed by a paranoid fundamental fantasy. It is a *passage a l'acte* by the individual or group frustrated by social elision of the symbolic function itself. An image haunts Žižek's texts: in it, a racist skinhead eloquently discourses on the causes of his own violent predilections while planting a jackboot in the head of his victim.[18] Such cynical violence is the *outgrowth* of a techno-capitalist society, one in which "everything functions," as Heidegger admitted in a famous interview.[19] The culture of utilitarian/pragmatist "problem-solvers" is inevitably haunted by machine gun-wielding psychotic teenagers, biological terrorists, vicious skinheads, etc., etc.[20] The emergence and spread of such "senseless" viola-tions of the social contract points to the repressive limitation within which terror becomes such a dominant force – the prohibition which today forbids agitating for a fundamentally different world.

And, of course, it's not too big a leap from the multiplication of such acts within a cynical reality to their *effect* upon that reality – the release of a kind of sadism in the social body. As the paranoid fantasy with its apparent per-versity completes its domination of social space, the sense of looming and inexplicable violence grows with it. We might, indeed, associate this sense of a peculiar "stain" on the very surface of reality with the classical paranoid mechanism of the persecutor-figure: such an "agent" allows an affective presence of the fundamental fantasy otherwise denied to the subject. By focusing the paranoid fantasy, it operates as a kind of defense mechanism, giving a limited outlet to the fantasmatically generated anxiety and, at least, temporarily preventing complete breakdown of the subject and its society. On the other hand, the paranoid structure refuses to grant a *full* focus to the figure of the persecutor, who thus remains the shadowy "secret agent" lurking everywhere and nowhere. For Žižek, such paranoid delusions – Black Helicopters, shadowy conspiracies, etc. – typify our world, where they act as a coping mechanism in the face of potential trauma. As Žižek puts it in *The Ticklish Subject,* "the typical subject today is the one who, while displaying cynical distrust of any public ideology, indulges without restraint in paranoiac fantasies about conspiracies, threats, and excessive forms of enjoyment of the Other" (Žižek 1999a, p. 362).

But, of course, such mechanisms also *fail* to cope and, in fact work in reverse – focusing anxiety and social aggression against the persecuting other. In other words, such social anxiety serves, above all, as trigger for a defense of *reality itself.* A social reality laced with nausea is prepared for "prophylactic" measures that would otherwise remain unthinkable. Žižek here calls our attention to the figure of the "terrorist," indicating the vicious circle of a "war on terror": in a society where the political is increasingly foreclosed, the possibility of political opposition also withers. Not only do political differences get reduced to subtle technical differences of policy but the very figure of the political "enemy" can no longer emerge.[21] Žižek claims that this foreclosure of political difference leads to the emergence of a kind of stand-in for the political opponent, a new kind of "enemy" in warfare, the "unlawful combatant" or terrorist. Such a figure (Žižek has in mind the Bush administration's definition for the prisoners taken in the Afghanistan war) is refused the legal status of a criminal or of an enemy combatant.[22] Because the fantasy now, in the "New World Order" is that the benevolent empire is *itself* a neutral force beyond politics, the terrorist must, by definition, be illegitimate. That violence puts her/him beyond all legal protections. The terrorist is an enemy, but an enemy without the legal rights of an enemy, an enemy who cannot be protected by any "neutral" law or force (the Red Cross, etc.) (Žižek 2002b, pp. 93–94). As a result, we visit upon the terrorist the aggression that, as we saw above, leads to terrorism. Or, more precisely, the figure of the terrorist (the "scum", the "lowest form of life") is used to sublimate the anger at the loss of the political which might otherwise create pressure for change.

At a time when terrorist violence elicits numerous versions of calls for "increased security apparatus" (everything from the "war on terror" to censorship of popular music and mass incarceration), Žižek's analysis is particularly important: for it predicts that the "security" response is not only bound to fail but also destined to exacerbate the problem it claims to address. Security is always itself essentially "technical" – an effort to contain or control violence by technical means. As such, it reinforces the fundamental fantasy of a completed social fabric within which the behavior of individuals can be controlled. That means, of course, that the expanded security state is just another way of cutting off the possibility of a genuinely political social life. It's only another invitation to "senseless violence." Such is the predictable circle of terror: "senseless" acts of violence elicit sadistic social responses, which call forth additional terror.

It's important to notice that Žižek's explanation of contemporary social violence, while apparently in line with "postmodern" (Derridean, Levinasean, etc.) analyses, in fact marks a critique of and alternative to such accounts. Žižek always distances himself from Levinas (and his postmodern followers) because of the way that he (Levinas) puts "respect for the other" at the forefront of ethics, a respect which, he argues, "humanizes" the "face of the other," eliding the uncanniness of subjectivity from it.[23] The imperative, within a Levinasean ethics, is to "make room" for the "neighbor" whose humanity our chauvinism would otherwise violate. Žižek's question is implicitly whether this respect – ignoring the genuine, "monstrous" and "inhuman" face of subjectivity – doesn't domesticate alterity, leaving us with a new Other, one which now includes a "space of the excluded" in its totalized inventory of being.

If that is in fact the case, if this new Other is just another version of postmodern cynicism's homogeneous and infinite field inclusive of all difference, then we must suggest an alternative source for contemporary ideological violence. To put this more assertatively, Žižek claims that violence against an "other" representing "the Other" is a uniquely contemporary, cynical phenomenon, not an overall explanation of aggression. For him, the key to understanding violence today is not only the *fictionality* of the "Other" but also the sense in which we all *know* this fictionality *full well*. Ironically, "violence" against the absolute heterogeneity of the subject occurs in the very gesture of "respect," the gesture which creates a "place" for the other within an ideologically constituted reality.[24] Thus, the postmodern, Levinasean ethics turns out to be *exactly the wrong one* for today, an ethics whose consequence is more "acting out" rather than an address *to* acting out. By contrast, Žižek asks that we pay attention to the way that our cynical world provides a unique "host" for eruptions of violence against "neighbors."[25]

Another example from contemporary cinema, though one that, as far as I know, Žižek has not yet interpreted, can help clarify his position. Lars von Trier's recent film, *Dogville seems* to provide a perfect example of the postmodern idea of violence. The film tells the story of a small, poor American town of that name and, in particular, of a young writer, "Tom," who is convinced that he's figured out the cause of the town's malaise. Tom hypothesizes that the problem with Dogville is that its citizen's "don't know how to receive." He is proven right, it seems, by the arrival of a beautiful fugitive – appropriately named, "Grace" – whom the townspeople prepare to turn over to her persecutors. Stopped from this by Tom's harangue on the subject of "the gift," they are convinced by him to allow "Grace" into their lives, to have her do various "unnecessary" favors for them: so, Grace helps out at the local store, watches the children of the overworked mother, etc., etc. The film's point emerges in Grace's eventual fate: she becomes the increasing object of the townspeoples' aggressions, which build to a crescendo of murder and rape, leading to the town's very annihilation.

Thus, it seems that we have a perfect example of a violence sparked by a fear of alterity as it breaks into a closed community, and the answer to such violence would seem to be a renewed call for respect of "difference" and openness – a cycle typical of Liberal responses to the ethnic and racial violence that convulse the social body today. Indeed, readers have taken von Trier's choice for ending-credits of *Dogville* – a montage of images of lynchings of blacks from the American South superimposed on David Bowie's "Young American" – as pointing in precisely this direction.[26]

However, a closer understanding of the film reveals a more Žižekean understanding on the filmmaker's part. Here, we must return to the specific constellation indicated by Tom's "rule" (that the townspeople have forgotten how to receive) and the name of the fugitive ("Grace") sent as answer. What begins with Grace's small gifts to the townspeople in work she does for them soon becomes expectation. What begins as superfluity becomes necessity, with the result that "Grace" – constant reminder of gift itself, that something which cannot be placed within an economy of pleasures and needs – becomes the increasing object of hostility. Not only must she work ever more (so as to capture her excessiveness within a literal economy of labor), but this placement of her within the "economy" of Dogville is what subjects her to abuse.

Von Trier's most brilliant gesture here, though, involves Tom himself – for whom the "illustration" of his rule about the universal importance of accepting gifts, cancels the grace *in* Grace. Of course, he falls in love with her, and is, in the end, unable to wait for her to respond to him. After all, she *must* love him for his recognition of "who she is." His betrayal of her is the decisive turning point in the film and its result, registered in the Picaresque structure of the film's narration, is to call into question the very possibility of an *economy* of human freedom, or, more precisely, to equate the pressure to conform with the breakdown of traditional normativity.

That is, it turns out that the *town* of Dogville is quintessentially postmodern – even cynical: its citizens, accepting of "difference," make no demands that anybody hold any particular set of beliefs. But *this* is precisely the source of the one demand they *do* make – that everybody conform to *Law* itself, to economy in the broadest sense. Grace can be superfluous, unnecessary to them, but this lack of necessity must be immediately commodified, bought and sold, rewarded or withheld from her or from the citizens. As one character, Chuck, puts it, "we just don't have enough to support a freeloader." In this, Tom, with his rule for excess, is no exception at all: quite the contrary, his position perfectly illustrates the film's insight about the cynical, postmodern origins of conformism: precisely when no substantial identity maintains social reality – when there's no communal persona to which individuals are supposed to conform – then what does not "belong" within the social totality first threatens to emerge in its purity, as "grace."

But it is *this threat* against which the entire social apparatus acts as defense, with Tom as its leader. Conformism is, above all, the pressure to displace "grace" – the marker of the "not all," the rupture in social totality – into a substantive container of excess. The excessiveness of her position must become *her* excessiveness. One of the most interesting things about Grace's reception in Dogville is the citizens' lack of curiosity about her: they could care less about who she is, because it is their self-appointed task to produce her "identity" out of the role (as *excess*) that she plays in the town. She becomes the mysterious symbol of all that they *are not* and *don't need*. Thus, under their domination she becomes a "scapegoat," the site of both their lust and their hatred.

Here we find a uniquely *cynical* form of social violence: indeed, it's vital to see how this violence reverses even traditional psychoanalytic models for aggression. In Lacan's older model, the bond is between aggression and a basic "lack" in reality. Thus, for example, the master signifier is affixed at that point in the subject's experiential matrix where "something's missing," where it seems that reality itself is inadequate. This privileged signifier thus marks a site of primordial ambivalence, naming both my "love" or ideal and my "hatred," the *unattainability* of my ideal. Within such a context, the "symbolic" task must be to break the logjam of identity – to deflect the hole in Being into articulation. Put differently, the *answer* to aggressivity (an answer supplied by the Lacan of the 1950s) is the symbolic itself – the sublimation of the "death drive," its diversion from imaginary "captation" and obsession, into the endless *articulation* of desire by language systems. In the Derridean version of such a response, we must rework *différance*, developing new sites for the "other" who otherwise provokes violence. In any case, it's a matter of taking advantage of the symbolic order's lack of closure to open new spaces within it.

Grace, however, encounters in Dogville a reality *without substantial lack*, a world which has no "identity" because it is missing "nothing" – except, of course, "gift" or "grace" itself. That "everything without lack" is exactly what cynics "know." Grace is pure excess to the cynical social totality of Dogville. In such a situation and as such an excess, Grace is a kind of "mark" for pure aggression, even when, nominally, as in the case of Tom, she's "loved." The townspeople *can't* accept grace per se but only its commodified simulacrum (the "useful" Grace). And their violence to her excessiveness is reenacted over and over in their violation of *her*. In this she stands for the fundamental transformation of human behavior ongoing in our world today.

And this means, too, that we lose the "therapeutic" affect of the symbolic order per se; for it is the precisely in the desire to "find a place" for Grace (the other) within this cynically totalized reality that violence subsists. The inhabitants of the town come to visit the violence of paranoia upon her precisely in re-weaving the fabric of their "culture" to make room for her (in coming up with "jobs" for her, in "finding a place" for her). The lesson is that the language of "difference," multiculturalism, etc. belongs together with – is inseparable from – the "racist" violence it supposedly opposes. They are simply two different faces of the same violence. Every call for tolerance and understanding, every revisionist "re-weaving" of social space so as to open it to difference, simply reinforces the condition that elicited violence in the first place. The "economy" of openness demands the enslavement of "Grace."

Over-identification and revolution

All of this suggests, what is most difficult to accept about Žižek but also most compelling in his work, that for him there is *no way out* of postmodern violence *short of revolution*; only if the very economy of the paranoid fantasy and its perverse signifier is overturned can we break the circle of paranoid/cynical sadism. Žižek's consistent (and persistent) work as a critic has been largely directed to pointing this out, to yanking the rug out from under all forms of "realistic" address to the problems of a cynical world. For him, the games played by postmodern theorists, which aim to subvert power by subtly shifting its symbolic bases, simply amount to ideology itself, ineffective "solutions" that cover over the deeper issue, and, in so doing, exacerbate the problem. It is with this in mind that we can understand how Žižek has

resurrected the *stance* of the traditional Leftist with regard to "Liberal com-
promises," demonstrating how they inevitably exacerbate the condition
they intend to remedy. This *ethos* or attitude as much as Žižek's substantive
re-conceptualization of dialectical materialism and ideology critique places
him solidly in the tradition of Marxist critical theory.

On the other hand, regarding the *level of address* at which ideology critique might make a difference, Žižek has more in common with postmodernists than he does with Marxists. If, that is, we make the question, "how
is it that criticism of ideology can make a difference?" we must recall his
rejection of the idea that simple "enlightenment" might help. This is, after
all, precisely the issue that led to Žižek's critique of Sloterdijk – to his discovery of a cynical ideology. To repeat the argument I articulated above
from *The Sublime Object of Ideology*, by definition no amount of "knowledge,"
no surfeit of enlightenment, can peal back the façade of today's ideology.
For Žižek, as a result, the genuine critic of ideology is not the theorist who
discovers truth.

As to who this critic *is*, Žižek repeatedly finds her in the one who
"over-identifies" with an official ideology.[27] To understand the kind of
critique Žižek associates with such philosophers as Pascal, Malbranche and
Kierkegaard as well as with writers and artists like Brecht, Kleist or the
Slovenian rock group Laibach, let's turn to over-identification's possible
operation in the rituals of politics.[28] In such cases, over-identification
depends upon the "spectacular" nature of symbolic empowerment. Covering over the fact that all political power is actually *produced* by those who are
ruled (the king is a king because we treat him as one and not vice-versa
[Žižek 1989, p. 146]) is the magnificence, brutality or sublimity of the ruler
(the king, the Dictator, the Party, etc.). Of course, the "proper" acknowledgement (and reinforcement) of power involves some form of humility on
the part of the subject: in the fantasy here, she is "nothing," the ruler "everything," etc., etc. However, in such self-abasement, one might already discern a note of discord, of parody, and in that note lies the possibility for
over-identification; for what happens when the "excremental" identity of
the subject in relationship to the ruler becomes *too obvious*, when, she *really*
insists upon being seen as a "piece of shit"? What happens when the sadism
involved in *actually* reducing the subjected to "nothingness" is acted out in
front of power?

For Žižek the obviously inconsistent combination of Stalinist, Nazi and
Blüt und Boden themes invoked in *Laibach's* response to late Yugoslav Communism amounts to such an over-identification, as does the odd behavior
of "Jack," (Ed Norton) in *Fight Club*. In this last (and favorite) Žižekean

example, the key to an entire drama of self-beating is contained in a single scene, where Jack "bottoms out" by responding to an upbraiding in his boss's office by "beating the crap" out of himself, throwing *himself* through coffee tables, etc., etc. (See, Žižek 1997, p. 72.) As Žižek puts it in *Revolution at the Gates*, "the unbearably painful and embarrassing effect of the scene" derives from its exposure of a sadistic "disavowed fantasmatic truth" – namely, that the normal reality of the late capitalist world the film depicts depends upon such a sado-masochistic exclusion of the subjected from power (Žižek and Lenin 2002, p. 252).

The genuine critic of ideology is thus the "proletarian" subject. That subject alone confirms the sado-masochistic contract underlying her/his nullity before power, and is thus able to *paralyze* the operations of the fantasy – just as Jack's self-punishment (in *Fight Club*) paralyzes his boss or as demonstrators defuse police abuse by similarly starting to beat themselves (Žižek and Lenin 2002, p. 252). The model is of ideology critique directly *as* revolutionary act and of the proletarian *as* the critic.[29]

But this model indicates a deep problem – namely, that, even among Žižek's list of over-identifiers are a series of philosophers (Pascal, Malbranche, Kierkegaard) for whom criticism takes the form of a "truth" embraced rather than a transformation enacted. That is, in each of these cases, "over-identification" comes in the form of a philosophical insight *demanding* a "crazy" act rather than *in the act itself.* Like Žižek (and therein lies the rub), each of them delivers an *argument for* over-identification rather than an impulse toward it – an argument whose distancing form mitigates against any actual over-identification. Or, to put this in other words, the critic of ideology is more recognizable as the traditional intellectual *representative* of the proletariat rather than as the proletariat itself. In his very reliance on sources like *Fight Club* – which is, after all, either a filmic *representation* of ideology critique or itself constitutes such criticism *as* representation – Žižek seems to admit a basic unclarity here.

And certainly such unclarity extends to the entire range of "ideological" phenomena that we've seen Žižek to discover throughout this chapter: that is, Žižek's ideology critique uncovers basic structures of selfhood and social structure in late capitalist societies. While these discoveries may *call for* transformation they do not yet involve it. In giving a *picture* of our contemporary world, they expose a *truth* underlying it, a truth which self-consciously distances the recipient from any actual transformative act. Here, it would seem that we must distinguish between ideology critique and the act of the revolutionary.

Thus, in Žižek's account of ideology critique, a vital distinction – about both the addressee of Žižek's imperative and the level of address at which that command operates – gets muddied. That's a fact which, first of all, explains why we can discover in his thought the critic both as proletarian actor, as the mad hero of "over-identification", and as philosopher – as the distanced addressee of a complex theory of contemporary society. The final part of *Žižek and Heidegger* argues that this unclarity plays a vital role, positive *and* negative, in the genesis of Žižek's thought. Leaving behind Žižek's sketch of contemporary reality from part 2, part 3 now turns to both the virtue and the vice underlying this split between two "positions," both of which he embraces as his own.

Part III

The split subject of history

Chapter 5

Splitting history: Žižek on utopia and revolution

At the end of the last chapter, I wrote of a basic unclarity in Žižek's ideology critique when it comes to the double question of his *mode of address* and his *addressee*. Swinging back and forth between an *exemplary* work aimed at a proletarian reader, a subject directly transformed by the writer's gestural act, and, on the other hand, an *argumentative* textuality, a science demanding philosophical appropriation, Žižek's thought on ideology, in particular, seemed divided. His writing assumes *two* readers, and, what's more, two readers with mutually canceling reading practices.

If, now, we make this doubleness our more general theme, the following chapters home-in on different ways that it mediates our relationship to Žižek's texts. In *this* chapter, we will see the overwhelming fecundity of an aspect of his thinking *just beyond* his control; my claim will be that Žižek's best work often approaches, but fails to articulate, the rupture we've underscored at a performative level – circling around the substantive issue of his address to the reader. That is, we find the difficult bond between act and knowledge of the act serving as a kind of "red thread" in many of Žižek's most provocative texts, and our task must be to demonstrate how this thread, unacknowledged, organizes those arguments. In the final chapter, we'll reverse the coin, turning to the issue of performative contradiction and relating it Žižek's impatience with self-referential questions of voice and address.

Perhaps the best sites for investigating issues of split or rupture in Žižek are those places where he explicitly makes them the theme of his writing. And most vital of these sites is the introduction of *The Parallax View*, a text which frames that book's project in terms of the idea of "parallax gap" – "the confrontation of two closely linked perspectives between which no neutral common ground is possible" (Žižek 2006b, p. 4).

Having introduced this concept, however, Žižek quickly blocks its most obvious, "Kantian" understanding, an interpretation which would conceive of parallax as transpiring in a completed universe of multiple perspectives, between which there simply is no translation. This conceptual move should be quite familiar to my reader at this point and demands little commentary; except that Žižek's *answer* to the Kantian interpretation – he names it "dialectical materialism" – itself introduces a second level parallax which *doubles* Žižek's explanation. In other words, we have here a text which *performs* the very phenomenon it describes. In order to trace this doubling in Žižek's introductory text, let's follow two paths leading from the essay's very title – "Dialectical Materialism at the Gates." First of all, of course, that title alerts us to the *praxical* nature of philosophy for Žižek, its self-understanding as intervention rather than mere "knowledge." Žižek describes parallax gaps as something to be "practiced" in a fashion designed to produce maximum discomfort, by producing an "unbearable" effect (Žižek 2006b, p. 13).

The context of Žižek's "praxical" argument about parallax is indeed a discussion of philosophy and its origination in pre-Socratic and Socratic Greece in the philosopher's inability to identify with the "particularity" of the local community, its substantial national or ethnic identity. According to Žižek, accused of simple disloyalty (one might think of Socrates' trial here), philosophy developed a shocking response: instead of merely giving up on identity (and thus verifying accusations of nihilist atheism) these philosophers transformed identification, suggesting a new, "universal" identity. Nor, in Žižek's understanding of it, is such identification simply a new, Enlightenment-style, "universal religion." In tracing this new identity, Žižek claims that it derives from the subtraction of substantial particularity from the triad of "singular, particular, universal." Philosophy suggests an identity which itself has the form of a parallax gap, a direct binding of singular and universal without the *content* provided by *particular* community. In the philosopher's proposal, the universal is both absolutely singular – so singular that we cannot characterize it – and absolutely general. What falls out are the characteristics, the "particulars," by which an individual can be *one member* of a broader class, both like and unlike others. (See, Žižek 2006b, pp. 7–8.)

More important than Žižek's narrative here, is the *end* it supports, namely, a view of human activity *as* act, as literally a confrontation with the incompleteness of the lifeworld. In uniting the thoroughly unredeemed singular with the lofty universal, the philosopher practices what Hegel calls "infinite judgment" – an existential face-off with the impossibility of totalization. Thus, in Žižek's ultimate example of "philosophy" from the introduction to

The Parallax View, he gives us several pages of Hegelian argument (the loftiest and most abstract form of philosophy) but devoted to a dialectical logic of sexual acts (moving from *coitus a tergo* to "fisting"), a passage meant to illustrate the irreducible necessity that the "concrete negation" implicit in parallax shifts can only be "practiced."[1]

In other words, the "singular-universal" of philosophy lies in its *shock-effect*, its ability to defeat expectations for a universal *content* – to restrict such content to the absolutely singular, so singular that it defies language (which, even in *naming*, assumes substance).[2] We have here a practice comparable in many ways to that of those aesthetic avant-gardes from the early twentieth century which practiced collage and montage as a way of exposing the ideology behind culturally sanctioned representation.[3] In the proximity of radically heterogeneous objects (think of Breton's umbrella and sewing machine on an operating table!), one is forced to acknowledge the limits of knowledge itself, its failure at the specific point of the singular.

On the other hand, if we rest *merely* with such a praxical rejection of knowledge, then we end up unintentionally underwriting a theoretical *aestheticism*, a reduction of revolution itself to the momentary effect of rupture. Žižek, aware of this, also proposes another understanding of "dialectical materialism," one which stands in direct contradiction to the first. To understand this other approach, we might follow Adrian Johnston's tracing of it in a brilliant interpretation of *The Parallax View*, an understanding for which "parallax gap" is also a way of reconsidering Marx's theory of historicity (Johnston 2007a). In the course of the introduction, Žižek elaborates on the theme that Johnston picks out, suggesting that the key today is to catch up to the increasing "materialism" of contemporary science, its ability to explain, for example, human behavior in terms of genetic characteristics or the structure of the brain. The problem, of course, is that both the analytic philosophical interpretation of such materialism and the self-understanding of science conceive it reductively – leaving no space for any meaningful discussion of non-material phenomena. Or, as Johnston puts it, these accounts "assume that the outcome of folding mind and matter into each other is a becoming-material of the mind, namely, a naturalization of the spirit," an approach in which "the mind comes to resemble the brain conceived of as just another part of the physical world as depicted by the cause-and-effect laws posited by the natural sciences at larger-scale levels above the quantum domain" (Johnston Forthcoming). One natural result of such reductivism is what Žižek calls "idealist obscurantism," that is, an effort to "save" some space for the "spiritual," through one or another "reservation" ("value," "belief," etc., etc.) from full objectification by science.

Spirit leaves some space "beyond" or outside of the material realm as the space of the subject.

As we've seen before, in response to this arid choice between reductivism and idealism, Žižek's dialectical materialism offers an alternative. He maintains the thesis of a material "origin" for all phenomena but now adds to this what we've already seen in reference to Heidegger, an "incomplete" conception of material ontology itself. It is a thesis which leaves room for the development of an autonomous, extra-material dimension from the "gaps" or "lacunae" within a natural, material dimension – reserving a possibility for a *transcendental* account of subjectivity, through its *genesis from* the material. That is, the dimension in which we can *know* ontological completion is the restless and chaotic dynamism of nature, a dynamism that gives birth to subjectivity itself. Žižek's story about nature here amounts to a science of history, of the emergence of historicity.

Thus, the *two* accounts of dialectical materialism sandwiched into the few pages of *The Parallax View's* introduction suggest the full scope of Žižek's praxical insight, which is here revealed to concern nothing other than the limitation and possibility of a praxical philosophical science, a knowledge of practice. Stretched between an irreducible *negation* of the field of knowledge, the field of representation, and an *alternative* knowledge belonging to it, we might hazard that dialectical materialism transpires when those two irreconcilable "concepts" of the material in fact touch. Such touching, such "enactment," does not remove their heterogeneity, but it does allow a transformation which, from either perspective alone, remains strictly impossible. Indeed, that is what Žižek *really* means by that overly pregnant term he pulls from Lacan, the "act." The act, for Žižek is the materiality of human life as exemplified both in the irreducibility of practice to knowledge and in the material historicity of knowledge itself. Only when these two senses of the term come into contact can we hope for significant human change.

Revolution: the impossible

Nowhere does the parallax gap between two epistemological constitutives of "act" play itself out more richly than in Žižek's various addresses to the related questions of utopia and revolution – addresses which sometimes seem scattered and even contradictory, but, which, such will be my contention, actually hide precisely the kind of hitherto un-illuminated thinking that we discovered in our examination of the *The Parallax View's* introduction. Here, though, the *appearance* is often of bald contradiction between

Žižek's own various views. That's particularly the case when we ask the simple question as to where Žižek stands with regard to utopia. On the one hand, at stake for him with this issue is the very possibility of radical change, of a change beyond what's conceivable within the ideologically produced boundaries of every "realism." Thus, in a recent filmed lecture, *The Reality of the Virtual,* Žižek goes so far as to suggest that our very "survival" as human beings depends upon a re-igniting of utopian possibility in response to our cynical world. "The future will be utopian," comments Žižek, "or there will be none" (*Reality*).

On the other hand, Žižek himself criticizes that particular "utopian imaginary" at work in various postmodern thinkers as well as in contemporary techno-capitalism and even rejects the possibility of any utopian "image" at all. Indeed, one could go so far as to suggest that, given certain understandings of the word, "utopia," Žižek's entire critique of contemporary political theory turns on his demonstration of the ideological nature of "utopian thinking."

Of course, the first step in unraveling any terminological confusion here demands that we distinguish between a utopian *impulse* as it's revealed in revolution and the utopian *imaginary*. The important thing here is not to mistake Žižek's rejection of such an imaginary with a condemnation of utopia, per se – to carefully distinguish between "utopia" and "utopia." Or, if you like, we must pass beyond the positing of utopian "images" to some more essential task of the imagination.

Still, even with such a clarification of the language by which we refer to utopia, a problem remains for us as interpreters of Žižek. That problem follows from the duelling demands that the fruits of revolution remain absolutely unknown prior to it (so as to guarantee their freedom from previous ideology) and that we be able to form immanent criteria to distinguish *genuine* revolution from its *pseudo*-cousins. Thus, Žižek confirms Fredric Jameson's theoretical model according to which utopia *originates* in the revolutionary act rather than in any prior historical dialectic. In *Organs Without Bodies,* Žižek argues for the unanticipated nature of the utopian revolutionary moment, a moment in which revolutionaries are forced to the "reinvention" of "the very modes of dreaming" (Žižek, 2004, 211). The key here is that we can only *form the dream* for which such experiments give evidence *in the wake of* the disruptive "Event."

But, alternatively, Žižek *also* demands that we distinguish genuine revolution, using, among other things, utopian "self-invention" as setting apart the real thing. That is, he gives us criteria for knowing whether a given revolution deserves the name. However, doesn't this amount to, if you like, a "meta-imaginary," of the utopian – a symbolic substitute for the traditional image of the "good life" forbidden as ideology? That Žižek conceives of utopian novelty as somehow *ingredient* to an overall revolutionary spirit would suggest that we can come to know and desire precisely those sorts of social change which fulfill this criterion, that they come to act themselves as a new utopian "imaginary."

So, it cannot be for Žižek simply a matter of defeating the utopian "imaginary" in favor of another kind of utopian "impulse." The contradiction here demands a more substantive investigation of the utopian issue as it attaches to Žižek's revolutionary program. To that project, we now turn.

In a sense, the *anti-utopian* Žižek simply radicalizes a move repeatedly made by Marx and Engels: from the *Communist Manifesto* of 1848 through the *Anti-Dühring*, when they explained the program of Marxist communism in contrast to the "utopian socialism" of others. Now, obviously this reference to the utopian nature of earlier socialisms was not meant to suggest that Marxists eschew "utopia" in the sense of the possibility for radical change. Rather, the notion was that exercises in *imagining* a better world, always conceived from within the enclosure of our ideologically saturated reality, inevitably fail to be sufficiently radical. In effect any vision produced from within such a society necessarily carries within itself the limited historical situation of the visionary.

The next step here for Žižek would be to see that and why Marx and Engels *themselves* failed to live up to their critical insight about the ideological nature of utopian thought. If – so their implicit reasoning went – from within the confines of our historical situation, we cannot imagine a redeemed world, then it might still be possible to deduce at least the form of such redemption from the present. In other words, we might say that some particular structural element in capitalist society is responsible for the maintenance of oppression, the failure of utopia to have realized itself heretofore, and on that basis we could project "communism" as the condition in which we would *subtract* that structure. Such is the gambit of "scientific socialism." As Žižek puts it, with communism, "everything remains as it was: only the means of appropriation have been transformed" (Žižek 2000, p. 17).

The remaining "form" of utopia, then, would simply be the industrial (and "rationalized") means of production. And, here's the trick, that form could then provide the "content" of a revolutionary moment: the end or *telos* of revolution would be the emergence of a society in which the means of appropriation and distribution would reflect the "rationality" of the new, industrialized, means of production. *Voila!* The nineteenth- century "science" of socialism could claim to discard the utopian imagination while in fact using it to maintain the picture of the industrial workers' revolt.

At this point, we would do well to remind ourselves of the lesson we already saw Žižek draw from his life in the Soviet-era Eastern Block – namely that "really existing socialism" was itself nothing, a construction of capitalism, the ideological "inherent transgression" of capital itself. On the one hand, this means that, when stripped of the injustices and inqualities of capitalism, the wheels of production grind to a halt. Communism simply cannot reproduce the wonders of the bourgeois industrial world, the world in which "all that is solid melts into air" in a perpetual phantasmagoria of Romantic proteanism. On the other hand, though, Žižek's comment indicates that for him the entire "formalist" method of Marxist utopianism fails; in the final analysis, Marx and Engels are not able to locate in industrial productivism a genuinely revolutionary utopia, a form beyond the ideological determination of capitalism. The utopia they do find is *still* determined by the capitalist fantasy.

Soviet-era Marxism might be a dead letter today, but we should not therefore decide that the residual "deduction" of utopia it represents has dried up as a source of Leftist thought. Effectively, Žižek's response to Ernesto Laclau, Chantall Mouffe and other "postmodern" political theorists is to see their work as merely repeating the "formalist" failure of Marx and Engels.[4] In its most recent manifestation, since his 2000 *Auseinandersetzung* with Laclau and Butler printed in *Contingency, Hegemony, Universality*, Žižek's criticism of Laclau and Mouffe takes the form of a rejection of "democracy" (even in its "radical" manifestation) as potential utopian signifier. This critique of the democratic ideal, a departure from Žižek's earlier position, provides the site for his self-clarification on the possibility of *any* Leftist "imaginary."[5]

The first step in following Žižek's argument must be to understand why today's Leftist imagination *necessarily* takes the form today of "democracy" – why the democratic trope is so powerful. And the easiest way to grasp that is to follow Laclau and Mouffe's own justification for their choice of democracy as the key "ideal" of a post-Marxist Left. The argument is precisely for a rejection of the teleology of history implicit in "scientific socialism." *Hegemony and Socialist Strategy* asserts that since there is no utopian "end of history," we must get beyond the illusion that political movements tend logically toward the realization of a single, universal vision. Such a transcendence of traditional essentialism precisely leaves room to imagine the efficacy of the disparate and often unrelated "identity" movements of the "new Left." In other words, the pluralizing response to our query about the radical democratic imaginary is absolutely vital to Laclau and Mouffe's defense of such movements.

But if the fundamental insight following from the fall of Soviet-Marxism is the lack of a universal identity and end of history, this insight, when applied also to individual and society, serves Laclau and Mouffe as more than historical precondition for the emergence of a new theory.[6] More strongly, the impossibility of closing social identity (the identity of a person, a people, a group or a nation) justifies asserting the ultimately political nature of all societies. Neither I nor we can ever finally know who we are: indeed, the reason for this impossibility is that identity is indeterminant. There is no complete identity either for individual, group or society. Politics takes place in the undetermined interstices of social identity. To say that society is structurally prevented from knowing or being itself is just to say that identity is a matter of political struggle rather than of some kind of deduction. And that assertion of openness, in turn, serves as another condition for the possibility of the formation of particular "social imagineries" today.

For Laclau and Mouffe, this transcendental can and does become at least part (the general form) of the "radical democratic imaginary"; for a democratic society is definitionally one which "makes itself" – which structurally acknowledges its indeterminacy. In effect, the "democratic revolution" that Laclau and Mouffe (following Claude Lefort) identify with modernity itself involves a self-realization of the "truth" of society's lack of truth.[7] In a sense the historical particularity of the "radical democratic imaginary" just refers to the various guises in which the ideal of a society radically open to ceaseless re-definition can emerge. As Laclau puts it, a consciousness of the impossibility of identity can be "important for democratic politics" in that it "involves the institutionalization of (a society's) own openness and, in that sense, the injunction to identify with its own impossibility" (Žižek, Laclau and Butler 2000, p. 199).

"Democracy" is the ideal of a society in which the god of history is dead, which *knows* that it is free. Because of this, it is the only ideal that *can* survive the tide of cynicism, the only one that can mark the end or goal of history: history, all along has been moving toward the social form in which *there is no* content – the identity of *lacking an identity*. But that means that all particular identities, while negotiated *through* democratic structures, are, in the end, subsidiary to those structures, those forms. Of course, for Žižek the irony here should not be lost: democracy's "content" is liberation from such ends only at that same time that it emerges as the "truth" of history, as the obvious end of every incomplete ideal of historical identity. Or, to put this differently from Žižek's perspective, democracy is actually the *least* open of social forms, the social form in which the identity of "openness" leads to the greatest actual pressure to conform. A democratic society doesn't only provide a "home" for differing communities, maintaining the "open society" of Liberal dreams: it can only do that by also maintaining a *framework* within which such differences are coordinated. "Incompleteness in principle" *is* such a framework, one which takes the form of that "neutral" field we have previously associated both with "Law" itself and with the capitalist field of exchange. What we "believe in," when we believe in anything, is this space of "equal" rights, of Democratic "procedures," etc., etc.[8]

This returns us to "The Reality of the Virtual," where Žižek rejects utopia as *imaginary* and *symbolic* construct, but does so in order to embrace utopianism *in the real*. To explain this distinction, let's begin with the difference between "imaginary" and "symbolic" utopias, a difference which corresponds, more or less, to that between traditional, "dreams" and the formalist deduction suggested by Marx and Engels. Utopian socialists *imagine* a better world; scientific socialists *deduce* its content from the form of class conflict. Žižek explains what a "utopia in the Real" means with regard to Lacan's equation in *Seminar XI* of the Real and the impossible, suggesting that we call "utopian" precisely that action within the matrix of choices which offers itself as beyond possibility (see, Lacan 1981, p. 167). As he puts it there, "utopia" "means do what appears within the given symbolic coordinates as impossible." (*Reality*)

In analyzing Žižek's distinction here, we should begin again from his rejection of the Marxist method; that is to say, precisely what characterizes the impossible is its refusal to appear within the philosophico-utopian game (still played by Marxists) wherein the *content* of the good life is deduced from its *form*. The acts chosen for their impossibility are precisely those which disallow any such deduction. Žižek's example in the film, Nixon's trip to China, suggests this absolute opposition between any "vision" and the utopian effect. It also underscores the reason why utopia must be an *act* rather than a *thought* or an image. The key here is that, only when something is actually done, something actually changed, does the utopian dimension open.

Utopia emerges when, rupturing the symbolic fabric ("yes, Nixon, the old red-baiter, *can* talk with the communists . . .") an act produces *new possibilities,* not when it reinforces any previously framed ones. Which also explains Žižek's contention that the "impossibility" of the utopian act refers to its ability to "change the very coordinates *of* the possible." (*Reality*) In other words, precisely what produces a "utopian" moment in history is its unanticipated nature, and thus its ability change reality. We are moving in the direction of the possibility that the very *fundamental fantasy* underlying the social might shift.

But wait. To this point, Žižek's discourse disregards a matter central to his own concerns. It's not the case that "the impossible" in every situation *actually* produces new possibilities, *actually* transforms the symbolic world. Indeed, in the light of the failed "revolutions" of 1968 and 1989, Žižek himself has wielded the psychoanalytic distinction between genuine "traversing of the fantasy" and a mere "acting out" which, as we've seen, perversely reinforces society's underlying coordinates. We must admit that a certain *kind* of impossibility often fails to produce genuine change at the level Žižek desires. And, furthermore, it is precisely when we *know* that revolution lies in a present which is "impossible" that we enter a spiral of pseudo-revolution.

While this issue emerges in numerous places in Žižek's work, it is perhaps most clearly focused in his recent debate with the thinker to whom he is otherwise closest, Alain Badiou. At least in Žižek's interpretation of him (whose accuracy or adequacy is a matter of some dispute, which I won't address here), Badiou structures his view of history through the merely logical contrast between a "truth-event," which produces revolutionary eruption and an otherwise structurally static "order of Being." Occasionally the entire fantasmatic edifice of reality crumbles, producing a revolutionary change and liberation from the constraints of prior ideology.

The problem with such an emphasis upon the "evental" – immanent, present – rupture of being is that it unintentionally re-asserts the totality of the history it disrupts. In an odd but vital passage from *The Parallax View*, Žižek raises a problem with Badiou's view, one that, interestingly, he imputes to Jacques-Alain Miller (his sometime teacher and training analyst) as well as to Badiou himself (see, Žižek 2006b, p. 307). Paraphrasing Lorenzo Chiesa, Žižek asks what he calls a "key question of Lacanian political theory," namely, whether or not psychoanalysis must reach the "resigned conservative conclusion that every revolutionary upheaval has to end up in a new version of the positive order . . ." (Žižek 2006b, p. 306). To the extent that revolution represents an unsupported act, an unanticipated and impossible "event" rupturing an otherwise whole "order of Being" (to use Badiou's theoretical vocabulary) such a conclusion seems unavoidable; for the very *knowledge* of history represented in such a structure (fanatasy/act/fantasy or order of Being/event/order of Being) precisely forbids any "progress" and ironically condemns history to a classical closed-cycle.

Given such knowledge, one must inevitably arrive at an essentially conservative politics: what happens when I *know* that the revolution in which I participate is a mere break or rupture in a soon-to-be-re-established fabric of reality? Doesn't this subvert every effort to revolt, either undercutting it entirely (since we share the "worldly wisdom" telling us that, in the end, it will make no difference) or transforming revolution into a neo-Aristotelian project of restoring some fictional "balance" missing under current conditions? Doesn't this cynical wisdom suck the very energy out of every revolution? The effect is bound to be revolutionary paralysis: revolution can change everything . . . except what matters. We have thus arrived at the crisis reflected in the return to a closed historicism from an ironically "open" affirmation of human spontaneity which, nonetheless, has the effect of confirming the futility of human practice (Žižek 2006b, pp. 206–207).

In other words, we get the cynical situation facing us today, above all, in the wake of the theories of revolutionary rupture emerging after May 1968. When it knows itself only as such, revolution, the pure moment of a radical rupture, fails. The "impossible" becomes merely the impossibility inscribed *within* the symbolic texture of reality, the "inherent transgression" allowing reality to maintain itself. We can see this structural boomerang particularly clearly when it comes to the question of the "present"; the purely dimensional moment of historicity which comes to represent revolutionary immanence, becomes, when posited as the end or purpose of political activity, anything but revolutionary. To aim at a "revolution of the present" is to forego revolution itself, to place it safely within the boundaries of a repeating and stable historical structure.

This problem allows us to understand a move Žižek makes in *For They Know Not What They Do*'s final chapter, a radical reflection on historicity (repeated numerous times since), within which he refuses to place the act of liberation in the *present*. Refuting, the "common wisdom" that sees the *past* as determined but sees the present, the "moment of decision" as free, Žižek writes there,

An act is never fully "present", the subjects are never fully aware that what they are doing "now" is the foundation of a new symbolic order – it is only afterwards that they take note of the true dimension of what they have already done. The common wisdom about how history *in actu* is experienced as the domain of freedom, whereas retroactively we are able to perceive its causal determination, is therefore idiotic after all and should be reversed: when we are caught in the flow of events, we act "automatically", as if under the impression that it is not possible to do otherwise, that there is really no choice; whereas the retrospective view displays how the events could have taken a radically different turn – how what we perceived as necessity was actually a free decision of ours. In other words, what we encounter here is another confirmation of the fact that the time of the subject is never "present" – the subject never "is", it only "will have been": we never *are* free, it is only afterwards that we discover how we *have been* free." (Žižek 1991, p. 222)

Žižek can only save the revolutionary potential of the act by rejecting its immanence, the utopia of the present. The supposedly revolutionary desire to "live in the present" is, in fact, an unconscious subversion of the historical subject's revolutionary potential.[9]

The labor of the act

OK, rewind the film. Let's go back to the question of how Žižek legitimates a utopian impulse. To save the utopian act, Žižek must consider its historicity, which means, also, that he must betray the purity of the vision he frames in "The Reality of Virtual," proposing a "content" of the utopian moment. He must add something to the characterization of the utopian/revolutionary moment as simply the "impossible" hole in the symbolic fabric of reality. Happily for us, though, this theoretical betrayal on Žižek's part also itself corresponds to *another* vital way that he approaches the set of issues around utopian thought and revolutionary change, a manner which emerges nicely in his *answer* to Badiou's antithesis between "Being" and "Event."

Equating Badiou's projection of history on the basis of the "Order of Being/Event of Truth" pair with the way that way the political universe must be conceived in order to reproduce the Liberal's fear of "totalitarianism," Žižek writes:

the fear of the impending 'ontologization' of the proper political act, of its catastrophic transposition into the positive order of Being, is a false fear that results from a kind of perspective illusion: it puts too much trust in the substantial power of the positive order of Being, overlooking the fact that the order of Being is never simply given, but is itself grounded in some preceding Act. *There is no Order of Being as a positive ontologically consistent Whole*: the false semblance of such an Order relies on the self-obliteration of the Act. In other words, the gap of the Act is not introduced into the Order of Being afterwards: it is there all the time as the condition that actually *sustains* every Order of Being. (Žižek 1999a, p. 238)

In some sense, of course, this is simply a repetition of what we've seen to be Žižek's basic ontological insight. However, Žižek follows up this passage with a practical result of this understanding, one which applies specifically to the problem of revolution. We should measure revolution, Žižek suggests, based upon its success in founding new institutions. He insists that every successful revolution must happen twice, that it depends upon the revolutionary's "follow through" beyond the mere feast of destruction with which the world of the old regime falls. Eulogizing Lenin, Žižek takes up the idea that "the fundamental lesson of revolutionary materialism is that revolution must strike twice" (Žižek and Lenin 2002, p. 8).

To cease revolution after the first moment is to re-assert a false erasure of the Act by which the Order of Being, Ontology, is constituted at all. Not only do we thus falsify the nature of reality but we also hide the nature of the Act, turning it into a mere instantaneous "event" by granting *it* a completion that really it lacks. An Act (the trace of subjectivity) only exists insofar as it *acts upon* the Real, producing a reality. Thus, Žižek writes that "the test of the true revolutionary, as opposed to this game of hysterical provocation, is the heroic readiness to endure the conversion of the subversive undermining of the existing System into the principle of a new positive Order which gives body to this negativity – or, in Badiou's terms the conversion of Truth into Being" (Žižek 1999a, p. 238).

And here we might reference a basic line of traditional leftism, namely that the worker shapes nature, *using* its residual "resistance" or opposition as the opportunity to produce both world and self.[10] For both Marx and Hegel, what distinguishes human beings from animals is what Marx calls our "species being," namely *consciousness* of our own activity as it bears upon an object that we shape. As Hegel writes in his *Aesthetics*, at its most radical this self-consciousness means that we *produce ourselves* through our labor, that it is only through our awareness of the difference *we* have made in the world that we can *be* selves. "Only by means of this effectual activity is he no longer merely in general, but also in particular and in detail, actually aware of himself . . . " (Hegel 1975, p. 256).

Of course, what I'm suggesting here is that the revolutionary is ironically an archetypal worker, the one whose act forms a new world. Recall that Žižek's key insight about ideology – "for they know not what they do" – invokes the insubstantial nature of subjectivity. The deed, the Act, is nothing. It only *exists* insofar as it *works upon something*. If, for the most, part this action registers itself in the projection of the fantasy sustaining reality, in revolution, where both constituted self and reality crumble, it emerges more forcefully as the construction of *new* institutions, *new* forms of life. If you like, the very conceptual space in which "things fall apart" is the space of a revolutionary work, the space of the *time* in which such work occurs, transforming "stuff" into meaningful life-forms. Instead of a revolutionary time conceived as "the 'exception' that characterizes the transition from one 'normality' to another" we have an excessive historicity later "gentrified" by the imposition of a falsifying fantasy (Žižek 1991, p. 195). The extended "time" of revolution – what for Badiou and others only appears as an instantaneous "break" or "cut" in history – already testifies to this "constructive" dimension. It is for this reason that Žižek can write that in revolutions, we are "already free even as we fight for freedom; we are already happy even as we fight for happiness" (Žižek and Lenin 2002, pp. 259–260). That is, the very time and very act of the revolutionary already in a sense marks the new vision, the new world that can emerge from it. The "energy" fueling the revolution is already, in theory, the energy for constructing a radically different *form* of reality, one not dependent upon guilt.

This is the origin of Žižek's sympathy for Trotsky, his claim that Trotsky's ideal of "perpetual revolution" marks the "primordially repressed" moment in Soviet history (admissible to neither Communists nor anti-Communists) and thus embodies "that which is worth redeeming in the Leninist legacy" (Žižek and Lenin 2002, pp. 305–306). The key for Žižek, then, is the unity between the negating and constructing moments of revolutions, both subsumed under the sign of a "revolutionary way of life." As Žižek puts it in *The Parallax View*, where he again uses this "embodying" metaphor, "the new post-revolutionary order does not negate its founding gesture, the explosion of the destructive fury that wipes away the Old; it merely *gives body* to this negativity" (Žižek 2006b, p. 382).

Consider for a moment Žižek's discovery of this measure for the "authenticity" of revolutions – a way of distinguishing between pseudo-revolutionary "acting out" (with its Fascist or aestheticist potential) and moments of genuine transformation: does a "revolution" remain satisfied with having brought down the old regime, or does it move from the "fury" of destruction to institution building? Only the revolution which insists that the destructive moment is *incomplete* without the moment of construction, only the revolution which struggles to overturn the very social form of the old world by replacing it with a new set of conventions and practices is real (see, Žižek 1991, p. 190).

Most famously, Žižek refers us back to the case of Lenin in 1917; as he tells it in *Revolution at the Gates*, a collection of Lenin's intra-revolutionary writings with commentary, the situation created by the February revolt *seemed* to call for a halt to revolutionary activity. Žižek reminds us that, after February, "Russia was the most democratic country in the whole of Europe, with an unprecedented degree of mass mobilization, freedom of organization and freedom of the press." Nonetheless, Lenin's "greatness" lay in his refusal to cease agitation, to let well enough alone: indeed, for Žižek, such an acceptance of the new *status quo* would have meant a fundamental *betrayal* of the revolution, one which would have subtracted from it its very "revolutionary" nature. Žižek embraces *this* Lenin (the Lenin who writes and acts between February and October, 1917) as a figure for his general theory of what I might call the *historicity* of revolution.

What does Lenin know that forces him to continue? What constitutes the "science" of the Party? Not, Žižek assures us, the stereotypical omniscience in which "the Party is always right." In order to explain this in his Lenin text, Žižek focuses on *the* Brecht play which *seems* to plump down *for* such a view of "scientific socialism." In the celebration of the Party from *The Measure Taken*, Brecht apparently embraces such a position when he praises the party as having "a thousand eyes." However, Žižek's closer reading of this poem indicates that something other than a mere equation of the Party with God is at stake here (a something, by the way, which grants the figure of the "thousand eyes" its full, paranoid scope!): in Žižek's interpretation, the "rightness" of the Party lies not in its omniscience about matters of "content" – these *need* the intervention of individual interpretations to decide – but simply in its formal demand for *collective self-determination:*

... The authority of the Party is not that of determinate positive knowledge, but that of the form of knowledge, of a new type of knowledge linked to a collective political subject. The only crucial point on which the Chorus insists is that if the young comrade thinks that he is right, he should fight for his position *within* the collective form of the Party, not outside it – the Party needs him even more than its other members. What the Party demands is that we agree to ground our "I" in the "we" of the Party's collective identity: fight with us, fight for us, fight for your truth against the Party line *–just don't do it alone,* outside the Party. (Žižek and Lenin 2002, p. 188)

With these last ideas – revolutionary "follow-through" and collectivism – we have turned one hundred and eighty degrees away from our earlier conclusion, the conclusion that defined utopia for Žižek as the "impossible." In our prior analysis, the dialectic of history led us away from any deduction of utopia's content and toward a pure moment of rupture. The trope of impossibility simply names the remainder of utopia after the subtraction of both imaginary and symbolic modes from it. Today, such was Žižek's implicit argument, the same winnowing which earlier forbad any utopian imaginary extends to Marx's own discovery of utopian content in the *forms* of class struggle.

Now, starting from the possible aestheticism of a utopia of impossibility – from, that is, the *insufficiency* of Žižek's first definition – I've reached a point of reversal. We've now followed Žižek's construction of an argument starting again from Marxist (or, more generally, modernist) utopianism but now leading us ironically to a *form*, a form of collective labor, opening new possibilities in a manner which is never simply present. In other words, we return precisely to the *symbolic* model utopia of Marx and Engels, the utopia whose failure produced Žižek's own candidate, the utopia of the Real.

The problem is, though, that, taken alone, *this* utopia, the utopia of a radicalized labor, fails the *other* Žižekian test, the test of conceptual *impossibility*. Once we have any of the formal ideas definitive of genuine revolution for Žižek, we *lose* the sense that the act is unimaginable. Here, an example would help.

Take the work of Michael Hardt and Antonio Negri, authors of two key texts in contemporary political theory, *Empire* and *Multitude*. Hardt and Negri have attempted an alternative rescue of Marxism to Žižek's, one that repeats the Marxist deduction from a utopian form in contemporary production. Instead of rejecting the Marxists' symbolic logic of utopia, Hardt and Negri argue that Marx and Engels simply came *too soon*, that the form of production in industrial capitalism was not yet anarchic *enough* and so the revolution that they proposed was also still too hierarchical: as Žižek puts it, for Hardt and Negri "the limitation of Marx was that he was historically constrained to centralized and hierarchically organized, mechanical, automatized industrial labor, which is why his vision of "general intellect" was that of a central planning agency" (Žižek 2006a, p. 119).

In the place of such containment, such still "mechanical" centralization and unification, Hardt and Negri propose that today's globalized techno-capitalism opens the possibility to liberate labor in its uncontainable and anarchic self-creativity. Today's capitalism has unleashed forces of life (now "bio-power," to borrow another term from Foucault and Deleuze) that it (capital) struggles to contain and that can overcome it. Effectively they locate two qualities of contemporary labor which seem to win it this potential – its "virtuality" (the production of ideas and processes rather than things) and its de-centered multiplicity. Today's labor is network-like, rhizomatic, etc. And its "subject" is the irreducibly plural "multitudes" rather than the proletariat. To oversimplify a little (but not too much!), Hardt and Negri argue that today's completed, globalized capitalism, offers a unique opportunity to finish the history projected by Marx and Engels, to de-capitate capitalist "Empire" and replace it with the plural and non-totalized "multitudes." All that's necessary to derive Hardt and Negri's approach from Marx's is to translate "immaterial" or "communicative" for "industrial" labor – while getting rid of the obvious positivistic falsehoods of the nineteenth-century "science of history" and adjusting the theory of class in accord with these changes.

Complicating this story is, of course, the very nature of the means of production dialectically liberated; for, as good Deleuzians, Hardt and Negri are exquisitely aware of the irony of producing a unified historical narrative about a unified subject (Marx's "Proletariat") engaged in a linear historical movement. As a result, much of both *Empire* and *Multitude* is devoted to revising the Marxist hypothesis with regard to each of these modes. We not only lose the linear historical necessity of "Scientific Socialism" but also find revolution reconceived on a model of the "emergence" of new organisms within the life-sciences (The "Snake" versus the "Old Mole" of Marx) With the death of the center comes the possibility for revolutionary movements without boundary, margin or center. Thus, we get a new analysis and strategy of revolutionary action, one for the age of the internet and other mediatic events.

Still, for all their postmodern emphasis upon de-centering and emergence, Hardt and Negri remain, in Žižek's view, as unsuccessful as was Marx in genuinely liberating the historicity of labor. For Žižek, Hardt and Negri remain "too much Marxists" precisely to the extent that they think labor so framed – whether by an historical theory or a Party structure – can ever deliver its revolutionary potential. Žižek develops this argument in several places but most forcefully in a recent essay on Lacan's Seminar XVII, "Objet a and Social Relations."[11] There he notes that the very *narrative* by which Hardt and Negri claim to protect the act of labor from substantialization has the opposite effect, that it transforms that act into a traditional, "proletarian" subject. For all their care to *complicate* it – to find a new immanent form of power present in "empire" to construct an open history and a new subject for that history, the story remains basically unchanged. It is a *single story* because it is a story about a single (particular) subject and must remain so in order to maintain its rhetorical/political power. Why is it tempting to return to the Marxist view of history, as Hardt and Negri, despite all protests to the contrary, do?[12] Because such a return allows us to say what *single thread* in the corrupt world of capital holds redemptive power. Because doing so allows a glimpse of the *content* of a better world connected (immanent) to ours but distinct from it. Or, as Žižek puts it, Hardt and Negri "continue to rely on the rhetorics of the One, the sovereign Power, against the multitude" (Žižek 2006a, p. 121).

Now, without having to repeat Žižek's critique of Marxist historicism, of that symbolic utopia which displaced its imaginary predecessor, it should be clear at this point that *Empire* and *Multitude* repeat the failure of such a view of history. That is, the way in which the rhetoric of multiplicity gives birth to a narrative unity simply repeats the breakdown of the illusion that we have really seen labor "beyond" its corrupted form. In imagining an unlimited productivity without the oppressive social relations – poverty, exploitation, class – constitutive of capitalism, both Marx/Engels and Hardt/Negri fall prey to the mirage that they have really transcended the capitalist fantasy. In both cases, the subtractive method fails. The utopia of labor turns into just another way to locate the "inherent transgression" of capitalism, the key to its maintenance of ideological hegemony.[13]

In other words, precisely in giving us an imaginable "content" of a post-revolutionary world – even the content of its labor – Hardt and Negri fail to think critically about our world at all. For all Žižek's admiration of them as thinkers attached to a genuine political movement (the anti-globalization protests of Seattle and beyond), in the end he must condemn Hardt and Negri as little better than mouthpieces of techno-capitalist ideology.

More vitally from the viewpoint of my argument here, Žižek's critique of Hardt and Negri suggests the insufficiency of *his own* characterization of "authentic" utopia as revolutionary collective labor. That is, after all, precisely what *Empire* and *Multitude* propose by way of a contemporary revival of Marxism. In other words, so long as we understand the end or goal of revolution *only* in the terms of such radical historicity, we will fall into the trap that Žižek has exposed with his *other* critique of utopia, the critique which leaves us with the category of "the impossible." As soon as we think to derive the content of utopia from its form, as Hardt and Negri's Marxism still does, we find ourselves back within the perverse ideology of the paranoid fundamental fantasy, back within the terrain of what revolution must traverse to deserve the name. And doesn't the same argument count, too, for the utopia of collective labor that *Žižek* has allowed to blossom in his recent commentaries on revolution? Aren't Žižek's encomia to the labor of Lenin, Robespierre or Mao, if taken alone, simply exercises in the ideology of utopian imagination?

Unfolding revolution: where does Žižek stand?

Now, to be clear, my intention here is *not* to accuse Žižek of becoming a Marxist ideologue. Far from it, I'm raising, instead, the question of what prevents him from suffering the fate he so powerfully detects for Hardt and Negri. And the answer to that question is, of course, that Žižek *supplements* his formalist understanding of utopia – his concept of it as revolutionary, collective labor – with his characterization of it as *impossible*, as defying the grasp of imaginary or symbolic activity. Indeed, in an apparently complementary way, this just reverses our earlier discovery, wherein the utopia of the impossible needed a formal supplement to keep from sliding into mere immanence. It would seem, altogether, that we must construct a compound definition between these *two* approaches: *for Žižek, utopia takes up the possibility of a revolutionary, collective historicity by means of an act aimed at the point of impossibility within symbolically constituted reality.*

But, for all of its apparent encyclopedic virtue, this compound approach also soon falls apart; for the two ends of the definition *contest each other.* They cannot be thought together within any normal dialectical process. That is, *to the extent* that the winnow of history, post-Marx, forbids the deduction of any form of utopia – a form which would then provide the content of the utopian imagination – we cannot admit the form which Žižek, in the second argument, uses to distinguish utopian historicity. Utopia is only admissible as the "impossible." On the other hand, *to the extent that* we *must* posit the utopia of collective labor in order to prevent translation of "impossibility" into an aestheticized "present," we cannot accept Žižek's thesis of a utopia of the "Real": in other words, because we can deduce the content of utopian historicity from its form, we must forego the thesis of utopia's "impossibility." The material movement of work is precisely not "unimaginable," but has provided stuff for a particular symbolic, philosophical imagination since Schiller and then Marx redeemed it, and, as a result, it simply cannot be unproblematically joined with Žižek's radical Lacanian formula. Or, put differently, there can be no marriage of Žižek's anti-formalism and his formalism.

We are, then, in a situation rather like the one that Žižek underscored with regard to Heidegger's finitism. My book began from Žižek's reconsideration of finitude – his discovery in it of a an irreducible doubleness. Recall that his reading of *Being and Time* demanded that we understand such doubling in terms of an historical narrative involving two moments or even stages. Heidegger's virtue, the "positive" virtue of a philosophy of finitude, lay in his movement beyond a mere Kantian skepticism and into a characterization of Being itself with the incompleteness which, previously, we had only attributed to our knowing.

A first effort to understand what Žižek's two approaches to utopia would suggest that we might adopt a similar historicism. The obvious insight here – one that I've mentioned above in my discussion of Badiou and Lenin – would be that the two arguments represent pre- and post-revolutionary perspectives, that before the revolution we can only detect the possibility of utopia negatively (as "the impossible" rupture or break in the symbolic fabric of reality) whereas *after* the revolution we can re-conceive history itself materially. Indeed, it turns out that the radical historicity we've discovered under the name of "collective revolutionary labor" has been at work "all along," and thus that this historicity forms a possibility for the content of utopia.

Now, of course, the *danger* inherent in such a sequencing of "viewpoints" on history – a danger to which Žižek himself succumbs at moments and particularly in his Heidegger interpretation – is that we consider the second "moment" an adequate "synthesis" of the truth contained in the first: according to such an understanding, *actually*, the materialist possibility of a radically different social form has existed "all along as possibility." It was just impossible to discern within the old reality. However, a moment's reflection reveals that Žižek's argument against Hardt and Negri's Marxist historicity also forbids this naïve solution. No discovery of a stable underlying structure, even if it is a structure of pure "becoming," can suffice to understand the necessity of revolutionary break. Return here to Žižek's insistence that genuine subjective freedom demands the reinvention of the *past*, the production of *new* possibilities for human life. We can't say that utopia is "always already there" in the form of a potential to be realized without compromising this truth of its unanticipated nature.

One of Žižek's most brilliant insights concerns this very *aporia* to which we have now brought the question of history. I've referred previously to this idea, particularly in Chapter 2 when I discussed Žižek's interpretation of *Minority Report*. We might best reinject it as it emerges in *The Puppet and the Dwarf*, where it appears as a reinterpretation of Walter Benjamin's conception of history, the idea referenced in the very title of Žižek's book. What if, Žižek asks, the "ordinary 'historical' notion of time" were wrong? For the most part we operate within a common-sense, Leibnizean understanding of history, one in which "there are multiple possibilities waiting to be realized," but "once one of them actualizes itself, others are cancelled." The key to such a view is, of course, that "possibility precedes choice: the choice is a choice among possibilities" (Žižek 2003, p. 160).

Against this universe of Leibnizean "monads," Žižek proposes that we conceive historicity as "the notion of a choice/act that retroactively opens up its own possibility," or as he puts it alternatively, "the idea that the emergence of a radically New retroactively changes the past" (Žižek 2003, p. 160). As we saw in Chapter 2 in the case of "Anderton" from *Minority Report*, Žižek is here invoking the odd set of phenomena that result from the subject's imbrication within objective causality, "the self-referentiality of knowledge" of a predetermined train of events (Žižek 2006b, p. 208). However, the effect of such "inner loops" within the "apparent straight line" of determined history is importantly twofold: on the one hand, they indicate that, from within a "commonsense" pre-revolutionary historicism, it remains unprecedented: as Žižek puts it, "we cannot establish the time of the explosion of the Event" by locating any predictive "objective criteria" (Žižek 2003, p. 135). On the other hand, however, the event itself brings with it a *different historicity*, one which, in hindsight, is/becomes a structurally stable characteristic of revolutions.

Or, as Žižek puts it in *The Puppet and the Dwarf*, his anti-Leibnizean theory of historicity is really just another way of conceiving the act as "unthinkable" – an alternative to the limited conceptualization of it as "impossible" in *The Reality of the Virtual*. (See, Žižek 2003, p. 160.) Now such "unthinkability" refers to more than what violates the fantasmatic fabric of social reality: it also refers its own logical self-immolation. For Žižek, "revolution" stands for the *possibility* of an *unprecedented* act – an act which is, prior to itself, *impossible* and thus can only occur insofar as it creates its own possibility.

So, we must say instead that the utopia of and in revolution both is and is not a potential structural for human existence, that it both awaits *discovery* by a political "science," and demands *creation* by a revolutionary act. Which is, first of all, strictly to equate Žižek's full treatment of revolutionary utopia with the central theme of *The Parallax View*. As we already saw, for Žižek the existence of a "parallax gap" is indicative of "the confrontation of two closely linked perspectives between which no neutral common ground is possible," and, in dedicating an entire division of *The Parallax View* to "the revolutionary parallax," he himself indicates that it makes up one such *topos* (Žižek 2006b, p. 4). Moreover, the structure here both mirrors and adds something to the *additional* understanding of "parallax" we derived above through a close reading of *The Parallax View's* introduction. That interpretation suggested that the heterogeneity at stake here concerns above all the epistemological question, the question of how and to what extent the essential issue provides an object for a potential science.

One way to put our finger on what "utopia" adds to our earlier understanding of parallax might lead one last time through Marx's theory of history. Couldn't we say at this point that the "epistemological/ontological" issue here really concerns, above all, *historicity?* That is, the underlying heterogeneity in our investigation of Žižek's theses about utopia has really divided between, on the one hand, an "impossibility" which boils down to the dimensional, a-historical presentness of subjectivity, and that essentially non-present historical dimension, the subject as *labor.* Above all, Žižek's thought pursues and assumes this division between these two historicities, *both* of which are necessary to constitute the possibility of a genuinely revolutionary act. And this splitting is, such is my argument, the great *strength* of Žižek's approach to the question of revolution and utopia, a virtue that he does not himself sufficiently acknowledge.

In concluding, we might re-formulate this last assertion, (regarding the central role of historicity in understanding the "performative" dimension of parallax in Žižek), suggesting now that Žižek's thought about utopia is a way of remaining *loyal to Marx.* We saw above that both the thesis of utopia's emergence as "impossible" and the idea of a utopian form of collective labor are of Marxian provenance. The only problem, we might now say, with that perspective lies in the efforts of Marx and Marxists to *marry* these demands, to *overcome* the essential heterogeneity of a parallax gap, substituting for it the power of a unified insight: the "subtractive" method amounted to precisely that, defending "productivism" as both the site of presentness and of the alternative historicity of labor. In other words, implicitly for Žižek, Marx *should have* insisted upon the full force of a contradiction: utopia both is inaccessible as form and is *pure* form, the form of labor. Utopia, in the end, is "impossible" in another way than Liberal theorists since Popper and Berlin have been proposing but also in a different manner than the one that Žižek suggests in "The Reality of the Virtual": it is impossible because its reality subsists in the inconceivable confrontation of those absolutely heterogeneous perspectives – one might almost say, those *subjects* – which Žižek's *two* approaches to it delineate.

Chapter 6

The pervert and the philosopher (as witnessed by) the theologian and the analyst

I began *Žižek and Heidegger* with a discussion of Žižek's commitment to philosophy as a pursuit of truth, his disdain for postmodern views of thought which, claiming only to be "interventions," eschew taking the risk of saying something. In such a spirit, he makes the following comment in a recent interview:

> I believe in clear-cut positions. I think that the most arrogant position is this apparent multidisciplinary modesty of 'what I am saying now is not unconditional, it is just a hypothesis,' and so on. It really is a most arrogant position. I think that the only way to be honest and to expose yourself to criticism is to state clearly and dogmatically where you are. You must take the risk and have a position. (Žižek and Daly 2004, p. 45)

At a first take, we might say that Žižek is demanding that we take the ultimate stake of theoretical work (in general) and his work (in particular) to lie in the exposure of a truth, albeit, in Žižek's case, a strange and often paradoxical one. Above all, this commitment forbids the kind of hyper-reflexivity about voice and discursive structure that typifies much post-structuralist writing. Žižek does his best to present the truth, full stop; and all secondary concerns about the "imperial" authorial voice or related matters be damned.

On the other hand, though, Žižek's work, which claims the mantle of a *praxical* philosophy, is all about *doing things with words* (to borrow Austin's phrase). Indeed, a closer analysis of Žižek's statement above from *Conversations with Žižek* indicates this praxical concern, since his measure for theoretical work lies in whether or not the theorist is willing to "take the risk" of embracing a position. Read thus, the success of Žižek's writing depends upon its ability to forward revolutionary change – at every level, from the individual through society.

In the tension between these *two* Žižek's lies the story of the following chapter, a story which, as we will see, takes shape around the by-now-familiar issue of *perversion*. The question I raise below is the following: what happens when Žižek's commitment to truth – to the presentation of truth – actually *blocks* the effectiveness of his arguments? What happens when the presence of Žižek's clear theses inhibits the revolutionary end they propose? Because, as it turns out, such collision is no rarity but occurs at certain key moments in his project, these questions will raise more than merely "academic" concerns.

Let me return to the end of the last chapter – to Žižek's introduction of an "unthinkable" concept of historicity, one adequate to the odd, double narrative of revolution and utopia that I traced in the chapter's body. Recall that the idea of an act which would "pull itself up by its own bootstraps," creating its own possibility, served my larger narrative precisely by adding to the ways in which utopia is "the impossible" for Žižek.

Now, returning one last time to this question of the revolutionary act's historicity, I want to suggest that Žižek's presentation of it nonetheless betrays its content at the *performative* level, the level I invoked at the end of the Chapter 4 of *Žižek and Heidegger*. Isn't what Žižek *does*, in proposing the act's absolute self-creation, precisely to assert its *possibility* by giving us a theoretical frame within which to understand its impossibility? That is, the "act" of framing the revolutionary moment's historicity (self-creating, unanticipated) posits it as *possible*, as *a possibility* among others. Many things *could* happen, among them a self-creating act . . . And this, in turn, prevents us from confronting the act's absolute heterogeneity, its radical impossibility. Žižek's presentation of his shocking insight limits its "shock."

A related example might help to clarify my point. Consider the following passage from *The Parallax View*, where Žižek tells the story (from Somerset Maugham) of the servant on an errand in Baghdad who "meets Death." The servant is so terrified by Death's fixed gaze at him that he immediately returns home, begs his master for a horse and permission to ride to the city of Samarra – which the master grants him. But the master, concerned for his servant, also himself seeks out Death at the market and, in Žižek's words, "reproaches it for scaring his faithful servant." Death, surprised, answers, "But I didn't want to scare your servant. I was just surprised. What was he doing here, when I have an appointment with him in Samarra tonight? . . ." (Žižek 2006b, p. 207)

Of course, just as is the case with the story of Oedipus, we usually read this narrative as illustrating the unavoidability of fate: the very thing the servant does to avoid Death leads him into its arms. The story, then, would seem to teach us to become fatalists. But for Žižek there is an opposite lesson here – one that it shares with numerous "time-travel" narratives – which is that destiny *already includes our consciousness of it* (see, Žižek 2003, p. 135). Such a conclusion, however, leads Žižek to a radically different "moral" than the one usually attached to such tales, namely that, *because it includes our knowledge about it,* the story actually opens up a hole in fate. The problem is just that the servant refuses this path. It is a moral that Žižek explains in regard to the Samarra anecdote: "What if," he suggests, "the message of this story is not that our demise is impossible to avoid, that trying to twist free of it will only tighten its grip, but the exact opposite: accept fate as inevitable, and you will break its grasp on you?" (2006b, p. 207)

I might translate Žižek's odd interpretation here as follows: our real *experience* of unfreedom emerges from our inability to accept the choices and conditions of choice we face. "If only we could escape," we complain, betraying our efforts to "twist free" of fate, our hidden belief in the arbitrariness of reality. Still, on the other hand, as we saw in Žižek's underscoring of "anticipatory resoluteness" in *Being and Time,* eschewing such self-pity, or simply leaving behind the game in which we imagine another possible life as our own, we can *decide.* Thus, if we just quit trying to assert our freedom (over and against our circumstances) we will in fact free ourselves.

No matter how compelling it is, my claim here would be that Žižek's insight about the Samarra anecdote produces the "perverse" effects of knowledge that we saw to be operative in his "Benjaminian" interpretation of historicity: the key idea, that consciousness punctures a closed causal loop, splits into two *contradictory* propositions: on the one hand, the imperative is to *act as though there was no way out* of fate's declarations, a command backed up by the way that fate's declarations already take into account our struggles against it. On the other hand, though, Žižek suggests that we accept fate *because* doing so will liberate us. His very inclusion of such consciousness within destiny leads us to a *secret perverse knowledge* of freedom, a knowledge whose very purpose is to "get around" fatalism.

This is not to say that the advice to "quit struggling with fate" is *wrong,* quite the contrary, this advice contains Žižek's (and Heidegger's) first-level wisdom about finitude. Nor is it incorrect to suggest that, *in fact, coincidentally,* following such a course has a liberating effect. The problem lies, rather, in Žižek's insistence upon the simultaneous combination of these propositions. Insofar as we *know* that the hidden effect of our fatalism will be the undoing of fate, any "acceptance" here becomes a mere ruse. When Žižek couches his advice in his knowledge of its effects, he undoes those effects.

Not that, on the other hand, one could really avoid this moment of perversity. After all, Žižek's central insight about modernity, about the modern subject, binds it precisely to such "knowledge of our freedom." "In truth" we need the argument that our action will further liberation, in order to *motivate* our act, our decision, at all. As a result, not just Žižek but all of us seem to be left with the essentially perverse imperative, "if you want to be free, give up on freedom!" By Žižek's own insight, such a commandment must fail, since we cannot forget, cannot give up on it, so long as it forms our *purpose*.

Recall that, in my interpretation of *Being and Time* in Chapter 1, I suggested a splitting of Dasein between its "inauthentic" and "authentic" forms, between the Dasein torn by existential guilt and the "resolute" Dasein who responds to such guilt. Short of proposing such a solution here – proposing, that is, that the subject who ceases trying to evade fate is not the same as the one who believes in freedom – there seems no way out of Žižek's dilemma. Knowing the truth of our freedom prevents us from attaining it.

Christianity and perversity in *The Puppet and the Dwarf*

We could find a convenient example of what I'm proposing – and one, ironically, that plays around the very question of perversity in Žižek – in the *subtitle* of Žižek's *The Puppet and the Dwarf*. It announces the book to be about "The Perverse Core of Christianity," though any serious reading of Žižek's intention soon discovers within the text itself just the opposite, Christianity's *non-perverse* core.[1] Like Žižek's previous theological essay, *The Fragile Absolute*, whose subtitle promises to tell us why "the Christian tradition is worth fighting for" (Žižek 2000), *The Puppet and the Dwarf* attempts to rescue Christianity from its "perverters." Indeed, the framing question for Žižek in this book is, *can Christianity be pried apart from the perverse form in which it has been institutionalized so as to provide an alternative to the cynical belief dominant within the post-modern world?*[2] That Žižek answers this question affirmatively would suggest that there is, in fact, another "core" of Christianity than the perverse one and that *The Puppet and the Dwarf* aims to elucidate and valorize precisely it.[3]

Things in *The Puppet and Dwarf* are not, in fact, even as clear as that: we do *also* get the story of Christianity's perversity, but the marginalization of that narrative is itself significant. In fact, the real confusion here concerns the extent to which "Christianity" can be fully understood as a "belief system" at all. To grasp this, follow through on Žižek's analysis of how Christianity can have a "non-perverse core." To arrive at this, *The Puppet and Dwarf* first frames an argument much like the one by which Heidegger's understanding of finitude is preferred to Descartes' mere skepticism, a version of the Kant-Hegel refrain to which we've been thoroughly familiarized at this point. Perhaps Žižek's clearest articulation of this framing in the context of *The Puppet and the Dwarf* involves an old Soviet-Era joke: "Rabbinovitch" wants to emigrate from the Soviet Union. In his interview with the emigration official, he gives two reasons for his desire: "'First, I'm afraid that, if the socialist order disintegrates, all the blame for the Communists' crimes will be put on us, the Jews.' To the state bureaucrat's exclamation, 'but nothing will ever change in the Soviet Union! Socialism is here to stay, forever!' Rabbinovitch calmly answers: 'That's my second reason!'" (Žižek 2003, p. 77)

The key to this joke and the logic that it announces is the necessity that a certain situation be "read twice," first from the perspective of those engaged in it and then, again from a viewpoint including the speaker's "position of enunciation" (Žižek 2003, p. 87). That is, Rabbinovitch first articulates his desire, his dissatisfaction, from the discursive set of possibilities available for a Jew in dialogue with a Soviet official – the fear of anti-semitism as the brutal force held at bay by the "necessary discipline" of Soviet governance. The official's response, and Rabbinovitch's twist on that answer, reveals the way that discursive position distorts what can be said. It reveals the "truth" of Rabbinovitch's desire – to get out from under the repressive Soviet system – in a way that can only emerge after this source has first appeared in distorted form.

The claim in *The Puppet and the Dwarf* is that the "core" of Christianity amounts to the second iteration of the Other's non-existence, the iteration including the position of enunciation of the believer. Žižek finds the first or Kantian insight in the central "doctrinal" moment of Christian theological history, the doctrine of "original sin" and the history it traces out before and short of Christ's sacrifice.[4] Such a doctrine locates a "missing" or "lacking" element in cosmological totality precisely at the point of the human will. For Christians, the "sin of Adam" (pride, self-assertion) is the *form* of sin itself – so that no "sacrifice" by any of us could atone for it. As I already discussed it in Chapter 3, the idea here is that *we ourselves* are the unruly and extraneous element in an otherwise "whole" creation, the exception which allows every created element to enjoy a pre-given place in a cosmos. As in the dialectic of finitude, here, too, pre-history first delivers truth as *our* limit or failure.

The knowledge of this failure is, of course, perverted by the fantasy formation that it sustains: instead of making manifest the incompleteness of being, it simply multiplies our guilt. For Žižek, this opens the opportunity marked by his Pauline version of Jesus, a Jesus who proves his "Father" impotent to "save him" from death when he calls out to him in despair upon the cross ("Father, why have you forsaken me?") God can't save Jesus because he (God) *doesn't exist.* There simply is *no force* to the universe guaranteeing that everything will "turn out" in the end.

This atheism of the dying Jesus allows, as a kind of "second blow" the Fall to appear as what it "really" always was – an assertion of the essential, meaningless *non-totality* of the universe (see, Žižek 2003, p. 126). Žižek's Jesus wants us to see that, precisely because, actually, this universe *is* incomplete, we had to posit our "sinful" selves as exception to any totalized cosmos in order to maintain the fantasmatic illusion of totality. Jesus teaches that the very idea of a divine reality against which we sin is an illusion reproduced in the gesture by which we first free ourselves (as sinners) from it. In other words, the "fictionality of the Other" sustaining fantasy can only first appear *as* fantasy. For Žižek, Jesus does not come to "redeem us" from Adam's Fall but only to help us "shift our subjective position," our perspective, so that we could see "that it [redemption] is already there" in the Fall – that there never was a "cosmos" from which we rebelled (Žižek 2003, pp. 86–87). In a precise mirroring of the logic of finitude in Heidegger, Christianity, as "non-perverse" enterprise, means for Žižek this knowledge or insight translating the form of our own limitation into the *content* of a lack in Being itself.

The interesting thing about this theological structure, really, is how Žižek constantly reasserts it throughout *The Puppet and the Dwarf* (and indeed, through all of his theological work), but only at the same time that he obviously struggles with its insufficiency. If Žižek is right, things *ought* to be clear: Christianity, once rescued from its various orthodoxies, delivers us a doctrine, a body of knowledge, sufficient to truth. The only task thus would seem to be critique of various theological "deviations" and defense of what is certainly a radically Protestant version of Christian dogma. But Žižek knows *full well* that no such sufficient doctrine exists, that there really couldn't be an adequate theology. It's for this reason that he must so insist, in the last lines of *The Puppet and the Dwarf*, that Christianity, to "save itself" "has to sacrifice itself" (Žižek 2003, p. 171). And it's here, too, that we must insist upon the significance of the subtitle of *The Puppet and the Dwarf* as symptom of Žižek's muddle: in some sense, Christianity *is* perverse to the core.

But what could this mean? In what sense is Christianity *essentially* perverse for Žižek? Return to a site I've discussed before, Žižek's (and Santner's) retelling of *Moses and Monotheism*, their common view of Judaism as the religion of the Kafkaesque Law (Žižek 2003, pp. 128–129). With the sadistic imperative that indicts us before the "court" of Law, with an order whose content – whose specific demands – we are never allowed to know, we find a freedom that we don't want. If I can't know what God commands me to do, I am, as Žižek puts it, "thrown back into myself, compelled to assume the risk of freely determining the coordinates of my desire."[5] That is, as I indicated above, we are liberated by the *necessity* that, in the face of an unspecified, infinite demand, we choose *for ourselves*. And, furthermore, this liberation is *shared* and, as such, marks the birth of that new form of community, the collective. For Žižek, the dialectical virtue of Judaism lies in its introduction of such collectivity, of a new kind of social being.

Notice, though, that in such choice we are made free, paradoxically, by the very existence of the Other – albeit in its sadistic, supplemental form. Without the Other and its unreasonable and unfathomable imperatives – without the Law before which we are inexplicably and indefinitely called – we never can take the leap to form a collective, even the "Collective of the Holy Spirit." Nor can the authentic moment here be reduced to *any belief or knowledge*; rather, it lies in an act *produced* in response to the Other's demand – albeit a demand which throws us back on ourselves.

Seen thus, as Žižek *does* see it at various points throughout *The Puppet and the Dwarf*, the problem with *Christianity* is that, for all of its theological acumen, *as a belief system* it is essentially unable to reflect this demand. Seeing things in this way allows us to understand a number of passages in *The Puppet and the Dwarf* where Žižek attacks postmodernity's pluralistic or new age efforts to renew religious traditions. Precisely in their avoidance of anxiety before the Law, Buddhist meditators or "nice" modern Christians avoid that traumatic aspect of religious tradition which opens the radical possibility of modern freedom.[6] In this light, one might argue here that, for Žižek, Christianity remains necessarily perverse, *precisely insofar* as it delivers the hidden formula of atheism, insofar as it is too enlightened, too nice: that is, in giving birth to the illusion that we might "get beyond" belief, get beyond the Other, it actually paralyzes us all the more effectively in our effort to act. Žižek knows that, knows that the religion of "atheism" he openly embraces automatically becomes its own opposite when we come to believe in it as a sufficient basis for our actions. In other words, when it's a question of *how* one should act rather *what* the truth is, Žižek's analysis dubs "perverse" exactly what seemed the path away from perversity from the perspective of his epistemology. The "Perverse Core of Christianity" is precisely Christianity's hidden atheism, its non-perversity.

The case of Christianity thus illustrates the difference between the two models of operation in Žižek's texts – as presentations of a truth and as efforts to produce an effect on an interpreter. Christianity is *non-perverse* as a truth but, at least at an initial pass, *perverse* as it effects us. Furthermore, Žižek also seems to propose *another* Christianity, one which subsists precisely in order to betray its own truth – which comes full circle to evade perversion through a decisive act. Recall those last words of *The Puppet and the Dwarf* with their invocation of *sacrifice*: isn't their implicit proposal (that Christianity can only "save itself" insofar as it "sacrifices itself") that the *truth* of atheism must sacrifice itself to produce the *revolution* it espouses? Of course, this religious language is particularly central to Christianity, the belief based on endless reenactment of a particular sacrifice.

I can explain what I mean here by returning to the problematic with which I began this chapter, the issue of a *performative* contradiction between form and content in Žižek's doctrine of the act's historicity – a historicity without precedent or anticipation, one which opens a "new past." Now, the reader will recall that the contradiction here comes in the very act by which Žižek announces his insight, a *form* that implicitly reintroduces the act into a totalized field of possibilities, betraying the radical novelty that is its *content*. At this point, though, we might extend the question of performativity yet further, all the way, in fact, to the point of self-reflection. That is, we can *also* say that Žižek's performative contradiction *helps* him make his case for the *unthinkability* of the act. What better to boggle the mind – to resist "thought" – than a full-scale contradiction between "what I say" and the "way I say it"?

Which as much as to suggest, when we treat Žižek's *discourse about* the historicity of the act as itself a kind of act, a way of directly *confronting us* with the unthinkable, the problem of perversity seems to melt away. To the extent this performative contradiction actually *helps* Žižek to *make* his point – that the act occurs beyond the historical categories by which we comprehend it – the fact of his own self-contradictory "deed" in thinking it ceases to be a problem. We might then, try reading Žižek "against the grain" of his own desires, seeing his texts *precisely* as interventions, as efforts to directly *change* the world rather than to understand it.

More than this, the redemption above of a second-level, non-perverse Christianity opens up several possibilities for understanding how Žižek pursues such textual action. First of all, if Christianity "redeems itself" by "sacrificing itself," we can suddenly see Žižek's own role as precisely one *of* sacrifice: *he* takes on the (perverse) knowledge of historicity *for us*. In his function as "vessel of the truth" of atheism, we have literally a kind of *imitatio Christi*, a priestly function or, even, a kind of "sin eating." Žižek "suffers" (we'll have to adjust this word below) so we don't have to.

There's also another, related, set of metaphors by which we could understand Žižek's texts as themselves "acts," themselves effort to produce change rather than to share knowledge, and that is, of course, the language of psychoanalysis, of the relationship between analyst and analysand.[7] If we cannot read Žižek as philosophers communicating with a "master philosopher" – if what we come to know in that relationship actually protects us from becoming what we should be – then perhaps we should admit that we are *analysands* and that Žižek is our *analyst*. Perhaps to the extent that both Žižek and we take on those roles we are able to escape perversity; perhaps psychoanalysis marks the path of "sacrifice" open to us. Let me now turn to this language of analysis, hoping to gain from it a deeper understanding of how Žižek might model the efficacy of his texts.

The desire of the analyst

In his early exposé, "Enjoy your Žižek!," Robert Boynton reports Žižek's own following account of his incomplete training analysis with Jacques-Alain Miller:

> It was my strict rule, my sole ethical principle, to lie consistently: to invent all symptoms, fabricate all dreams . . . It was obsessional neurosis in its absolute purest form. Because you never knew how long it would last, I was always prepared for at least two sessions. I have this incredible fear of what I might discover if I really went into analysis. What if I lost my frenetic theoretical desire? What if I turned into a common person?[8]

A telling analytic moment if there ever was one – even if it comes in the form of a ruse to avoid such telling moments. *What* does it tell us?

First of all, it suggests that, even when he is supposed to play the role of the analysand (since an essential part of becoming an analyst is to oneself undergo a thorough analysis), Žižek is unable to do so. He cannot let go of the psychical economy, "Žižek", the economy responsible for his "frenetic theoretical desire," the structure which differentiates him from the "common person." It's worth noting that the passage I've quoted above continues with a detailed account of how Žižek was able to maintain his practice of lying while on the couch, how he was able to fool Miller. He geared what he said to Miller's own fascinations, for example, obsessively reporting (nonexistent) dreams about Bette Davis' role in *All about Eve*, whose title character shared the name of Miller's daughter. In other words, Žižek seduced *Miller* into a transference relationship, subverting the analytic situation by making *himself* the analyst.[9]

Žižek the analyst: such a characterization certainly goes some way to explaining the obstinate stability of the "self," Žižek, through countless books and a couple of decades – the analyst even when he should be an analysand.[10] Many scholars have noted the development of Žižek's work since 1989: and, indeed, there have been changes of focus, allegiance and, to some degree, of doctrine. On the whole, though, we should marvel at the obstinate and unchanging nature of "Žižek." Today, he's still telling the same jokes (the Chicken, "Lenin in Warsaw," etc.) that launched his international reputation with *The Sublime Object of Ideology* – and finding much the same meaning in them. We might here observe the odd parallel between Žižek and the figure of the sadistic but eloquent skinhead to which he's returned over and over – Žižek's symbol for, among other things, the inefficacy of interpretation in our world, for the clean separation between what the subject "knows" and its behavior. Don't we witness something akin to that skinhead (with his thuggish behavior combined with a sophisticated theoretical explanation of why he behaves as he does) in Žižek's own work, which for years has been singing the praises of revolutionary change from a theoretical "position" that has remained remarkably static, remarkably unable to *undergo* radical change? Žižek tells us endlessly of the cause, demands that we transform ourselves for it but himself remains a model of stability. Žižek is immune to classical analysis. *He* need not fear the exposure of his symptom, which will resist interpretive resolution in any case.

Given this personation of "the analyst," any effort to understand Žižek's texts should explore how they might function *as* analyses of the reader. As prelude to such an exploration, we must recall what he has to say about the analytic relationship, the relationship between analyst and analysand. Let's go back a little bit. The interesting thing about psychoanalysis, and particularly about *Lacanian* psychoanalysis is that it isn't just another symbol system (like Christianity) for conceptualizing issues of belief and knowledge. Quite the contrary, analysis emerges in, and is a way of responding to, the peculiarity of a world in which we "know the fictionality of the Other" – know that we have "made up" the very idea of a position from or for which we might enjoy omniscience. In other words, analysis belongs to a world in which the perversity of the knower becomes an issue. Up to this point, we've effectively been asking whether Žižek demands that we *know* the fictionality of the Other including my role in producing this fantasy – even if my knowledge limits the efficacy of its insight; or whether he demands that we *live* beyond our selves in a way that actually attacks the fantasy of the Other, even if without knowing what it does. The drama of an analysis is, of course, that it *casts* the two sides of this now familiar Žižekian choice, placing them in the dual roles of analyst and analysand. We might say that the efficacy of analysis depends upon a strict division of labor between an analyst who *knows* (but cannot, as a result, herself change) and an analysand, who changes (but only insofar as she *does not know* what she is becoming). In other words, the analytic relationship, largely pushed into the background of Žižek's explicit concerns, actually rehearses the structure of his thought as a whole, perhaps even *forms* that structure.

To provide content to this claim, let's flesh out the way that the roles of the analyst and the analysand correspond to the two sides of the Žižekian divide, beginning with the analyst – who does not lose her status as bearer of "Truth" with the resolution of the transference. Quite the contrary, key to Lacan's approach to analysis in *Seminar XVII* ("The Other Side of Psychoanalysis") and to Žižek's Lacan is the diagram of the "four discourses," a diagram in which the "position of the analyst" sites "knowledge" in the "position of Truth." Žižek comments here that this "knowledge" is irreducible to the "supposed" expertise which originally draws the analysand into transference but rather also includes a "non-scientific" dimension, a "knowledge that concerns the subject (analysand) in the truth of his subjective position" (Žižek 2006a, p. 115). In other words, the analyst "knows" in theory the insubstantiality of the subject that is its "truth" (as opposed to the truth of this particular analysand's symptom!) and knows, further, how to draw the analysand to an "act" affirming this very insubstantiality.

According to Žižek, such knowledge grants to the analyst a certain "enjoyment" in the analytic relationship. Indeed, for Žižek the analyst becomes exemplary in his *success* within the economy of perverse enjoyment, "profiting" from his labor in eliciting a revolutionary change in the analysand. In a recent essay, "Neighbors and Other Monsters,"[11] Žižek uses Henry James' novel, *The Lesson of the Master* to illustrate this economy of the analysis. In the novel, the old "master," Henry St. Georges advises his younger friend,

Paul Overt, that becoming a great writer demands giving up love and particularly the love for his beautiful fiancée. After Overt takes his advice, leaving the young woman, St. Georges marries her. When confronted by Overt, St. Georges, surprisingly, defends himself, claiming, in Žižek's words, that "he will not write again, but Paul will achieve greatness" (Žižek 2004b, p. 152).

This is the basis for Žižek's claim that St. Georges appears "as a true analyst" in the narrative, "one who is not afraid to profit from his ethical choices." Žižek's essay then turns to an analogy between St. Georges, Jewish Law and the analyst. As we've already seen in several places, Judaism for Žižek represent a new relationship to Law and prohibition, one wherein Law is separated from any transcendence it might represent: one follows the Law because it *is* the Law, infinite in itself rather than representing the divine. On the one hand, the Jews are like every other "nation" – transfixed by a master signifier, pursuing an identity held in place by a name. On the other hand, "the Law" *qua* identity challenges the very economy of fantasy and master signifier; if the Law *is* the divine (and not simply a symbol or path *to* it), then that is as much as to deny the existence of an Other *beyond* our world. All there is *is* the Law.

As we've already seen in a couple of places, within the practices of Judaism, this tension in the very status of identity can best be understood in terms of what it does to the usual economy of prohibition and enjoyment: usually we *oppose* Law and enjoyment, or think of enjoyment as transgression of the Law. Within Žižek's Judaism, however, Law *is* enjoyment, *is* its excess beyond finite understanding and representation. Žižekian Jewish Law leads naturally to the universe of Kafka, a universe in which the Law, as divine, exceeds all finite instantiations of it: Law corresponds with the command to "obey!" in which we are not allowed to know just *what* we are to do. Thus, the two sides of an ambiguity: first, we get the implicit *denial* of the Other visible, for example, in the passage from the Cabbalist, Isaac Luria, in which the entire universe is constructed (literally) from the letters of the Torah. There is "no God" beyond the text of the Law. Here, we might also mention the famous *mishna* of the "pardes," in which a court of great rabbis defy a "heavenly voice" in their judgment of the Law's application, declaring "it's not in heaven anymore!" On the other hand, this very construction transfers the excess of the Other *into the body of the Law*, which then becomes a site for an enjoyment no longer opposed to *following* the rules: to live a "holy" life is to excel in "enthusiasm" for following the "mitzvoth" (commandments), even down to the smallest details of personal hygiene or sexual regimen.

If we return to the question of analysis, the import of this analogy should be clear: the analyst is like the Jew: she *knows* the Truth of the Other's fictionality, indeed, her role is to *be* this Truth for the analysand, but because, like the Jew, she maintains an *identity*, because, as bearer of knowledge for an other, she holds onto a *self*, she is forbidden the analysand's liberation. Precisely because of this limitation, she is granted an enjoyment parallel to Judaism's enjoyment of the Law, an enjoyment *in* the body of the Law rather than beyond it. Thus, St. Georges' virtuous theft of Overt's fiancée. The analyst, after all, gets to "have" the knowledge of the Other's fictionality, a truth which she "enjoys" as it emerges in endless interpretive variety through the analysand's symptoms.

On the other side of the room lies the analysand. Actually, the "couch" metaphor here is inapt, because – for Žižek, following Lacan – the analysand is the *active* partner in the analytic relationship, the one whose act creates decisive change. Indeed, the repeating figures in Žižek's discussions of analysis play with the image of the analysand as almost a suicide, a most decisive "actor." Thus, we have the position of Overt in the James novel, a position "destined" for genuine creativity. But, of course, it is creativity with a price – namely, a certain blindness, an inability to "hold onto" reality sufficiently to enjoy it. That is why Žižek returns ever and again to the metaphor of the analysand's act as a "'suicidal' gesture" in which she/he "step(s) out of the symbolic" order of constituted fantasy, a gesture in which the very "consistency" of reality is threatened (see, for example, Žižek 2004b, p. 140). Though it is not *literally* suicide that's at stake here, but rather a destruction of the band-aid covering over the incompletion of reality, the difference here is dangerously subtle – as indicated by one of Žižek's favorite examples, the end of David Fincher's *Fight Club*, where Ed Norton's "Jack" frees himself from his paranoid delusional double by shooting himself/his double in the head. Indeed, Žižek insists that we cannot abridge the violence of this act without denuding it of its liberating potential (see, for example, *Reality*).

Now, the *Fight Club* example is helpful because it presents perhaps Žižek's most vivid images of the analysand's path to an *act* beyond knowledge. Indeed, this is contained in the central metaphor of the film, a metaphor already activated at the end of the film's opening shot, where Jack has his gun in mouth ready to kill himself. To free oneself *is* to do violence to, to even do away with one's "self." That is, *Fight Club* substitutes *beating oneself* and even killing *oneself* for any kind of self-knowledge. Recall that the film largely evolves in the psychotic relationship between Norton's Jack, a narcoleptic yuppie, and his delusional double, "Tyler" (Brad Pitt). Pitt, as Tyler Durden, pulls Jack away from his conformist life as corporate clone into an increasingly desperate and dangerous underworld, an underworld whose thematic unity is provided by the "fight clubs" that the two found together – clubs dedicated to ritualized fighting between bored workers. Rejecting the various ideologized pastimes and identities offered to pacify them (Jack's prior hobby was redecoration from the Ikea catalogue), these men choose a kind of direct contact with the Real by way of beating the pulp out of each other.

For Žižek, *Fight Club* contains a profound insight about how we might challenge the otherwise *unchallengeable* and unconscious structure producing our very reality. One must understand, first of all that all of the "sadistic" violence in the film *turns out* to be masochistic – that the "fight clubs" and all of their spin-offs are actually venues for unconsciously beating *oneself* up. Tyler is really Jack's psychotic double; they are one person. When Tyler beats up Jack (or *vice-versa*), actually we are (unbeknownst to the audience at the time) witnessing acts of self-mutilation.

As the film progresses, Jack (through his double, Tyler) "kills" his identity, such as it is, as a "worker," a "young, urban professional" (symbolized by the catalogue furniture he obsessively collects for his condo) and a "civilized" (that is, in the parlance of the film, "docile") man. In the words of Tyler, he "bottoms out," losing all that had previously held together his identity. In other words, Jack becomes the "universal" subject Marx envisioned with the term "proletariat," the one who has been emptied of all substantial humanity in subjection to capitalist reality (Žižek and Lenin 2002, p. 252). "Nothing to lose" here means no longer needing to participate in the ideological activities by which we support the consistency of ourselves and reality – prepared for revolution – a preparation Jack reveals at the end of the film when he does away with Tyler by shooting himself and then is able to watch the detonation of the bombs by which his group hopes to destroy the techno-capitalist order. In this way, Žižek tells us, Jack "also liberates himself from the dual mirror-relationship of beating: in this culmination of self-aggression, its logic cancels itself; Norton will no longer have to beat himself – now he will he able to beat the true enemy, the system" (Žižek and Lenin 2002, p. 253).

While Freud introduced the idea of "transference" as the agency of analytic therapy, our primary interest lies with Lacan's translation of Freudian thought. Still, since understanding that transformation demands a minimal discussion of Freud, let's begin with the observation that "transference" historically arose as a way out Freud's deadlock on the issue of knowledge. In the period of his association with Breuer, Freud became aware that his initial theory of the "talking cure" as practiced with hysterics was inadequate, that the hysterical symptom might survive discovery and that the analysand's *knowledge* of the origins of the symptom was not effective in curing hysteria. It was in this context that Freud proposed that the "talking cure" rested on *transference*, an erotic bond between analyst and analysand which re-injected ("transferred") the erotic disturbance in the patient's behavior into a situation *internal* to the analysis. Responding to an erotic incapacity in her/his life, the hysteric or neurotic reproduces within the transference relationship with the analyst the symptom blocking the formation of non-pathological erotic attachments. The success of analytic therapy, then, depends upon the identification and resolution of these issues within the safe laboratory of the analytic situation.

The interesting thing about Lacan's approach to the transference is that, in a complex manner, it returns to the bond between love and *knowledge*, precisely the tie that Freud sought to break. What, for Lacan, leads the analysand to fall in love with the analyst in the first place? Precisely the fact that the analyst is the "subject-supposed-to-know," supposedly possessed of the secret knowledge of the analysand's "illness," his/her sickness. In other words, the transference relationship is predicated on the medical myth endemic in our society, the myth that there is an "expert" who enjoys a complete knowledge, a knowledge "in the Other," of what ails me. Indeed, because of this starting point, Lacan playfully calls the transference relationship "philo-sophical" a "love of knowledge," although its goal is not the *attainment* of knowledge but only (Alcibiades-like) of the affections of the knower. From a Lacanian perspective, in fact, the analysand's real *goal* is the maintenance of her/his ignorance, or, better, of the "mystery" protecting the "knowledge in the Other." Rather than seeking a successful "relationship" with the analyst, the analysand really wants to reproduce the reality – the viewpoint of the fantasmatically constituted Other – within which the symptomatic failure of the erotic has been constructed. Which is as much as to say that the analyst comes to occupy the site of the "master signifier" for the analysand.[12]

Thus, the "resolution" of a transference within a Lacanian context depends upon the dissolution of the analyst's status as location of occult knowledge about the analysand's symptom. This suggests, what I've already discussed in earlier chapters, the problematic status of "interpretation" in Lacanian analysis: we are about as far as we can be from the classic Freudian picture of an analytic situation in which the "doctor" solves the mystery of the "patient's" symptom. The analyst must precisely cure the analysand of the syndrome by which the analysand makes her/himself into a "patient," one who is the *object* of knowledge. Effectively, the analyst uses the patient's desire, a desire *reversing* the dynamics of objectification, to begin this transformation of the analysand. "Resolution" of the transference occurs when, in a final *use* of the analysand's identification with the analyst, the analyst's status as "master signifier" breaks down (see, Žižek 2006a, p. 115). That is, there, where I look to the secret of the Other, I realize that there is "nothing," just another person who him/herself lacks certain knowledge. At this point, the very consistency of the reality guaranteed by this Other is threatened: perhaps reality itself is *not*, in the sense that I have taken it to be – that is., as guaranteed by a possible totalizing knowledge. The situation of the analysand, leaping into the precipice of an "act" challenging the very existence of the Other (the fantasy, the master signifier, etc.) seems to model perfectly the situation of the revolutionary, able to embrace a different kind of transformation.

In *The Plague of Fantasies*, Žižek points out the necessity of extending the path I've already suggested, which leads away from "interpretation" in resolving an analysis. In fact, we throw away the picture of the analysand, as "making sense" of her symptom at all. Depending as it does on the very end of Lacan's career, this addendum to our understanding of the efficacy of analysis demands we amend our vocabulary significantly. For most of his life, claims Žižek, Lacan belongs in a solidly existentialist tradition, one which conceives the goal of therapy in terms of *authenticity*. As Žižek explains it, *this* Lacan underscores the role of "truth" for the analysand. Emphasizing the hysterical symptom, the symptom which "tells the truth in the guise of a lie," the Lacan of the 1940s through the mid-1960s sees analysis as moving toward the analysand's need to acknowledge the "lie" she/he has been living. It is the lie of my own desire hidden in the hysterical symptom; for example, when I say "'I hereby close this session'" instead of "I hereby open this session" in a public speech, I let slip this repressed wish or desire (Žižek 1997, p. 37). Analysis aims at authenticity to the extent that its goal would coincide with the analysand's acknowledgement or knowledge of that repressed desire.

For Žižek, however, the very last period of Lacan's life, when he was working through the implications of the idea, introduced earlier in the 1960s, of a "fundamental fantasy", rejects both the existentialist ideal and any intersection of truth and analytic progress (Žižek 1997, p. 37). Here, the key movement takes us *away* from the overlapping of truth and knowledge, to a condition in which the "truth" enjoyed by the analyst is rigorously divided off from a new, "a-subjective" knowledge on the part of the analysand. To understand this, begin from the distinction between a "symptom" – unconscious, yes, but theoretically resolvable through and into knowledge – and that "fundamental fantasy" which, constructive of reality itself, remains inaccessible to consciousness "because it is in itself non-subjectivized, ontologically prior to the very dimension of truth" (Žižek 1997, p. 37).

As we've already seen, the fundamental fantasy simply *cannot* be "subjectivized," integrated into an honest or authentic interpretation of the subject's "life story." Contrary to such interpretation, the "construction" of the fundamental fantasy in an analysis has more the character of a transcendental posit (of what "must be the case") than of a discovery. Žižek (and Lacan) even go further, proposing that the construction doesn't actually "represent" any reality at all, that, to quote Freud, the fantasy has "never had a real existence." (*Plague*, p. 36) Furthermore, the defining quality of the "constructive" narrative is that it *cannot be* "made sense of" by the analysand, that it seems irreducibly "crazy," to her, even after its presentation within the analysis.

There is nothing uplifting about our awareness of this 'factor': such awareness can never be subjectivized; it is uncanny – even horrifying – since it somehow "depossesses' the subject, reducing her or him to a puppet-like level 'beyond dignity and freedom'. (Žižek 1997, p. 8)

In the shift from what Žižek calls an analysis centered on desire to one which uncovers the workings of "drive," (i.e., the "death drive" of Freudian provenance), we find a second model for its efficacy which no longer places the analysand "in the truth" about her/himself. Of course, what now counts as the analysand's "knowledge," is also correspondingly different; it's not just that such knowledge lacks the pleasure of theoretical epiphany, rather, it lacks even the "transparency" we associate with truth. Here, once again, *Fight Club* is useful, as Jack's "traversal" of the fantasy, his exposure of it, is by no means accompanied by any process of insight. In other words, here the end of Žižek's thought is not theoretical at all, no *truth* about the nature of history or truth, but, once again, that very act which produces reality from the impossible Real. In *Fight Club*, the "analysis" has clearly reached its term at the film's end, when Jack is able to "shoot" Tyler and blow up the capitalist infrastructure of the city. The actualization of a knowledge beyond conscious truth subsists in freeing the analysand from the circle of aggression which makes up the fantasmatic basis of reality. More, we cannot map a straight path from "truth" *to* such "knowledge" – cannot claim that the attainment of the "truth" of finitude forms a simple *prolegomenon* to a liberating act. The act is, must be, in some basic sense, "blind," and the very impulse to present it *as* a truth betrays it.

Let's begin from that last image, the image of the analyst and the analysand working (according to Žižek's proposal) in radically divergent directions. The problem here is the fundamental *inequality* between these two roles. What I mean is this: certainly Žižek's model can help us to make sense of the analytic situation, but this splitting of tasks between an analyst granted "truth" (or "knowledge in the position of truth" in the language of the slightly earlier Lacan) and an analysand endowed with a blind but practical "knowledge" falls apart when applied to the relationship between Žižek's texts and his readers. More precisely, the analysand's trauma threatens to become merely *perverse* in the case of the reader of a theoretical text, a *play* with risk rather than the real thing.

The key here lies in the bond within an analysis between "traversing the fantasy" and transference: the former can only take place on the back of the latter on the basis of the positing and subversion of the "subject-supposed-to-know." Only when the analysis itself subverts any "expertise" with regard to my symptom, undercuts even its *possibility*, is the road open for the peculiar, non-epistemic "knowledge" resolving the analysis. But the experience of reading Žižek *cannot* in fact substitute for such a transference relationship. One way to see this would be to insist that the very focus of almost any reading of a theoretical text must be "what the author is trying to say" – a focus that Žižek's own dense but lucid writing only intensifies. It is a practical demand which undercuts any passage beyond such interpretation: reading Žižek demands that we retain a "master," one whose prophetic knowledge we pursue.

My last assertion here demands a brief aside, a momentary return to the question of Žižek's style; for it is in that aspect of his work that he implicitly gives fodder for the reader's effort to "resolve" a transference relationship with him. Specifically, to understand how Žižek's writing might support such a claim we might reference the site I discussed at the beginning of the last chapter, the introduction of *The Parallax View*, where I discovered, a "meta-gap" of sorts *in Žižek* between two "dialectical materialisms" – one of which presents a "doctrine" for understanding history and nature and the other of which, the "singular universal," subsists precisely in style, the philosopher's ability to produce "shock effects." Žižek describes this second characteristic of his writing in the language of aesthetic avant-gardism, a kind of "montaging" of serious dialectical analysis with radically "inappropriate" content; so, for example, we get a discussion of Hegel delivered as analysis of "fisting."

That kind of stylistic "collage" of high and low is a trick, of course, that Žižek self-consciously maintains throughout his work.[13] He mentions this aspect of his style in *Conversations* as part of his Oedipal struggle with *Heidegger*, where he argues that rejection of "Heideggerian pathetic style" underlies his own "absolute compulsion to vulgarize things," a compulsion which leads him to "jump suddenly from the highest theory to the lowest possible example" and choose topics consistently from popular culture, the scatological, the sexual (Žižek and Daly, p. 44). In other words, as a sometime Heideggerian himself, Žižek feels compelled to "drag in the mud" the (in any case, "Earthy") Heideggerian discourse of the peasant, its location of an untouchable "Thing."

The very language of "collage" here – of heterogeneous discourses "placed together on a table" to paraphrase Breton – indicates the necessarily limited hold that Žižek's writing can offer for a transference; that is, Žižek's "wild" forays into popular culture only appear *at the same time* and *in the same gesture* as his most intense and controlled philosophical explorations. Indeed, it's a good bet that the more bizarre and "inappropriate" the example, the more "serious" and precise the Žižekean discussion it accompanies. Or, to put this differently, the "digressive" nature of his texts – their movement from philosophical concepts to "examples" from popular culture to other concepts implied by those examples, etc., etc. – really determines that they will retain a quite traditional narrative structure, wherein everything revolves around "what Žižek has to say" in a fashion that never allows doubt that there *is something* we seek but also never finally raises the veil (for author or for reader) on that hidden "treasure." Indeed, the only "space" Žižek allows for a hermeneutical disappearance of his authority is the one from which we began in the the preface to *Žižek and Heidegger*, the one where the reader simply pulls the plug on Žižek, declaring him a charlatan who doesn't really say anything; such a solution, however, amounts to no "resolution" at all, since it maintains Žižek's "mastery" in reverse: Žižek becomes what he is, for example, for Ian Parker, a *dangerous* poseur, the pied-piper who leads theorists away from "serious" commitments.[14] In other words, still a master, but now a "dark" master! There's never a possibility in Žižek's writing that we will leave the controlled textuality of the master's discourse, never support for a genuine "disappearance" of the writer/ analyst so as to clear the way for the reader/analysand's act.[15]

Or, to put this last point differently, Žižek's texts put the reader in a *perverse* position rather than a genuinely transformative one. To the extent that we follow Žižek's occasional desire to be *read* as analyst, we must argue against the potential success of such an analytic process. After all, the *attentiveness* Žižek demands of his readers (in itself, a *virtue*, don't get me wrong!) maintains a stable symbolic framework, one which forbids the very "crazy act" for which he argues. In this situation, the voice of Žižek is fundamentally reassuring, stabilizing; by demanding our interpretive attention, it prevents real change. Instead, we face the peculiar "both/and" of the pervert, the promise that we can have "revolution without revolution," that we can fantasize about radical change while identifying with the framing voice of the master, the voice whose stability itself stands in the way of such transformation.

Indeed, we might go so far as to suggest that, when applied to Žižek's own texts, the model of analysis which proposes a split between the "knowledge" of the analysand and the "truth" of the analyst proposes nothing other than perversion itself – the reassuring bond between the "blind" reader and the writer who "sees" for her. The analysand can rest assured that the analyst understands her "truth" – a perverse reassurance which forbids the very transformative effects at which psychoanalysis aims. And we might reinforce this by noting that the *actual* effect of all those "low" examples in Žižek's work is to support such an economy: as we learn to "play" like he does, we come to identify with the space of perversion which Žižek's style "pictures" for us, becoming comfortable in the pervert's universe, that Newtonian infinite, centerless, homogeneous space in which, precisely, "nothing is sacred."

To be clear, I am *not* proposing that Žižek for the most part plays the role of a perverted analyst in relationship to his readers. Quite the contrary, my real intention here is only to close the door that Žižek opens when the issue of the perversity within his own theoretical text leads him to a quandary. *If* Žižek takes the position of analyst in his texts, then he remains a *failed* analyst. Thus, because the model Žižek proposes for his text's "act," leads back to exactly the same problem, we can't leap from Žižek the theorist to Žižek the analyst, cannot close our eyes to the issue of "performative contradiction" in the interests of what Žižek's work "does." Whether we see his writing as a site of truth or a provocation makes no difference: in either case, we face Žižek's occupation of a perverse position in his battle against the perversity of the contemporary world. There's no easy way out of this challenge to the very manner in which he does philosophy.

Conclusion: Žižek *ex Machina*

Throughout this chapter I have explored the question of how Žižek's texts would have us respond to *them*, or, to put it even more directly, how *he* would have us respond to *him*. It turns out that we can take *neither* of the roles that Žižek's writing proposes for us, can be neither philosophers nor analysands in relationship to his texts, without falling into perversion. As a result, we have been torn between the impossibility that Žižek could effectively guarantee our knowledge that we are free and, alternatively, that he could certify the success of our own act.

It's now time to examine the hidden prejudices behind my questions, behind this *demand* that we attribute to Žižek. Why, after all, should we accept his proposals? Why accept his "offer" of a guarantee?

Of course the simple answer to these queries is that we fall into Žižek's proposals because he makes them so compellingly: with his profound thought about freedom he tempts that part of us that demands to *know* we *are* really free. With his radical conception of a transformative act, he entices us to *make sure* that we really can change ourselves and our world. Which is all simply a way of admitting that we (or," I," let me make no assumptions here!) *have* unwittingly entered into a transference relationship with Žižek: indeed, isn't exactly that what we do when we take up the demand facing us in his texts, the demand to be "read carefully" – parsed, reconstructed, made sense of? To respond to such an imperative is precisely to admit a neurotic concern for what Žižek, or more precisely, "Žižek" (the textual system he produces), "thinks."

This is the deeper support for my suggestion above that something in Žižek invites us to consider him the reader's "analyst" – this despite the fact that Žižek's few pronouncements on the subject would discourage such an understanding of him.[16] In his unique combination of lucidity and difficulty, the ability to produce the sense of a definite meaning just out of the reader's grasp, Žižek writes in precisely the way that sets him up as the "writer-supposed-to-know" – a relationship with his reader that we might, in order to differentiate it from full-bore analysis, call a "philosophical transference".

The answer to the questions that I raised above about just how we (I) get into a situation where we find ourselves responding to Žižek's perverse textual positioning is double: on the one hand, Žižek artfully *puts us there*. On the other hand, in accepting Žižek's challenge, *we* put ourselves there and in a fashion which, following from *what* he has to say, invites us to pull ourselves out, to "resolve" the "philosophical transference."

Let's tarry for a moment here with the first idea, the idea that something about the way Žižek writes asks us to take the position of transference in relationship to his texts. Indeed, precisely this combination of Žižek's "placement" of his readers and their necessary complicity in this siting explains, I think, the attitude of many of his most angry critics, like Ian Parker or Paul Bowman: their outrage, I would suggest, is precisely at the unreasonableness of the demand to enter such a "philosophical transference" in order to get what Žižek is saying. If one would be critical of him in any case, and if Žižek is always telling us that one should write clearly, at least one could be spared the demand to have a "relationship" with him just to criticize his theses!

We might find also find here a good explanation of Žižek's rocky relationship with so many of his colleagues in political theory, a rockiness more extensive than could be explained alone by Žižek's frequent critiques of their positions. In recent years, as Žižek's influence has increased within the academic world, so, too, has his political isolation within it. At this point we are in a position to suggest why that might be the case: is there not, after all, something *structurally* undemocratic in Žižek's thought? Not in the sense, of course, that he doesn't embrace the deepest aspirations of democratic life but rather because he does, indeed, speak from the analyst's view of the analysand or the Party leader's *take* on the Proletarian subject? Moreover, isn't there something shocking today in Žižek's very willingness to posit a kind of fundamental division between the position of the analyst/leader – the one who, in some sense, "knows" – and everyone else? Thus, in his critique of "democracy" Žižek really *is* announcing a radical departure from everything represented by today's "post-Marxist" situation, including emphasis upon "consensus" in process and "difference" between individuals and groups. This way of placing himself makes Žižek a *threat* to almost all positions in today's theoretical world. And, of course, it also precludes the possibility that *Žižek* might really learn from any of those positions. There really can be no dialogue with "Lenin". [17]

But enough complaining! It is, in fact, to the limits of such complaint that *Žižek's truth* brings us, the truth which corresponds with our realization the *we* produce the demands Žižek seems to "make" on us. The *insight* underlying both the seduction of Žižek's "truth" and the temptation to follow his proposal to "act" is that there *are no guarantees*. Recall the point from which I set out in *Žižek and Heidegger*, the image from *Being and Time* of Dasein choosing to take its *lack of knowledge* about some situation facing it *as* the "situation" itself. As Heidegger puts it, in such a "resolute decision" "the situation is only through resoluteness and in it" (Heidegger 1962, H. 300/ J&M, p. 346). Which is just to say that something happens to and for Dasein precisely in the moment it ceases to require an explanation for the choices facing it (choices which always seem "unfair," etc.) or a guarantee that giving up on its demands for explanation will lead to a "right choice."

In this context, we might say that unfreedom lies in exactly the Other we reproduce constantly through and as the addressee of our complaints and demands. We are free, then, when we act in such a way as to cease reproducing that addressee. Which is what Žižek really *means* when he says that we liberate ourselves by "accepting fate." The interesting addition we've made to this picture in the current chapter is that we seem to have entered an odd bargain with Žižek himself (meaning both that he's offered and we've accepted the offer) to put *him* in the position of that Other, that addressee of our complaints and demands. We've made him the one who knows why I face the situation I do and the one who could change it.

Given the very truth that motivated us to enter into it, that bargain is absurd! It amounts to a demand for certainty about the lack of certainty. Still, one might suggest that it is also a *necessary* pact or, at least, an important moment; for it circles around what we can now see to be the irreducible existential quality of the "decision." How might Dasein, knowing itself to be free, nonetheless, evade engaging anticipatory resoluteness?

Two related strategies suggest themselves: either Dasein could lose itself in the quest for a kind of knowledge that would eliminate the necessity of actually *doing* anything, a pure "truth" sufficient in itself; or it could leap into a "blind" acting out, a way of letting somebody else take responsibility for my freedom. But, of course, these two possibilities correspond precisely to Žižek's two perversities, the two positions that that he takes when we read him. And, we could take this a step further and recall what our argument in this chapter has traced out, namely, the rigorous manner in which, having originally opened them, Žižek *closes* each of those doors by seeming to open the other; when we wish to know our freedom (without practicing it) we find that we cannot act upon it, that we are paralyzed. When we wish to be led to an act, without freely choosing it, Žižek shows us the perversity of that desire, too. Indeed, we can now see that the double addressee of his work that we've traced since Chapter 4 of this book – both critic and proletarian or philosopher and analysand – corresponds to the mutually exclusive ways in which we can avoid our freedom; and Žižek's persistent task has been to play each "inauthenticity" off of the other.

In a sense, then, Žižek has been both successful philosopher and analyst all along. In his vision of finitude, of the decision which ontologizes doubt, he has guided us toward our essential freedom. In his insistence upon our unmediated responsibility for such choice he has helped us to make it.

Both of these aids are, however, impossible or only become possible when we frame them with the gesture of saying, "who gives a shit about what Žižek wants?" In other words, we must resolve the "philosophical transference" which Žižek so artfully helps us to establish, dissolve our desire to address the demands of his textual machine. So long as we fail to remember this, so long as we only accept the "help" his fruitful texts offer, he remains *the* essential pervert for us, claiming to fill the void of the act.

Which is to bring us to the question of whether Žižek *is* a pervert or an analyst?

Of course, the *proximity* of analyst and pervert is an important issue in Žižek as well in wider Lacanian circles, particularly as it emerges in Lacan's *Seminar XVII: The Other Side of Psychoanalysis.*[18] We could summarize the current chapter of *Žižek and Heidegger* as a demonstration of this intimacy, this sense that, at least with regard to what I've been calling Žižek's "philosophical analysis," the two phenomena are like the two sides of a single coin. As he himself puts it in an essay on this very question, the analyst *is* a pervert to the extent that he cannot "reduce himself to the void," that he remains "something" for the analysand/reader (Žižek 2006a, p. 115). But flipping that coin depends not only on the analyst – on Žižek in this case – but also on the act of the reader/analysand. What results is a double test, an ordeal for both analyst and analysand, writer and reader, one whose outcome is never predetermined.

If there's a broader lesson here, it would be that we have not in fact wandered so far from Heidegger as it might at first seem. The complexities of Žižek's meditations on predestination, mind and causal determinism should blind us no more than the twists and turns of his thought about the revolutionary act. In every case, what's at stake, what remains at stake through all the changes Žižek is able to ring, is finitude. While Žižek may have turned Heidegger on his head, we can still recognize the reversed idol. Žižek's virtue comes in helping to complete Heidegger's task, a task which, so long as he remained "right side up" he could only fail to accomplish.

Notes

Preface

1 For Myers, this starting point is Žižek's predilection for "rhetorical" questions of the form "does it not . . . ?" (Myers 2003, p. 4); for Parker, Žižek's stylistic dependence upon jokes of a certain kind; (Parker 2004, p. 1); and for Butler, the question of Žižek as *performer* (Butler 2005, p. 2) With regard to the question of the cogency of Žižek's writing, Paul Bowman takes the criticism yet a step further, arguing that "Žižek merely picks up some familiar emotive terms – 'capitalism,' 'the system' – and deploys them *as if they are already fully understood* and as if they simply *must* be taken to be millenarian signifiers of pure evil." (Bowman and Stamp 2007, p. 40)

2 It's important to note a couple of recent exceptions to this tendency, exceptions which suggest an improving picture in the study of Žižek. The first is the appearance of the online *Journal of Žižek Studies*, which, in addition to publishing some of Žižek's own recent work, has also sponsored serious critical scholarship. The other exception, himself a frequent contributor to the *Journal for Žižek Studies*, is the person of Adrian Johnston, whose *Žižek's Ontology* (just published as I write these words) promises to reshape this area of scholarship. See Johnston 2008.

3 Here again Parker's approach can be taken to stand for a general tendency when he suggests that Žižek's glide from discipline to discipline, discourse to discourse, is fatally flawed in its erasure of the disciplinary specificity of the fields he crosses. In other words, Žižek is condemned both for being *too* interdisciplinary (for ignoring the specificity of the various fields to which he claims to contribute) and not interdisciplinary *enough* (since, participating in such a broad range of discussions, he obviously can't have any one thing to say).

4 The Conference: *St. Paul Among the Philosophers*, was held at Syracuse University, April 14–16, 2005 and sponsored by the Departments of Religion and Philosophy there. I should also note that the "Žižek-as-Rock-Star" trope has reverberated quite a bit in the broader media culture. See, for example, Rebecca Mead's 2005 Žižek-exposé in *The New Yorker* (Mead 2005).

5 "Heidegger's greatest single achievement is the full elaboration of *finitude* as a positive constituent of being-human – in this way, he accomplished the Kantian philosophical revolution, making it clear that finitude is the key to the transcendental dimension. A human being is always on the way toward itself, in becoming, thwarted, thrown-into a situation, primordially 'passive', receptive, attuned, exposed to an overwhelming Thing; far from limiting him, this exposure is the very ground of the emergence of a universe of meaning, of the 'worldliness' of man. It is only from within this finitude that entities appear to us as 'intelligible',

as forming part of a world, as included within a horizon of meaning – in short, that we take them 'as' something, that they appear as something (that they appear *tout court*)." (Žižek 2006b, p. 273)

[6] I am aware here that I shift from the original context of Žižek's assertion: the point for Žižek is not that *texts* lack the position of a "Last Judgment" but rather that *life* does. If the reader will bear with me, though, the difference *made* by this difference between meaning in texts and meaning in reality will return – albeit in a slightly different form. My argument is effectively that the situation of the reader has broader implications for "life" than Žižek allows.

[7] (Žižek 2004a, p. 48). We should also note here that part of Žižek's delight in the "buggery" metaphor comes in its convenience for distinguishing Deleuze (and implicitly himself) from Derrida: "Both Deleuze and Derrida deploy their theories through a detailed reading of other philosophers, that is to say, they both reject the pre-Kantian, uncritical, direct deployment of philosophical systems. For both of them, philosophy today can be practiced today only in the mode of metaphilosophy, as a reading of (other) philosophers. But, while Derrida proceeds in the mode of critical deconstruction, of undermining the interpreted text or author, Deleuze, in his buggery, imputes to the interpreted philosopher his own innermost position and endeavors to extract it from him. So, while Derrida engages in a 'hermeneutics of suspicion,' Deleuze practices an excessive benevolence toward the interpreted philosopher. At the immediate material level, Derrida has to resort to quotation marks all the time, signaling that the employed concept is not really his, whereas Deleuze endorses everything, directly speaking through the interpreted author in an indirect free speech *without* quotation marks. And, of course, it is easy to demonstrate that Deleuze's 'benevolence' is much more violent and subversive than the Derridean reading: his buggery produces true monsters." (Žižek 2004a, p. 47)

[8] See Chapter 4 of *Žižek and Heidegger* for a fuller presentation of Žižek's argument.

Chapter 1

[1] It's important to note Heidegger's ambivalence about the very term, "finitude" (*Endlichkeit*). While *Being and Time* uses "finitude" and its cognate, "finite" in order to indicate a basic existential structure of Dasein – its being-toward-death as its ownmost possibility – to which the existential "decision" of "resolution" "attests"; texts in the following years, (*The Basic Problems of Phenomenology* (1928) and *Kant and the Problem of Metaphysics* (1929)) cast some doubt on this terminological gambit (Heidegger, 1962, H. 259, R & M, 303) and (Heidegger, 1962, H. 97, R & M, 343). These later texts problematize "finitude," given its metaphysical origin in a theological relationship between "creator" and "creation." See, for example, *The Basic Problems of Phenomenology*: In Kant's understanding, "Being of a being must be understood . . . as being-produced, if indeed the producer, the originator also is supposed to be able to apprehend the substance, that which constitutes the being of the being. Only the creator is capable of a true and proper cognition of being;

we finite beings get to know only what we ourselves make and only to the extent that we make it." (Heidegger, *Basic*, p. 150)

[2] For references to Žižek's Heideggerian beginnings in the secondary literature, see Kay's *Žižek: a Critical Introduction* (Kay 2003, p. 2), Butler: *Slavoj Žižek: Live Theory* (Butler 2005, p. 10) and Parker, *Slavoj Žižek: a Critical Introduction* (Parker 2004, p. 4). Žižek himself discusses this background and its influence on him in one of the interviews with Glyn Daly included in *Conversations with Žižek* (see Žižek and Daly 2004, pp. 26–33).

[3] We should also note here another possible direction for interpreting the Žižek-Heidegger link, this one concerning the *traumatic* nature of human consciousness. In a recently published manuscript on Žižek, Adrian Johnston pursues the powerful thesis that Žižek's current interest in the Philosophy of Science can be traced back to *Being and Time* and to Heidegger's insight there that Dasein's reflection only takes flight on the wings of *failure* – specifically, the failure of the projects of the "ready-to-hand." Only when things "go wrong" do we gain the possibility for the specifically human response of *self-consciousness*. While I don't pursue this link between Žižek and Heidegger further, I acknowledge its importance for understanding the trajectory of Žižek's current work. (See Johnston 2007a.)

[4] It's worth noting here that Žižek's most extended interpretive discussion of Heidegger – in the first chapter of *The Ticklish Subject* – actually addresses *Kant and the Problem of Metaphysics* rather than *Being and Time*. While I've written about this interpretation elsewhere (see my unpublished paper, "Reflections on the Pre-Synthetic Imaginary: Žižek reads Heidegger reading Kant"), for reasons of clarity and succinctness, I've chosen here to stay with the more familiar territory of *Being and Time*'s analysis.

[5] (Heidegger 1962, H. 307–8/R & M, p. 355). Let me point out the significant ambiguity of the passage I here refer to. After binding resoluteness with *certainty*, Heidegger *seems* to back off from this position – precisely to what I'm here calling the "Cartesian" option: he *seems* to suggest that Dasein holds itself back from any identification with the situation. Such, indeed, is Robinson and Macquarrie's interpretation of a key grammatical ambiguity. Heidegger writes, *"Dies besagt aber: sie kann sich gerade nicht auf die Situation versteifen, sondern muss verstehen, dass der Entschluss seinem eigenen Erschliessungssinn nach frei und offen gehalten werden muss für die jeweilige faktische Möglichkeit. Die Gewissheit des Entschlusses bedeutet: Sichfreihalten für seine mögliche und je faktisch notwendige Zurücknahme."* Robinson and Macquarrie translate: "Such certainty must maintain itself in what is disclosed by the resolution. But this means that it simply cannot become rigid as regards the situation, but must understand that the resolution, in accordance with its own meaning as a disclosure, must be held open and free for the current factical possibility. The certainty of the resolution signifies that one *holds oneself free* for the possibility of *taking it back* – a possibility which is factically necessary." However, in a footnote, they add that one *could* also take the subject of "seine" ("its") to be actually *oneself* ("sich") instead of the "resolution". To make sense of the passage by Žižek's interpretation, though, demands that we embrace precisely the translation rejected by Robinson and Macquarrie: we "hold (ourselves) free" from the situation only to the extent that *we* may be "withdrawn from it" by death. Or, as Robinson and

Macquarrie are tempted to suggest, "the certainty of the resolution signifies that one *holds oneself free* for one's own *withdrawal.*" In other words, the situation's *necessity* stems from our free engagement with it.

6 The phrase is Parmenides', as quoted by Heidegger in his late essay, "The End of Philosophy and the Task of Thinking," in Heidegger 1977, p. 387.

7 Of course, the line of argument I trace here is not Žižek's *only Auseinandersetzung* with the approach in *Being and Time*: we should also mention the way that any Lacanian position such as Žižek's must train a basic suspicion on one of the basic premises of Heidegger's *phenomenology* – namely, its appeal to a vision of language "where (originally, *tb*) statements refer directly to their social context," so that the inauthenticity of Dasein's self-expression can be related to forgetting the experiential origins of metaphor. (Žižek, 2006b, p. 234). It's in that light, of course, that Heidegger considers the task of philosophy to be nothing other than the reanimation of the basic metaphors of a language or tradition (see, *Being and Time*, Section 44). For Žižek, on the contrary, "the first signifier is empty, a zero-signifier, pure 'form,' an empty promise of a meaning-to-come; it is only on a second occasion that the frame of this process is gradually filled in with content" (Žižek 2006b, p. 234). And he explains this pronouncement with Freud's famous statement that, "the secrets of the ancient Egyptians were also secrets for the Egyptians themselves"; that is, there is no "original meaning" in experience to which we might return. Quite the opposite, the *appearance* of such a meaning, embedded in the seeming "fallenness" of metaphor in language is what provides "the paradigm of how ideology works." (Žižek 2006b, p. 234)

8 See Heidegger1962, H. 271, R&M, p. 316: "Dasein fails to hear itself, and listens away to the 'They'; and this listening-away gets broken by the call (of conscience, *tb*.) if that call, in accordance with its character as such, arouses another kind of hearing, which, in relationship to the hearing that is lost, has a character in every way opposite. If in this lost hearing, one has been fascinated with the 'hubbub' of the manifold ambiguity which idle talk possesses in its everyday 'newness', then the call must do its calling without any hubbub and unambiguously, leaving no foothold for curiosity. *That which, by calling in this manner, gives us to understand, is the conscience.*"

9 Here, I must note a terminological difficulty: within Žižek's Lacanian discourse, Heidegger's notion of an "objectless" anxiety is mistaken. Anxiety indicates, not the lack of an object, but the presence of a particular object, *objet a*. While this distinction is important for understanding the specific *praxical* bond that Žižek identifies between analysis and revolution, it need not enter our considerations here (For more on this, see Žižek 2006b, p. 198, and Žižek 2006a, pp. 116–119).

It's also worth noting the parallel between Heidegger's and Freud's anxiety accounts, both of which distinguish between some form of fear (or phobia), as object-directed and anxiety, as too overwhelming to attach to a particular object. In Freud's version, the consistent note sounded from his letters to Fliess (1896) through *Inhibitions, Symptoms and Anxiety* is the traumatic nature of anxiety. Because, as he puts it in *The Ego and the Id*, "in anxiexty our fear is of being overwhelmed or annihilated," "what it is" that is feared "cannot be specified." (Freud 1974, p. 57) It is only when, later, we are able to *anticipate* anxiety's onset, associating it with the presence of particular objects, that we can place it within an economy of the pleasure/reality principles.

[10] Locating its central articulation in Hegel's *Phenomenology of Spirit,* Alenka Zupančič articulates this "alternative" comic dimension in some detail, dwelling particularly on the way in which it answers the philosophy of finitude (see, Zupančič 2006).

[11] Both guilt and identity, as attested in Freud's *Ur-myth* for the founding of society from *Moses and Monotheism,* assume a socially constituted reality conceived from a totalizing perspective – some "whole" in which the individual is given a pre-ordained "place."

[12] See, for example, Karl Löwith's *Martin Heidegger and European Nihilism* (Löwith 1995) or Jürgen Habermas', *The Philosophical Discourse of Modernity: Twelve Lectures* (Habermas 1987)

[13] Žižek has long followed Miller and later Lacan in his defense of a radicalized modern subjectivism – in his readings of Hegel and Schelling as well as, most polemically, in the very thesis of *The Ticklish Subject,* whose opening sentences play with the language of "The Communist Manifesto" as follows:

> This book thus endeavours to reassert the Cartesian subject, whose rejection forms the silent pact of all the struggling parties of today's academia: although all these orientations are officially involved in a deadly battle (Habermasians versus deconstructionists; cognitive scientists versus New Age obscurantists . . .), they are all united in their rejection of the Cartesian subject. (Žižek 1999a, p. 2)

See my interpretation of this passage at the beginning of Chapter 3. See, also, my further discussion of Žižek's "perversion" of Marx and Engels text in Chapters 4 and 5 of the current book.

[14] See Žižek 2006b, p. 283: "Stalinist Communism was inherently related to a Truth-Event (of the October Revolution)."

Chapter 2

[1] This argument is only implicit in "The Question Concerning Technology," where the historical origins of *Ge-stell* are traced surely enough to the seventeenth century, but therein only to the rise of modern Physics. However, several other essays of Heidegger make the role of Descartes explicit. For example, in "The Age of the World Picture" (1938), the idea of "Enframing" is strongly paralleled by an idea with similar metaphorical carry – the notion of the "world picture" itself. For Heidegger, it is not the case that every time and place has its own "world picture." Quite the contrary, "the fact that the world becomes picture at all is what distinguishes the modern age" (Heidegger 1977a, p. 130) That's the case because, "world picture, when understood essentially, does not mean a picture of the world but the world conceived and grasped as a picture. What is, in its entirety, is now taken in such a way that it first is in being and only is in being to the extent that it is set up by man, who represents and sets forth." (Heidegger 1977a, pp. 129–130)

This passage comes as explication and further articulation of Cartesianism a couple of pages earlier: "We first arrive at science as research when and only when truth has been transformed into the certainty of representation. What it is to be is for the first time defined as the objectiveness of representing, and truth is first defined as the certainty of representing, in the metaphysics of Descartes." (Heidegger 1977a, p. 127) See, also, Heidegger's *Nietzsche*, vol. 4, *Nihilism*, (Heidegger 1991, pp. 105–110).

I am much indebted for his excellent reconstruction of the role of representation in Heidegger's critique of technology to Michael E. Zimmerman, *Heidegger's Confrontation with Modernity: Technology, Politics, Art* (Zimmerman 1990, pp. 182–190).

[2] In addition to the site from *Conversations* below, one might look to *The Plague of Fantasies*, where Žižek defends Heidegger on technology, claiming that Heidegger anticipates Lacan's insight by which modern science and technology "think in the Real" (see Žižek, 1997, p. 38). See, also, my discussion of this passage below.

[3] See, for example *Inhabiting the Earth: Heidegger, Environmental Ethics, and the Metaphysics of Nature by* Bruce Foltz (Foltz 1995).

[4] "But note what this scenario leaves out (that almost all popular views of evolution include as a defining feature). Natural selection talks only about 'adaptation to changing local environments'; the scenario includes no statement whatever about process – nor could any such claim be advanced from the principle of natural selection. The woolly mammoth is not a cosmically better or generally superior elephant. Its only 'improvement' is entirely local; the woolly mammoth is better in cold climates (but its minimally hairy ancestor remains superior in warmer climates). Natural selection can only produce adaptation to immediately surrounding (and changing) environments." (Gould 1996, p. 139)

[5] In a later moment from the same set of interviews, Žižek considers a slightly different scenario, one in which *parents* clone a child to replace one who has died. It is, to be precise, *this* clone which Žižek claims will be experienced as "monstrous" (see Žižek and Daly 2004, p. 92).

[6] It's worth noting here that Žižek seems to retreat from this finding in *The Parallax View*, where he cites recent studies indicating that the brain tends to "symbolize" such experiences, to replace them within the fabric of coherent, symbolic reality in "experiencing" them (see Žižek 2006b, p. 197).

[7] In *The Plague of Fantasies*, Žižek acknowledges precisely this insight *as* belonging to the Heidegger of the technology writings, suggesting that modern technology is the "Real of our historical moment" precisely to the extent that it "doesn't think," that its functioning is "inherently indifferent towards the historically determined horizons of the disclosure of Being" (Žižek 1997, p. 38).

[8] In a final ironic twist, we must note that Heidegger does rather better than does Žižek in acknowledging this ambiguity in modern technology. In "The Question Concerning Technology" he writes that "the essence of technology is in a lofty sense ambiguous . . ." using this as an argument for a "poietic" re-engagement with it (see Heidegger 1977a, p. 33).

[9] In fact, the question of historicism demands a far deeper treatment than I'm able to give it here, a treatment which I only afford the matter in Chapters 5 and 6 of *Heidegger and Žižek*. In the meantime, it's important to note that the *reason* why the

second moment supercedes the first – why Hegel, in a sense, displaces Kant – is that it contains the truth of what Žižek calls "parallax gap" or "antagonism" itself (see Žižek 2006b, p. 27 or Žižek 2003, p. 77). That is, Hegel presents us with the insight that the truth we seek is not the dark, inaccessible, noumenal "Thing" but rather the very insubstantial and therefore irresolvable tension *between* phenomenon and noumenon that Kant posits but then flees (Žižek 2006b, p. 25). Truth resides in the irresolvable conflict between two "truths," a conflict which, since it contains absolutely incompatible insights, also cannot be smoothed over into the static relationship between relative "viewpoints." The real superiority of Hegel for Žižek is that, by *operationalizing* this "gap" in the dance of dialectical negativity, he insists upon the insubstantiality of what the philosopher seeks, refusing its ultimate reification. In Hegel's historical dialectic, parallax is literally "en-acted," made to act. What is the "Real" constitutive of human reality? Not the inaccessible thing "behind the screen" of human experience, but the "distorting screen" "perceptible only in the shift from one (perspective) to the other" (Žižek 2006b, p. 26).

Chapter 3

[1] See Lecture XI in Habermas' *The Philosophical Discourse of Modernity: Twelve Lectures* (Habermas 1987).

[2] See the discussion of the Descartes-criticisms common to each of these thinkers in Teresa Brennan's, *History After Lacan* (Brennan 1993, p. 85).

[3] "Having denied that the 'object' has any will of its own, the foundational fantasy also denies the effects of the object upon the subject. These effects become far more significant as developing technologies permit the subject to construct a world of objects which fulfill its fantasies When the world is actually turned into a world of objects, when living nature is consumed in this process, the power of the fantasy, the extent to which it takes hold psychically is reinforced . . . As the repressed hallucination and the technology applied to commodities alike bind energy, they increase rigidity and fixity, and this in turn increases the need to project a fixity felt as a constraint that slows the subject down" (Brennan 1993, p. 14).

[4] "People as divergent in thought as Kant, Hegel, Husserl, and Lacan all agree that Descartes's 'error', if it can be so called, consists in substantializing this empty spot of cogito by turning it into *res cogitans*. Cogito marks a 'non-place', a gap, a chasm in the chain of being, it doesn't delineate a certain sphere of being to be placed alongside other spheres, it cannot be situated in some part of reality, yet it is at the same time correlative to reality as such." (Dolar 1998, pp. 15–16)

[5] I am indebted to Adrian Johnston both for this specific account of this distinction between "*savoir*" and "*verité*" as it is introduced in Seminar XIII and in general for his clear understanding of the role of Descartes in the Seminars of the 1960s. See, *Time Driven: Metapsychology and the Splitting of the Drive* (Johnston 2005, p. 70). Additionally, see below for Lacan's transformation of this distinction at the end of his life.

[6] In "Position of the Unconscious", Lacan writes that the subject is oddly lodged between not yet speaking and "an instant after" speaking, an observation that

Adrian Johnston translates as amounting to the claim that it is "pre-ontological" ("Position of the Unconscious," printed in Feldstein, Fink and Jaanus 1995, p. 269). (See, also, Johnston 2005, p. 63.)

7 For Žižek's account of this limit to psychoanalytic interpretation, see Žižek 1997, pp. 35–36.

8 In Seminar 11 (Lacan 1981) and, even more centrally in Seminar 13, Lacan also finds in the history of *pictorial perspective*, and specifically in the development of systematic linear perspective during the Italian renaissance the historical origin of Descartes' (and Pascal's!) subject. That is, Lacan realizes that the ground for the purely "doubting" consciousness of the *Meditations* was laid two centuries before in the painting, architecture and theory of Alberti, Brunelleschi and Fillarette, Leonardo, Piero and others.

9 See, for example, *Seminar XIII*, session 16 (May 4, 1966) (Lacan Unpublished a).

10 See, Eric Santner, "Traumatic Revelations: Freud's Moses and the Origins of Anti-Semitism" (Santner 2000). (See, also, Žižek's discussion of this article in Žižek 2003, pp. 128–129.)

11 One important question I don't take up here is how, given its at least historical origin in Freud as an individual event, such a fantasy can be "inter-subjective." That such is not really an issue within a Lacanian or Žižekian perspective is well argued by Adrian Johnston in his paper, "The Cynic's Fetish: Slavoj Žižek and the Dynamics of Belief," where he points out that "from a Lacanian perspective, there is no such

> thing as strictly individual psychology per se. The singular person scrutinized by psychoanalysis, in all the richness of his/her memories, identifications, fantasies, and patterns of comportment, is inherently intertwined with larger, enveloping matrices of mediation. That is to say, the individual is always trans-individual (along the lines of, for instance, Lacan's phrase 'in you more than you,' as well as Jean Laplanche's theme concerning the 'primacy of the Other' in psychoanalysis). (Johnston 2007, p. 64)

12 Žižek compares the relationship between fantasy and the Real (in Lacan's sense) to that between an absorbing fictional world (he uses Conan Doyle's Sherlock Holmes) and the "reality" it constitutes. Precisely what such fiction delivers is the illusion that, if we could but get a better view, the "holes" in Conan Doyle's description could be filled in by the object of his representation. We could actually find out what color the walls of 221b Baker Street were painted, how many deerstalker caps Holmes possessed, etc., etc. Of course, that's not really the case: the "world" of Holmes and Watson only exists to the extent that it was described. Žižek's thesis is that such is the case with *every* human world. It is "fantasy," that gives us the sense of a fully constituted ("ontological") *reality*, by symbolically weaving the Real so as to cover over its incompletion. "What if our social reality is 'symbolically constructed' also in this radical sense," asks Žižek, "so that in order to maintain the appearance of its consistency, an empty signifier (what Lacan called the master signifier) has to cover up and conceal the ontological gap" (Žižek 1999a, p. 56)?

13 "The fundamental fantasy provides the subject with the minimum of being, it serves as a support for his existence – in short, its deceptive gesture is 'Look, I suffer, therefore I am, I exist, I participate in the positive order of being'" (Žižek 1999a, p. 281).

14 In a passage from his recent book, *The Fragile Absolute*, Žižek articulates this point in relationship to sexual fantasy: "one should not" Žižek writes, "confound this 'primordially repressed' myth ('fundamental fantasy') with the multitude of inconsistent daydreams that always accompany our symbolic commitments, allowing us to endure them." In order to make this distinction, he then elaborates on two predominant forms of (heterosexual) fantasy today –Peter Hoeg's idea, from *The Woman and the Ape*, "of a woman who wants a strong animal partner, a potent 'beast', not a hysterical impotent weakling" and the notion of the "cybernetic" lover from male fantasy, the "perfectly programmed 'doll' who fulfils all his wishes, not a living being." The point of this excursion into gendered sexual fantasy is that, in this context, the level of the *fundamental fantasy* could be metaphorized through "the *unbearable ideal couple of a male ape copulating with a female cyborg*, the fantasmatic support of the 'normal couple' of man and woman copulating."

That is, the fundamental fantasy is the fantasy *of* an Other in both senses of the genitive: it is the fantasmatic projection of an Other whose perspective includes all possible perspectives (in this case, the female and the male of the couple). On the other hand, reality is conceived (by us) as the Other's viewpoint or fantasy (Žižek 2000, pp. 65–66).

15 See "On Learned Ignorance" (Nicholas of Cusa 1997, p. 161).

16 Another way to put this insight is that, in a modern context, God is "outside" of the universe only in the sense that he is outside of *time*: Žižek reminds us of Descartes' and Malebranche's version of the divine as simply the arbitrary and irrational author of a closed time. As Žižek puts it, "the properly modern God is the God of predestination" (Žižek 1999b, p. 20).

17 As we will see in more detail in the next chapter, such paranoia at the level of the fundamental fantasy also explains our obsession with conspiracy theories. As Žižek puts it in an essay on *The Matrix*, "The problem is not that ufologists and conspiracy theorists regress to a paranoid attitude unable to accept (social) reality; the problem is that this reality itself is becoming paranoiac" (Žižek 2002, p. 249).

18 See Miran Božovič's introduction to Jeremy Bentham's *Panopticon Writings*, where Božovič argues that Bentham's own reference to the panoptic tower's presence within the panopticon prison as "like a God" must be understood at the level of fantasy. The panoptic gaze (in which every point is watched from everywhere) certainly takes the place of the fantasy of transcendence; that is, like the old God, this new one allows the constitution of the Real as reality. Still, Žižek's analysis allows us to see the essential difference between the new God and the old. (Božovič 1995)

19 "The relativization of our sociology by the scientific collection of the cultural forms we are destroying in the world – and the analyses, bearing truly psychoanalytic marks, in which Plato's wisdom shows us the dialectic common to the passions

of the soul and of the city – can enlighten us as to the reason for this barbarity. Namely, to employ the jargon that corresponds to our approaches to man's subjective needs, the increasing absence of all the saturations of the superego and ego-ideal that occur in all kinds of organic forms in traditional societies, forms that extend from the rituals of everyday intimacy to the periodic festivals in which the community manifests itself. We no longer know them except in their most obviously degraded guises." (Lacan 2005, p. 99) (See, also, Žižek 1997, ftn. 34, p. 43)

[20] Another important metaphor in Žižek's work emphasizes at this point the emergence of an alternative dominant father-figure – precisely the "irrational" Father who appears to replace the murdered "rational" Father of the Aristotelian/Medieval cosmos. Not only do we not know the "meaning" of our world (why things are as they are), but we cannot understand *what* we are supposed to do. In other words, the world of conscience corresponds closely to the universe of modern science, with its arbitrary origin and refusal of metaphysical speculation. In addition to the discussion at the beginning of the final chapter of *The Ticklish Subject* ("Wither Oedipus?"), see Žižek's history of Freudian "Fathers" up to and through *Moses and Monotheism* in Žižek 1999b, pp. 23–25. That text presents Žižek's clearest conceptualization of the modern Father as essentially opposed to the pre-modern one.

[21] See Todd McGowan, *The End of Dissatisfaction? Jacques Lacan and the Emerging Society of Enjoyment.* (McGowan 2004). Žižek most commonly refers to this as a "superego injunction to enjoy". See, for example, his essay, "*Objet a* in Social Links" (Žižek 2006a, p. 115).

[22] Žižek writes that "the ultimate *perverse* fantasy," lies in "the notion that we are ultimately *instruments* of the Other's *jouissance,* sucked out of our life-substance like batteries" (Žižek, 2006b, p. 313). See, also, "*Objet a*", where Žižek writes, "the pervert knows perfectly what he is for the Other: a knowledge supports his position as the object of his Other's (divided subject's) jouissance" (Žižek 2006a, p. 115).

[23] See for example, Alenka Zupančič, *Ethics of the Real,* (Zupančič 2000) and Slavoj Žižek, *Tarrying with the Negative: Kant, Hegel, and the Critique of Ideology* (Žižek 1993).

[24] See Žižek 2006b, p. 193 and Žižek 1999a, pp. 338, 354.

[25] This metaphor of a "sub-cutaneous" Other is literalized in another of Žižek's favorite contemporary films, David Fincher's *Fight Club* which opens with a tracking shot withdrawing from a microscopic perspective *inside* Edward Norton's skin. *Fight Club,* too, gives us a picture of a world produced by paranoid fundamental fantasy.

Chapter 4

[1] See, Lacan 1998. Žižek's most compelling and concise effort to grapple with Lacan's logic of the "not-all" comes in his essay "The Real of Sexual Difference" (Žižek 2002a).

[2] ". . . the direct global model of modern science is effectively 'closed' – that is to say, it allows for no beyond. The universe of modern science, in its very 'meaninglessness', involves the gesture of 'traversing the fantasy', of abolishing the dark

spot, the domain of the Unexplained which harbours fantasies and thus guarantees Meaning." (Žižek 1997, p. 160)

³ As recently as 2003, *The Puppet and Dwarf's* first chapter deals with belief in a cynical society, so-called "disavowed" belief. See, Žižek 2003, p. 5.

⁴ See Žižek's analysis in "*The Matrix:* or, the Two Sides of Perversion," for the fatal nature of understanding Neo as "The One" (Žižek 2002, pp. 255–259). The following comments on the idea of the "Superhero" interpret Žižek's intervention there.

⁵ "Crucial for the function of this One (Neo, *tb.*) is his virtualization of reality. Reality is an artificial construct whose rules can be suspended or at least rewritten – therein resides the properly paranoid notion that the One can suspend the resistence of the Real, ('I can walk through a thick wall if I really decide to . . .' the impossibility for most of us to do this is reduced to the failure of the subject's will)." (Žižek 2002, p. 257)

⁶ This particular immortality has been the theme of numerous filmic treatments in recent years but perhaps the best is still Roger Zemekis' *Who Framed Roger Rabbit.*

⁷ "When the mask (in the film of that name) – the dead object – comes alive by taking possession of us, its hold on us is effectively that of a 'living dead', of a monstrous *automaton* imposing itself on us – is not the less to be drawn from this that our fundamental fantasy, the kernel of our being, is itself such a monstrous Thing, a machine of *jouissance?*" (Žižek 1999a, p. 390)

⁸ Žižek reminds us that "what the pervert enacts is a universe in which, as in cartoons, a human being can survive any catastrophe; in which adult sexuality is reduced to a childish game; in which one is not forced to die or to choose one of the two sexes" (Žižek 2002, p. 265).

⁹ One weakness of *The Mask* is that it fudges this quality of the mask: while the film mines the "cartooned" quality of the masked character wonderfully to exploit Carrey's comic talents, it also insists on producing a kind of moral differentiation of the various characters who don the mask during the course of the film. Thus, the "bad guy"'s mask creates a *different* cartoon-character than does the mask when worn by Carrey himself (or, as it turns out, his dog!) A more courageous film would have made the wearer of the mask indistinguishable, no matter which character put it on.

¹⁰ "So we have a subject who is extremely narcissistic – who perceives everything as a potential threat to his precarious imaginary balance (take the universalization of the logic of victim; every contact with another human being is experienced as a potential threat: if the other person smokes, if he casts a covetous glance at me, he is already hurting me); far from allowing him to float freely in his undisturbed balance, however, this narcissistic self-enclosure leaves the subject to the (not so) tender mercies of the superego injunction to enjoy." (Žižek 1999a, p. 368)

¹¹ See Žižek's lengthy exploration of such a post-Oedipal universe in the last chapter of *The Ticklish Subject* (1999a), "Wither Oedipus?"

¹² "What is a cultural lifestyle, if not the fact that, although we don't believe in Santa Claus, there is a Christmas tree in every house, and even in public places, every December? Perhaps, then, the 'nonfundamentalist' notion of 'culture' as distinguished from "'real' religion, art, and so on, is in its very core the name for the field of disowned/impersonal beliefs –'culture' is the name for all those things we practice without really believing in them, without 'taking them

seriously'. Is this not also why science is not part of this notion of culture – it is all too real?" (Žižek 2003, p. 7)

13 See "Beyond Discourse Analysis" in Laclau's *New Reflections on the Revolution of our Time*. (Žižek 1990)

14 For a fuller treatment of the Žižek/Laclau debate, see my article, "The Failure of the Radical Democratic Imaginary: Žižek versus Laclau and Mouffe on Vestigial Utopia" (Brockelman 2003).

15 (Žižek 2004, p. 197). For Žižek, by contrast, "the economy is simply one among the social spheres. The basic insight of the Marxist critique of political economy ... is that the economy has a certain proto-transcendental social status. Economy provides a generative matrix for phenomena which in the first approach have nothing to do with economy as such." (Žižek and Daly 2004, p. 147)

16 For example, Žižek writes that, "the problematic of multiculturalism (the hybrid coexistence of diverse cultural life-worlds) which imposes itself today is the form of appearance of its opposite, of the massive presence of capitalism as (*global*) world system: it bears witness to the unprecedented homogenization of today's world" (Žižek 1999a, p. 218).

17 Thus, writing of contemporary efforts to battle racism, Žižek complains of *de-politicization*: "Today, however, the very terrain of the struggle has changed: the post-political liberal establishment not only fully acknowledges the gap between mere formal equality and its actualization/implementation, it not only acknowledges the exclusionary logic of 'false' ideological universality; it even actively fights it by applying to it a vast legal-psychological-sociological network of measures, from identifying the specific problems of every group and subgroup (not only homosexuals but African-American lesbians, African-American lesbian mothers, African-American unemployed lesbian mothers . . .) up to proposing a set of measures ('affirmative action,' etc.) to rectify the wrong. What such a tolerant procedure precludes is the gesture of *politicization* proper: although the difficulties of being an African-American unemployed lesbian mother are adequately catalogued right down to its most specific features, the concerned subject none the less somehow 'feels' that there is something 'wrong' and 'frustrating' in this very effort to mete out justice to her specific predicament – what she is deprived of is the possibility of 'metaphoric' elevation of the specific 'wrong' into a stand-in for the universal 'wrong'." (Žižek 1999a, p. 203)

18 See, for example, *The Ticklish Subject*, (Žižek 1999a, p. 203) or, also, "*Objet a* in Social Links," (Žižek 2006a, p. 113) where he writes: "What happens in psychoanalytic treatment is strictly homologous to the response of the neo-Nazi skinhead who, when really pressed for the reasons for his violence, suddenly starts to talk like social workers, sociologists, and social psychologists, quoting diminished social mobility rising insecurity, the disintegration of paternal authority, the lack of maternal love in his early childhood. The unity of practice and its inherent ideological legitimization disintegrates into raw violence and its impotent, inefficient interpretation. This impotence of interpretation is also one of the necessary obverses of the universalized reflexivity hailed by the risk-society-theorists: it is as if our reflexive power can flourish only insofar as it draws its strength and relies on some minimal 'pre-reflexive' substantial support that eludes its grasp, so that

its universalization comes at the price of its inefficiency, that is, by the paradoxical reemergence of the brute real of 'irrational' violence, impermeable and insensitive to reflexive interpretation. So the more today's social theory proclaims the end of nature or tradition and the rise of the 'risk society', the more the implicit reference to 'nature' pervades our daily discourse."

[19] Žižek writes of today's virtual technology that "when our entire social existence is progressively externalized-materialized in the big Other of the computer network, it's easy to imagine an evil programmer erasing our digital identity and depriving us of our social existence" (Žižek 2002, p. 245).

[20] On a related topic, Žižek writes that "the true horror of the slogan 'frictionless capitalism' is that although actual 'frictions' continue, they become invisible, repressed into the netherworld outside our 'post-modern', post-industrial universe; this is why the 'frictionless' universe of digitalized communication, technological gadgets, and so on, is always haunted by the notion that there is a global catastrophe just around the corner, threatening to explode at any moment" (Žižek 2006b, p. 278).

[21] Having written this, I hasten to add that Žižek does not *equate* the emergence of the political, as do his predecessor Carl Schmitt and many contemporary neo-Schmittians, with the framing of such "enmity." As Žižek explains in a contribution to a 1999 volume on Schmitt ("Carl Schmitt in the Age of Post-Politics" [Žižek 1999b]), Schmitt's understanding of society in terms of an irreducible antagonism between "Us and Them" is both a necessary and mistaken one: on the one hand, "the radicalization of politics into the open warfare of Us against Them discernible in different fundamentalisms – is *the form in which the foreclosed political returns in the post-political universe of pluralist negotiation and consensual regulation*"; (Žižek 1999b, p. 35) on the other hand, framing antagonism with the *substantial* nature of the enemy – or, indeed, modeling antagonism on the "external" model of "warfare" (i.e., a struggle *between* states) – amounts to a fundamentally Rightist diversion from the insubstantial antagonism at stake in revolutionary moments (Žižek 1999b, p. 27, 36).

[22] "In short what is emerging in the guise of the terrorist on whom war is declared is precisely the figure of the political Enemy, foreclosed from the political space proper" (Žižek 2002b, p. 93).

[23] ". . . For Levinas, the Other who addresses me with the unconditional call and thus constitutes me as an ethical subject is – in spite of the fact that this is an absolutely heterogeneous call which *commands me* and so comes from a *height* – the *human* other, the *face*, the transcendental form of neighbor as radical other." (Žižek 2004b, p. 145).

[24] This side of Žižek's argument tends to be lost in his polemical élan, which submerges it beneath the related argument in praise of "essential" ethical violence. That is, to use the example from "Neighbors and Other Monsters," for Žižek we should concentrate on the violence inherent in subjectivity, its "violation" of Being itself by tearing a hole in it.

[25] Perhaps the most focused version of such an argument takes place in a discussion of Levinas from *The Parallax View*, where Žižek brings Levinas' domestication of the neighbor together with the peculiar conditions of late capitalism, conditions

which favor the violent "eruption" of the "undead" excess of representation. As he puts it at the end of this discussion *"Pure Life is a category of capitalism."* See Žižek 2006b, pp. 113–118.

26 Von Trier's next film in the "America" series, *Manderlay*, expands upon the issue of race in such a cynical world. For more on this nexus, see my unpublished paper, "Spinoza's Dream: *Manderlay, Dogville* and Capitalism." (Brockelman Unpublished)

27 In addition to the passages I discuss below from *The Plague of Fantasies*, we should refer to a similar passage in *The Metastases of Enjoyment*, a passage in which Žižek in fact introduces the term, "over-identification" (see, Žižek 1994, p. 72). Parker traces Laibach's role in actually practicing over-identification, a role which underlies Žižek's later theorization of it. See, Parker 2004, p. 32.

28 See, *Plague*, pp. 71–81 where Žižek discusses and defends the critical potential of such over-identification.

29 Žižek appropriates the notion of such an act from Lacan, whose 15th seminar, *L'acte psychanalytique*, is devoted to it. Adrian Johnston provides an excellent description of those aspects of Lacan's concept which suit it for Žižek's understanding: "Lacan devotes the opening sessions of that year's seminar to delineating a distinction between an action' (l'action) and an "act' (l'acte). The former is simply some sort of natural and/or automatic process (for instance, the body's motor activities). The latter, by contrast, involves a dimension over-and-above that of something like a mundane material occurrence. A proper act has Symbolic repercussions: It transgresses the rules of a symbolic order, thereby destabilizing the big Other in revealing its flaws, inconsistencies, and vulnerabilities. Whereas an action is part of the normal run of things, an act disrupts the predictable cycles governing particular realities, forcing transformations of regulated systems in response to its intrusive irruption." (Johnston 2007, p. 87)

Chapter 5

1 "This, then, is the nontrivial sense in which I hope readers will find the present book interesting: insofar as I succeed in my effort to practice concrete universality – to engage in what Deleuze, that great anti-Hegelian, called 'expanding the concepts'" (Žižek 2006b, p. 13).

2 See Žižek's discovery of a Deleuzian version of the "singular-universal" in *Organs Without Bodies* (Žižek 2004a, pp. 14–15).

3 Adrian Johnston discusses Lacan's own similar understanding of "the act": "The Lacanian notion of the act, although lacking much in the way of conceptual specificity and theoretical details, involves two restrictions: One, an act cannot be anticipated and defined from within the framework of a given symbolic order, since it shatters the parameters of that same framework if and when it happens; Two, a subject does not actively perform an act, since subjectivity is, as Lacan indicates, a passive after-effect of such an event." (Johnston 2007, p. 87)

4 If the path from Žižek's essay on Laclau included in the latter's *New Reflections on the Revolution of Our Time* (1990) to *"Objet a* in Social Links" (2006) indicates

Žižek's increasing transparency about his critique of various forms of "post-Marxism" and "neo-Marxism," then it's vital to see a corresponding development in his understanding of the "imaginary" task of political theory. That is, for a long time, in fact even through the publication of *The Ticklish Subject* and *Contingency, Hegemony, Universality*, Žižek prevaricated about the basic "stance" common to engaged intellectuals today, a stance which binds together a possible revival of the Left with renewed "mobilizing global vision." On the one hand, consistent with his critique of theorists like Laclau and Mouffe, Žižek refused to himself project any such image of utopia. On the other hand, though, his own association with them, and, one suspects, his own desire to "engage," forced him to hold open the possibility of such "vision" as a pre-revolutionary *possibility*.

Nowhere, does this tension emerge more forcefully than in the rather painful set of exchanges between Žižek, Laclau and Judith Butler published as *Contingency, Hegemony, Universality: Contemporary Dialogues on the Left* (2000), a text in which Žižek utters the following commentary on the Left's dogmatic evacuation of every effort at radical change. Addressing Laclau and Mouffe's project, he writes: "Today . . . it is more important than ever to hold this utopian place of the global alternative open, even if it remains empty, living on borrowed time, awaiting the content to fill it in. I fully agree with Laclau that after the exhaustion of both the social democratic welfare state imaginary and the 'really-existing-Socialist' imaginary, the Left does need a new imaginary (a new mobilizing global vision)." (Žižek, Laclau and Butler 2000, p. 325)

5 The work of Claude Lefort, which explicitly draws out the "political" dimension of modernity, has been quite influential on Žižek. One can find frequent references to Lefort in Žižek's earlier writing particularly *The Sublime Object of Ideology* (Žižek, 1989) – references almost always in sympathy to precisely this bond asserted by Lefort between modernity and the political. In *The Sublime Object of Ideology*, Žižek interprets Lefort's account of the emergence of modern political forms (Democracy and Totalitarianism) precisely in terms of a dialectical progress. Modernity arrives, more or less, when the "fictionality" of royal power becomes explicit – when the illusion of a "natural order" legitimating political power is broken (see, Žižek 1989, p. 146).

6 For a fuller account of Žižek's early dialogue with Laclau and Mouffe, see my article, "The Failure of the Radical Democratic Imaginary: Žižek versus Laclau and Mouffe on Vestigial Utopia" (Brockelman 2003).

7 Žižek's recent critique of Democracy is certainly in part a rejection of Laclau and Mouffe's approach, but it is also a turning away from *Lefort's* fundamental concept – his praise of modern democracy as containing an acknowledged structural "empty place" preventing any institution or leader from *identifying with* the social as a whole: "The legitimacy of power is based on the people; but the image of popular sovereignty is linked to the image of an empty place, impossible to occupy, such that those who exercise public authority can never claim to appropriate it." (Lefort 1986, p. 279)

8 In a brilliant passage from his essay "Why Heidegger was Right in 1933," Žižek argues that democracy gives us the worst of traditional identity (chauvinism, etc.) while sacrificing the *passion* of political/ideological commitment. Arguing that it

is no accident that today's Left tends toward a merely Liberal bureaucratism – that the "ideal" of the European Union, for example, will never be able to inspire – Žižek sees the only place for passionate belief today to lie on the Right. What we can "imagine" through the lens of the democratic ideal today is hardly "utopian" in any genuine sense (see, Žižek 2007, p. 5).

⁹ In fact, this non-presence of the event of freedom is an important *Leitmotiff* throughout Žižek's writing since the early 1990s. See, for example, Žižek's analysis of freedom in today's cognitive science from *The Parallax View*. Freedom is "inherently retroactive: at its most elementary, it is not simply a free act which, out of nowhere, starts a new causal link, but a retroactive act of endorsing which link/sequence of necessities will determine me" (Žižek 2006b, p. 204).

¹⁰ Of course, the *locus classicus* for such an ideal of concrete labor is the Paris Manuscripts of Marx. See, Marx and Engels 1972, pp. 52–103.

¹¹ See, also *Organs without Bodies* which contains an extended but less focused critique of Hardt and Negri than "*Objet a*" (See, Žižek 2004a, pp. 195–201.)

¹² Žižek thus writes that "If anything, the problem with Hardt and Negri is that they are too much Marxists, taking over the underlying Marxist scheme of historcal progress" (Žižek 2006a, p. 125).

¹³ As evidence for this argument that Žižek sees Hardt and Negri as repeating the "deductive" mistake of Marx and Engels with regard to utopia, it's worth noting that the text in the "*Objet a*" essay repeats verbatim those several paragraphs from the *The Fragile Absolute* which conceive Communism as Capitalism's "inherent transgression" – differing *only* in substituting the names "Hardt and Negri" for "Marx" or "Marx and Engels." Compare Žižek 2006a, pp. 125–126 with Žižek 2000, pp. 17–18.

Chapter 6

¹ For a fuller version of my argument that *The Puppet and the Dwarf* turns on Žižek's ambivalence about the perversity of Christianity, see my article, "Polemical Ambivalence: Modernity and Utopia in Žižek's *The Puppet and the Dwarf*" (Brockelman 2007).

² (Žižek 2003, p. 16): "In all other religions, God demands that His followers remain faithful to Him – only Christ asked his followers to betray him in order to fulfill his mission. Here I am tempted to claim that the entire fate of Christianity, its innermost kernel, hinges on the possibility of interpreting this act in a non-perverse way."

³ See, "On Divine Self-Limitation and Revolutionary Love," where Žižek demands that we read the subtitle as ambiguous: "In a way, I'm sorry for that subtitle because some of my more vulgar materialist, anti-theological friends misread it and thought that I was saying Christianity is in itself perverse, and that I want to point to some perverse core in a negative way" (Žižek and Delpech-Ramey 2004).

⁴ For Žižek, the key here is to avoid a "perverse" construction of the Fall. The only way to do that is to see that "God does not first push us into Sin in order to create the need for Salvation, and then offer Himself as the Redeemer from the trouble into which He got us in the first place; it is not that the Fall is followed by

Redemption: the Fall is identical to Redemption, it is 'in itself' already Redemption. That is to say: what is 'redemption'? The explosion of freedom, the breaking out of the natural enchainment – and this, precisely, is what happens in the Fall" (Žižek 2003, p. 117).

5 ". . . Judaism in forcing us to face the abyss of the Other's desire (in the guise of the impenetrable God), in refusing to cover up this abyss with a determinate fantasmatic scenario (articulated in the obscene initiatic myth), confronts us for the first time with the paradox of human freedom. There is no freedom outside the traumatic encounter with the opacity of the Other's desire – I am, as it were, thrown into my freedom when I confront this opacity as such, deprived of the fantasmatic cover that tells me what the Other wants from me, without knowing *what* this desire is, I am thrown back onto myself, compelled to assume the risk of freely determining the coordinates of my desire." (Žižek, 2003, p. 129)

6 Thus, Žižek argues against the "enlightened" or non-fundamentalist versions of religion popular in our culture: "Against this attitude, one should insist even more emphatically that the 'vulgar' question 'Do you really believe or not?' matters – more than ever, perhaps" (Žižek 2003, p. 6). (See, also, the discussion of Buddhism in Chapter 1 of *Puppet.*)

7 "Žižek treats the world as a textual clinic in which the writer's task is to speak for and to social pathology. As his readers, *we* are that world, and in requiring us to make sense of his writings for ourselves, Žižek enjoins on us the difficulty of 'traversing the fantasy' and recognizing our subjection to the Real." (Kay 2003, p. 15)

8 "Enjoy Your Žižek!", by Robert Boynton (Boynton 1998). Reprinted in Kay 2003, pp. 12–13.

9 It is true that the Lacanian model of analysis gives a much more sophisticated view of the transference relationship as a *mutual* love-affair, but, even there, such mutuality limits the analyst's seduction in a way incompatible with Žižek's actions in his analysis.

10 Notice, in contrast, that, by way of contrast, Leigh Claire La Berge makes Žižek out as an *analysand*. Given Žižek's manifest inability to actually play the role of analysand, such a characterization seems far-fetched (see La Berge 2007, p. 11).

11 "Neighbors and Other monsters,"(Žižek 2004b, p. 175). I am indebted to Marc De Kesel for his suggestion of this as a site for understanding Žižek's construction of the analytic relationship. See his essay, "Transcendental Confusion: Žižekian Criticism and Lacanian Theory" (De Kesel 2007, pp. 111–113).

12 See, Lacan's Seminar, Book VIII, *Transference* (Lacan Unpublished). I am much indebted for my account of Lacanian transference to de Kesel's "Transcendental Confusion: Žižekian Criticism and Lacanian Theory" for my understanding of the matter. In particular, De Kesel notes that for Lacan the key to the transference lies in our identification of the analyst as expert: "This is what psychoanalysis has discovered and which made it redefine mental health care: more than his symptom, it is asking for help is itself which is the biggest problem for the analysand (or any other person asking for mental health care)" (De Kesel 2007, p. 118).

13 I give considerable attention to the question of the "shock effect" of collage and montage, its history in theory and practice in Chapter 4 of my book *The Frame and the Mirror: On Collage and the Postmodern* (Brockelman 2001).

[14] See my comments on Parker's *Slavoj Žižek: A Critical Introduction* in the Preface to *Žižek and Heidegger*.

[15] It's interesting in this light that Žižek not only identifies with the *analyst* but also with the political figure of the *revolutionary leader*. Indeed, as we saw in the last chapter, Žižek's essays on figures from Robespierre through Mao explore the relationship between the party leader and the proletariat, always preserving a similar "mastery" to that we examine here for the leader. See, for example, Žižek and Lenin 2002, p. 7.

[16] See, for example, his response to La Berge's essay in *The Truth of Žižek* where in his "response to my critics" he is dismissive of quick "characterological" dismissals of a writer. Of course, I am trying something a bit different here . . . (See Bowman and Stamp, pp. 208–209.)

[17] My thanks for this insight to Bruno Besana in response to a paper I delivered at the Jan van Eyck Academie, October, 2007.

[18] Žižek's essay '*Objet a* in Social Links' is an intervention in this debate, where he distinguishes the position of the analyst from that of the pervert on the basis of two "manifestations" of *objet a*:

> The difference between the social link of perversion and that of analysis is grounded in the radical ambiguity of *objet a* in Lacan, which stands simultaneously for the imaginary fantasmatic lure/screen and for that which this lure is obfuscating, for the void behind the lure. Consequently, when we pass from perversion to the analytic social link, the agent (analyst) reduces himself to the void, which provokes the subject into confronting the truth of his desire. Knowledge in the position of 'truth' below the bar under the 'agent,' of course, refers to the supposed knowledge of the analyst, and, simultaneously, signals that the knowledge gained here will not be the neutral objective knowledge of scientific adequacy, but the knowledge that concerns the subject (analysand) in the truth of his subjective position. (Žižek 2006a, p. 115)

Bibliography and References

Adorno, T. W. and Horkheimer, M. (1988). *Dialectic of Enlightenment.* J. Cumming, transl. Continuum: New York.

Adorno, T. W. (1984). *Aesthetic Theory.* C. Lenhardt, transl., G. Adorno and R. Tiedemann, eds. Routledge and Kegan Paul: London, Boston.

Agamben, G. (1993). *The Coming Community.* M. Hardt, transl. University of Minnesota: Minneapolis.

Benhabib, S. (1986). *Critique, Norm and Utopia.* Columbia University Press: New York.

Benjamin, A., ed. (1989). *The Problems of Modernity: Adorno and Benjamin.* Routledge: New York and London.

Benjamin, A. (1993). *The Plural Event: Descartes, Hegel, Heidegger.* Routledge: New York and London.

Benjamin, W. (1983). *Charles Baudelaire, a Lyric Poet in the Era of High Capitalism.* Harry Zohn, transl. Verso: London.

—(1969). *Illuminations.* Schocken: New York.

—(1978). *Reflections: Essays, Aphorisms, Autobiographical Writings.* E. Jephcott, transl., P. Demetz, ed. Harcourt Brace Jovanovich: New York.

Berman, M. (1982). *All that is Solid Melts into Air: the Experience of Modernity.* Penguin: Harmondsworth.

Bernstein, R. J., ed. (1985). *Habermas and Modernity.* MIT: Cambridge and London.

Boothby, R. (2005). *Sex on the Couch: What Freud Still Has to Teach Us About Sex and Gender.* Routledge: New York and London.

—(2001). *Freud as Philosopher: Metapsychology After Lacan.* Routledge: New York and London.

—(1991). *Death and Desire: Psychoanalytic Theory in Lacan's Return to Freud.* Routledge: New York and London.

Borch-Jacobsen, M. (1988). *The Freudian Subject.* C. Porter, transl. Foreword by F. Roustang. Stanford University Press: Stanford.

Borgman, A. (2005). "Technology." In *A Companion to Heidegger.* H. L. Dreyfus and M. A. Wrathall, eds. Blackwell: Oxford.

Bowman, P. and Stamp, R., eds (2007). *The Truth of Žižek.* Continuum Press: London and New York.

Boynton, R. S. (1998). "Enjoy Your Žižek! An Excitable Slovenian Philosopher Examines the Obscene Practices of Everyday Life – Including his Own." In *Lingua Franca,* 8. [Online]. Available at http://www.linguagfranca.com/9810/Žižek.html, viewed September 15,2005.

Božovič, M. (1995). "An Utterly Dark Spot." Introduction to Jeremy Bentham's *Panopticon Writings*. M. Božovič, ed. Verso: London.

Brennan, T. (1993). *History After Lacan*. Routledge: New York and London.

Brockelman, T. (Unpublished). "Spinoza's Dream: *Manderlay, Dogville* and Capitalism." Delivered at the Conference, "Slave to Freedom: on Lars von Trier's *Manderlay*." October, 2007.

—(2008). "Missing the Point: Reading the Lacanian Subject through Perspective." In *S: Journal of the Jan van Eyck Circle for Lacanian Ideology Critique*. Vol 1.1. [Online]. Available at : www.lineofbeauty.org

—(2008a). "Laughing at Finitude: Slavoj Žižek Reads *Being and Time*." In *Continental Philosophy Review*. Vol. 41, no. 4. Springer: Rotterdam and New York.

—(2007). "Polemical Ambivalence: Modernity and Utopia in Žižek's *The Puppet and the Dwarf*." In *Contemporary Political Theory*. Vol. 6, Issue 3. Palgrave: London and New York.

—(2003). "The Failure of the Radical Democratic Imaginary: Žižek versus Laclau and Mouffe on Vestigial Utopia." In *Philosophy and Social Criticism*. Vol. 29, no. 2. Sage Publications: London and Thousand Oaks.

—(2001). *The Frame and the Mirror: On Collage and the Postmodern*. Northwestern University Press: Evanston.

Bürger, P. (1984). *Theory of the Avant-Garde*. M. Shaw, transl. Foreword by J. Schulte-Sasse. University of Minnesota: Minneapolis.

Butler, R. (2005). *Slavoj Žižek: Live Theory*. Continuum: London and New York.

Copjec, J. (1994). *Read My Desire*. MIT: Cambridge and London.

—(2003). *Imagine There's No Woman: Ethics and Sublimation*. MIT: Cambridge and London.

Critchley, S. (2007). *Infinitely Demanding: Ethics of commitment, politics of resistance*. Verso: London and New York.

—(2002). *On Humour*. Routledge: New York and London.

Damisch, H. (1994). *The Origin of Perspective*. J. Goodman, transl. MIT: Cambridge and London.

De Kesel, M. (2007). "Transcendental Confusion: Žižekian Criticism and Lacanian Theory." In: Fabio Vighi and Heiko Felder, eds. (2007), *Did Somebody Say Ideology? On Slavoj Žižek and Consequences*. Cambridge Scholars Publishing: New Castle.

Deleuze, G. (1995). *Negotiations*. Columbia University Press: New York.

—(1993). *The Fold: Leibniz and the Baroque*. T. Conley, transl. and ed. University of Minnesota: Minneapolis.

Descartes, R. (1968). *Discourse on Method and Meditations*. F. E. Sutcliffe, transl. Penguin Books: Harmondsworth.

Dolar, M. (1998). "Cogito as the Subject of the Unconscious." In *Cogito and the Unconscious*. S. Žižek, ed. Duke University Press: Durham.

Dreyfus, H. L. (1992). "Heidegger's History of the Being of Equipment." In *Heidegger: A Critical Reader*. H. L. Dreyfus and H. Hall, eds. Blackwell: Oxford.

Ellis, B. E. (1991). *American Psycho*. Random House: New York

Evans, D. (1996). *An Introductory Dictionary of Lacanian Psychoanalysis*. Routledge: New York and London.

Feenberg, A. (2005). *Heidegger and Marcuse: the Catastrophe and Redemption of History*. Routledge: New York and London.

Feldstein, R., Fink, B. and Jaanus, M., eds. (1995). *Reading Seminar XI: Lacan's Four Fundamental Concepts of Psychoanalysis.* B. Fink, transl. SUNY Press: Albany.

Foltz, B. (1995). *Inhabiting the Earth: Heidegger, Environmental Ethics, and the Metaphysics of Nature.* Humanities Press: Atlantic Highlands.

Freud, S.(1974). *The Standard Edition of The Complete Psychological Works of Sigmund Freud.* 24 volumes. Hogarth Press and the Institute of Psycho-Analysis: London.

—(1974a). *The Ego and the Id.* In, J. Strachey, ed., *The Standard Edition of the Complete Psychological Works of Sigmund Freud, vol. XIX.* Hogarth Press and the Institute of Psycho-Analysis: London.

—(1974b). *Moses and Monotheism,* in, J. Strachey, ed., *The Standard Edition Of The Complete Psychological Works Of Sigmund Freud, vol. XXIII.* Hogarth Press and the Institute of Psycho-Analysis: London.

Gould, S. J. (1996). *Full House: The Spread of Excellence from Plato to Darwin.* Three Rivers Press: New York.

Guignon, C., ed. (1993). *The Cambridge Companion to Heidegger.* Cambridge University Press: Cambridge.

Habermas, J. (1987). *The Philosophical Discourse of Modernity: Twelve Lectures,* F. Lawrence, transl. MIT: Cambridge and London.

Hardt, M. and Negri, A. (2004). *Multitude: War and Democracy in the Age of Empire.* Penguin Press: New York.

—(2001). *Empire.* Harvard University Press: Cambridge and London.

Hegel, G. W. F. (1975). *Aesthetics: Lectures on Fine Art.* T. M. Know, transl. Clarendon Press: Oxford.

Heidegger, M. (1991). *Nietzsche,* vol. 4, *Nihilism,* D. F. Krell, ed. HarperCollins: San Francisco.

—(1982). *The Basic Problems of Phenomenology.* A. Hofstadter, transl. Indiana University Press: Bloomington.

—(1979). *An Introduction to Metaphysics,* R. Mannheim, transl. Yale University Press: New Haven and London.

—(1977). *Basic Writings: From Being and Time (1927) to The Task of Thinking (1964),* D. F. Krell, ed. Harper & Row: New York.

—(1977a). *The Question Concerning Technology and Other Essays,* W. Lovitt, transl. and ed. Harper & Row: New York.

—(1975). *Poetry, Language, Thought.* Albert Hofstadter, transl. Harper & Row: New York.

—(1962). *Being and Time.* J. Macquarrie and E. Robinson, transl. Blackwell: Oxford.

—(1962a). *Kant and the Problem of Metaphysics.* J. S. Churchill, transl. Indiana University Press: Bloomington.

Jameson, F. (1991). *Postmodernism, or, the Cultural Logic of Late Capitalism.* Duke University Press: Durham.

—(1988). *The Ideologies of Theory: Essays 1971–1986.* Volumes 1 (The Situation of Theory) and 2 (The Syntax of History). University of Minnesota: Minneapolis.

Johnston, A. (2008). *Žižek's Ontology: A Transcendental Materialist Theory of Subjectivity.* Northwestern University Press: Evanston.

—(2007). "The Cynic's Fetish: Slavoj Žižek and the Dynamics of Belief." In *The International Journal of Žižek Studies,* vol. 1.0, 2007. [Online]. Available at http://žižekstudies.org/index.php/ijzs/article/view/8/24, viewed April 15, 2008.

—(2007a). "Slavoj Žižek's Hegelian Reformation: Giving a Hearing to *The Parallax View*." In *Diacritics*. John Hopkins University Press: Baltimore.

—(2005). *Time Driven : Metapsychology and the Splitting of the Drive*. Northwestern University Press: Evanston.

Kant, I. (1987). *Critique of Judgment*. W. S. Pluhar, transl. Hackett: Indianapolis.

—(1958). *Critique of pure reason*. N. K. Smith, transl. and ed. Modern Library: New York.

Kay, S. (2003). *Žižek: A Critical Introduction*. Polity: Cambridge.

Kristeva, J. (1984). *Revolution in Poetic Language*. M. Waller, transl. With an introduction by L. S. Roudiez. Columbia: New York.

La Berge, L. C. (2007). "The Writing Cure: Slavoj Žižek, Analysand of Modernity." In *The Truth of Žižek*. Bowman, P. and Stamp, R., eds. Continuum Press: London and New York.

Lacan, J. (2007). *The Other Side of Psychoanalysis. The Seminar of Jacques Lacan*, Book XVII. R. Grigg, transl. and ed. Norton: New York and London.

—(2005). *Écrits:The First Complete Edition in English*. B. Fink in collaboration with H. Fink and R. Grigg, transl. Norton: New York and London.

—(1998). *On Feminine Sexuality: The Limits of Love and Knowledge*. The Seminar of Jacques Lacan, Book XX, *Encore*, 1972–1973. B. Fink, transl. and ed. Norton: New York and London.

—(1992). *The Ethics of Psychoanalysis, 1959–1960. The Seminar of Jacques Lacan*, Book VII. J.-A. Miller, ed., D. Porter, transl. Norton: New York and London.

—(1988). *Freud's Papers on Technique. The Seminar of Jacques Lacan: Book I*, 1953–1954. J.-A. Miller, ed., J. Forrester, transl. Norton: New York and London.

—(1981). *The Four Fundamental Concepts of Psycho-Analysis*. (Seminar 11). J. A. Miller, ed., A. Sheridan, transl. Norton: New York and London.

—(1968). *The Language of the Self: The Function of Language in Psychoanalysis*. A. Wilden, transl. Johns Hopkins: Baltimore.

—(Unpublished). *The Seminar of Jacques Lacan: Transference, 1960–1961*. (Seminar 8). C. Gallagher, transl. from unedited French Manuscripts.

—(Unpublished a). *The Seminar of Jacques Lacan: The Object of Psychoanalysis, 1965–1966*. (Seminar 13). C. Gallagher, transl. from unedited French Manuscripts.

Laclau, E. and Mouffe, C. (1985). *Hegemony & Socialist Strategy: Towards a Radical Democratic Politics*. Verso: London and New York.

Laclau, E. (1990). *New Reflections on the Revolution of Our Time*. Verso: London and New York.

Laplanche, J. B. and Pontalis, J. (1973). *The Language of Psycho-analysis*. Norton: New York.

Lear, J. (2000). *Happiness, Death and the Remainder of Life*. Harvard University Press: Cambridge and London.

Lefort, C. (1988). *Democracy and Political Theory*. University of Minnesota: Minneapolis.

—(1986). *The Political Forms of Modern Society: Bureaucracy, Democracy, Totalitarianism*. J. B. Thompson, ed. MIT: Cambridge and London.

Löwith, K. (1995). *Martin Heidegger and European Nihilism*, R. Wolin, ed., G. Steiner, transl. Columbia University Press: New York.

Lyotard, J. -F. (1990). *Heidegger and "the jews".* A. Michel and M. Roberts, transl. Introduction by David Carroll. University of Minnesota: Minneapolis.

—(1984). *Lessons on the Analytic of the Sublime.* E. Rottenberg, transl. Stanford University Press: Stanford.

Marcuse, H. (1991). *One Dimensional Man: Studies in the Ideology of Advanced Industrial Society.* Beacon Press: Boston.

—(1974). *Eros and Civilization: A Philosophical Inquiry into Freud.* Beacon Press: Boston.

Marx, K. and Engels, F. (1972). *The Marx-Engels Reader.* R. C. Tucker, ed. Norton: New York.

McGowan, T. (2004). *The End of Dissatisfaction? Jacques Lacan and the Emerging Society of Enjoyment.* SUNY Press: Albany.

Mead, R. (2005). "The Marx Brother." In *The New Yorker*, May 5, 2005.

Myers, T. (2003). *Slavoj Žižek.* Routledge Critical Readers. Routledge: New York and London.

Nancy, J. -L. (1991). *The Inoperative Community.* P. Connor, ed., P. Connor, L. Garbus, M. Holland and S. Sawhney, transls. Foreword by C. Fynsk. University of Minnesota: Minneapolis.

Nicholas of Cusa (1997). "On Learned Ignorance," In *Nicholas of Cusa. Selected Spiritual Writings.* H. L. Bond, transl. and ed. Classics of Western Spirituality. Paulist Press: Mahwah.

—(1997a). "On the Image of God," In *Nicholas of Cusa. Selected Spiritual Writings.* H. L. Bond, transl. and ed. Classics of Western Spirituality. Paulist Press: Mahwah.

Parker, I. (2004). *Slavoj Žižek: A Critical Introduction.* Pluto: London.

Salecl, R., ed. (2000). *Sexuation.* Duke University Press: Durham.

Santner, E. (2001). *On the Psychotheology of Everyday Life: Reflections on Freud and Rosenzweig.* University of Chicago Press: Chicago and London.

—(2000). "Traumatic Revelations: Freud's Moses and the Origins of Anti-Semitism." In *Sexuation*, R. Salecl, ed. Duke University Press: Durham.

Stavrakakis, Y. (1999). *Lacan and the Political.* Routledge: New York and London.

—(1997) "Green Fantasy and the Real of Nature: Elements of a Lacanian Critique of Green Ideological Discourse," In *The Journal for the Psychoanalysis of Culture and Society*, vol. 2, no. 1, Spring, 1997.

Torfing, J. (1999). *New Theories of Discourse: Laclau, Mouffe and Žižek.* Blackwell: Oxford.

Vattimo, G. (1992). *The Transparent Society.* D. Webb, transl. Johns Hopkins: Baltimore.

—(1988). *The End of Modernity.* J. R. Snyder, transl. Johns Hopkins: Baltimore.

Vogt, E. and Silverman, H., eds. (2004). *Über Žižek.* Turia und Kant: Vienna.

Weber, M. (1987). *Rationality and Modernity.* S. Lash and S. Whimster, eds. Allen & Unwin: London and Boston.

Wright, E. and Wright E., eds. (1999). *The Žižek Reader.* Blackwell: Oxford.

Ziarek, K. (2001). *The Historicity of Experience: Modernity, the Avant-Garde and the Event.* Northwestern University Press: Evanston.

Zimmerman, M. (1990). *Heidegger's Confrontation with Modernity: Technology, Politics, Art.* Indiana University Press: Bloomington.

Žižek, S. and Daly, G. (2004). *Conversations with Žižek.* Polity Press: Cambridge.

Žižek, S. and Delpech-Ramey, J. (2004). "On Divine Self-Limitation and Revolutionary Love" (Interview). *Journal of Philosophy and Scripture*, Spring 2004. [Online]. Available at: www.lacan.com/žižekscripture.html,September 10,2005.

Žižek, S. and Dolar, M. (2004). *Opera's Second Death*. Routledge: New York and London.

Žižek, S, Laclau, E., and Butler, J. (2000). *Contingency, Hegemony, Universality: Contemporary Dialogues on the Left*. Verso: London and New York.

Žižek, S. and Lenin, V. E. (2002). *Revolution at the Gates: A Selection of Writings from February to October 1917*. Verso: London and New York.

Žižek, S. and Robespierre, M. (2007). *Virtue and Terror*. (Revolutions). Verso: London and New York.

Žižek, S. and Trotsky, L. (2007). *Terrorism and Communism*. (Revolutions). Verso: London and New York.

Žižek, S. and Zedong, M. (2007). *On Practice and Contradiction* (Revolutions). Verso: London and New York.

Žižek, S. (2008). *In Defense of Lost Causes*. Verso: London and New York.

—(2007). "Why Heidegger Made the Right Step in 1933.", In *The International Journal of Žižek Studies*, vol. 1.4, Fall, 2007. [Online] Available at: http://žižekstudies.org/index.php/ijzs/article/view/64/129, viewed April 15, 2008.

—(2007a). *The Reality of the Virtual*. DVD Media. Olive Films, Producer.

—(2007b). "The Inexistence of the Big Other." In *Lacanian Ink*, vol 29., Spr. 2007. J. Ayerza, ed.

—(2006). *Interrogating The Real*. Butler, R. and Stephens, S., eds. Continuum: London and New York.

—(2006a). '*Objet a* in Social Links', in, J. Clemens and R. Grigg, eds, *Jacques Lacan and the Other Side of Psychoanalysis: Reflections on Seminar XVII/* SIC, 6. Duke University Press: Durham and London.

—(2006b). *The Parallax View*. MIT: Cambridge and London.

—(2006c). *The Universal Exception: Selected Writings*. Butler, R. and Stephens, S., eds. Continuum: London and New York.

—(2006d). *How to Read Lacan*. Granta Books: London.

—(2005). *Žižek!* DVD Media. A. Taylor, Dir. Zeitgeist Films: New York.

—(2004). *Iraq: The Borrowed Kettle*. Verso: London and New York.

—(2004a). *Organs without Bodies: On Deleuze and Consequences*. Routledge: New York and London.

—(2004b). "Neighbors and Other Monsters," in *The Neighbor: Three Inquiries in Political Theology*, S. Žižek, E. L. Santner and K. Reinhard, eds. The University of Chicago Press: Chicago and London.

—(2003). *The Puppet and the Dwarf: The Perverse Core of Christianity*, MIT: Cambridge and London.

—(2002). "*The Matrix*, or, The Two Sides of Perversion," in *The Matrix and Philosophy*. William Irwin, ed. Open Court: Chicago and La Salle.

—(2002a). "The Real of Sexual Difference," in *Reading Seminar XX: Lacan's Major Work on Love, Knowledge, and Feminine Sexuality*. S. Barnard and B. Fink, eds. State University of New York Press: Albany.

—(2002b). *Welcome to the Desert of the Real: Five essays on September 11 and Related Dates*. Verso: London and New York.

—(2001). *Did Somebody Say Totalitarianism?: Five Interventions in the (Mis)use of a Notion.* Verso: London and New York.

—(2001a). *On Belief.* Routledge: New York and London.

—(2000). *The Fragile Absolute – or, Why is the Christian Legacy Worth Fighting for?* Verso: London and New York.

—(1999). *The Fright of Real Tears: Krzystof Kieslowski.* British Film Institute: London.

—(1999a). *The Ticklish Subject: the Absent Center of Political Ontology.* Verso: London and New York.

—(1999b). "Carl Schmitt in the Age of Post-Politics." In *The Challenge of Carl Schmitt.* Chantal Mouffe, ed. Verso: London and New York.

Žižek, S., ed. (1998). *Cogito and the Unconscious.* Duke University Press: Durham.

Žižek, S. (1997). *The Plague of Fantasies,* Verso: London and New York.

—(1996). *The Indivisible Remainder: Essays on Schelling and Related Matters.* Verso: London and New York.

—(1994). *The Metastases of Enjoyment.* Verso: London and New York.

—(1993). *Tarrying with the Negative.* Duke University Press: Durham.

—(1992). *Looking Awry: An Introduction to Jacques Lacan through Popular Culture.* MIT: Cambridge and London.

—(1992a). *Enjoy Your Symptom.* Routledge: New York and London.

—(1991). *For they Know not What they Do: Enjoyment as a Political Factor.* Verso: London and New York.

—(1990). "Beyond Discourse-Analysis." In E. Laclau, *New Reflections on the Revolution of Our Time.* Verso: London and New York.

—(1989). *The Sublime Object of Ideology.* Verso: London and New York.

Zupančič, A. (2006). "The 'Concrete Universal," and "What Comedy Can Tell Us About It", in Žižek, S., ed., *Lacan: The Silent Partners.* Verso: London and New York.

—(2003) *The Shortest Shadow: Nietzsche's Philosophy of the Two.* MIT: Cambridge and London.

—(2000) *Ethics of the Real.* Verso: London and New York.

Index